Dos For Dummies

W9-BMV-460

For those times when you're even too lazy to read DOS for Dummies,
here is a quick reference of a few essential items.

Cheat Sheet

General stuff

This is the DOS prompt: C>

The DOS prompt may also look like this: C:\>

You can use upper- or lowercase to type at the DOS prompt.

Press Backspace to erase.

Press Esc (Escape) to cancel.

Press F3 to repeat the last DOS command.

Press Enter to send the command to DOS.

Lost and found

Where am I?

To find your current drive and directory, type the CD command (by itself). That displays the full name of your current drive and directory:

C> CD

C:\123\BUDGET

Above, the CD command tells you you're on drive C in the \123\BUDGET directory.

Where is it?

To find a lost file when you don't know its name, type this DOS command:

C> DIR /P

Look carefully at the list of files displayed. Is yours in there?

If you do know the file's name, type this command:

C> DIR \FILE1 /S

Press Enter and watch the screen for your file (named FILE1 above). DOS will display the directory where the file is located. You can then use the CD command to change to that directory.

To find a lost directory, type this command:

C> DIR *.* /A:D /S | FIND "SUBDIR"

Carefully type in that command, substituting SUBDIR above with your directory's name.

Sneaky DOS guide

To do this . . .	Type this . . .
Cancel a DOS command	Ctrl-C
Pause a long display	Ctrl-S
Turn on DOS's printer	Ctrl-P
Turn off DOS's printer	Ctrl-P
Clear the screen	CLS
Log from drive C to drive A	A:
Log from drive A to drive C	C:
Change directories to \DATA	CD DATA
Change to the root directory	CD \
List all files	DIR
List files in the wide format	DIR /W
List files with a page/pause	DIR /P
List a specific file, FILE1	DIR FILE1
Make a duplicate of a file	COPY FILE1 FILE2
Copy a file to another drive	COPY FILE1 A:
Copy a file to another directory	COPY FILE1 \OTHER\DATA
Copy a group of files	COPY *.DOC A:
Delete a file	DEL FILE1
Delete a group of files	DEL *.DOC
Delete all files	DEL *.*
Rename a file	REN FILE1 FILEONE
Rename a group of files	REN *.DOC *.BAK
Move a file (part 1)	COPY FILE1 C:\NEW
Move a file (part 2)	DEL FILE1
Move a file (DOS 6)	MOVE FILE1 C:\
Display a file's contents	TYPE FILE1
Format a disk in drive A	FORMAT A:
Format a disk in drive B	FORMAT B:
Format a low-density 5¼-inch disk	FORMAT A: /F:360
Format a low-density 3½-inch disk	FORMAT A: /F:720

. . . For Dummies: #1 Computer Book Series for Beginners

**COMPUTER
BOOK SERIES
FROM IDG**

Dos For Dummies

For those times when you're even too lazy to read DOS for Dummies,
here is a quick reference of a few essential items.

Cheat Sheet

Filenames

Filenames have two parts: The first part (the filename) can be from one to eight characters long. The second part (the extension) starts with a dot (period) and can be from one to three characters long.

The first part of a filename should be as descriptive as is possible with eight characters.

The second part of a filename should tell you what type of file it is: TXT for text files; DOC for documents; etc.

Filenames can contain letters and numbers, and can also start with a number. Filenames cannot contain spaces. The following characters are also forbidden in a filename:

. " / \ [ ] : * | < > + = ; , ?

The ? wildcard is used to match a single character in a filename.

The * wildcard is used to match a group of characters in a filename.

The *.* wildcard matches all filenames.

Pathnames

The root directory on every disk is named \ (backslash).

A pathname starts with the drive letter, a colon, and then the root directory:

C:\

Directory names in a pathname are separated by backslashes:

C:\123\AGENDA

A pathname never ends with a backslash (see above).

A filename can be the last item in the pathname; it must be separated from the last directory by a backslash:

C:\PROCOMM\DOWNLOAD\PROJECT.ZIP

Helpful info

✔ Always quit an application when you're done with it; return to DOS, then start your next program.

✔ Never turn off the computer when a disk drive light is on.

✔ Always turn off the computer when you're at a DOS prompt (C>).

✔ "Bad command or file name" means DOS doesn't recognize the command; check your typing, check for errant spaces, and then try again.

✔ "File not found" means DOS can't locate the file you've named; check your typing, check for errant spaces, and then try again.

✔ "Abort, Retry, Ignore" means something's amiss. If you can fix the problem, then do so (such as inserting a disk into the drive), then press R for Retry. If it's beyond hope, press A to Abort. Never press I for Ignore (or F for Fail if that option is listed).

. . . For Dummies: #1 Computer Book Series for Beginners

What the Press Says About DOS For Dummies®

"More than a publishing phenomenon, 'Dummies' is a sign of the times." — Steve Lohr, *The New York Times*

"This is the best book ever written for a beginner. I know. I have all the rest." — Clarence Petersen, *Chicago Tribune*

"If all this talk of memory and megabytes has given you a headache, take two aspirin and, in the morning, buy a copy of DOS For Dummies." — L.R. Shannon, *The New York Times*

"Gookin writes in a humorous, informal style that entertains as it teaches." — Craig Crossman, Nationally syndicated computer columnist

"DOS For Dummies is the ideal book for anyone who's just bought a PC and is too shy to ask friends stupid questions." — *MTV*, Computer Book of the Year, United Kingdom

"This is one of those rare techno-books where you literally can't wait to turn the page. The author starts off with his tongue firmly planted in his cheek and keeps the reader laughing all the way. At the same time, he never loses sight of the real reason the reader is here, and that is to learn DOS." — Bob Liddil, *Portable 100*

"Dan Gookin must have had a 'fly on the wall' positioned in my room because I found the 5,000 or so questions I have asked myself (and nearly everybody else) since I started using DOS neatly answered in this book." — Branko Djakovie, *Computer Buyer*, United Kingdom

"Most computer books are the same: rather boring and dry. DOS For Dummies strives to break that stereotype, and does a good job at it." — Gordon McComb, *PC Upgrade*

"This book doesn't skimp on information, or entertainment. Unlike most DOS instructional books that usually start by showing you how to format a disk, DOS For Dummies starts right at the beginning: How to turn on the computer." — Cheryl Kirk, *Anchorage Daily News*

"Despite the title, this book covers much more than an IBM computer's Disk Operating System (DOS). It tells you how to turn on a computer, things to ignore, and specific steps to take to get you through a variety of different programs. Best of all, it pokes good-natured fun at the computer industry and technobabble in general with chapter headings like "10 Things You Shouldn't Ever Do," and "10 Popular Programs (and How to Fake Your Way Through Them)." — Ron Mansfield, *Entrepreneur Magazine*

 ™

References for the Rest of Us

COMPUTER BOOK SERIES FROM IDG

Are you intimidated and confused by computers? Do you find that traditional manuals are overloaded with technical details you'll never use? Do your friends and family always call you to fix simple problems on their PCs? Then the *". . . For Dummies"*™ computer book series from IDG is for you.

". . . For Dummies" books are written for those frustrated computer users who know they aren't really dumb but find that PC hardware, software, and indeed the unique vocabulary of computing make them feel helpless. *". . . For Dummies"* books use a lighthearted approach, a down-to-earth style, and even cartoons and humorous icons to diffuse computer novices' fears and build their confidence. Lighthearted but not lightweight, these books are a perfect survival guide to anyone forced to use a computer.

> *"I like my copy so much I told friends; now they bought copies."*
>
> **Irene C., Orwell, Ohio**

> *"Quick, concise, nontechnical, and humorous."*
>
> **Jay A., Elburn, IL**

> *"Thanks, I needed this book. Now I can sleep at night."*
>
> **Robin F., British Columbia, Canada**

Already, hundreds of thousands of satisfied readers agree. They have made *". . . For Dummies"* books the #1 introductory level computer book series and have written asking for more. So if you're looking for the most fun and easy way to learn about computers look to *". . . For Dummies"* books to give you a helping hand.

IDG BOOKS

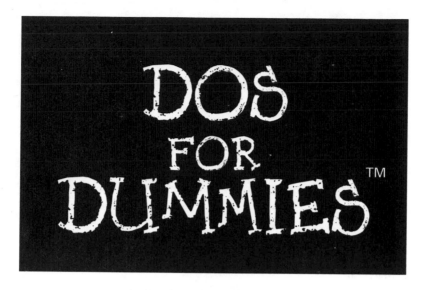

DOS FOR DUMMIES™

2nd Edition

by Dan Gookin

author of bestselling *WordPerfect For Dummies*
and *WordPerfect 6 For Dummies,*
and coauthor of *PCs For Dummies, Word For Windows For Dummies,*
and the *Illustrated Computer Dictionary For Dummies*

IDG
BOOKS

IDG Books Worldwide, Inc.
An International Data Group Company

San Mateo, California ✦ Indianapolis, Indiana ✦ Boston, Massachusetts

DOS For Dummies, 2nd Edition

Published by
IDG Books Worldwide, Inc.
An International Data Group Company
155 Bovet Road, Suite 310
San Mateo, CA 94402
(415) 312-0650

Library of Congress Catalog Card No.: 93-77181

ISBN: 1-878058-75-4

Printed in the United States of America

10 9 8 7 6

Distributed in the United States by IDG Books Worldwide, Inc.

Distributed in Canada by Macmillan of Canada, a Division of Canada Publishing Corporation; by Computer and Technical Books in Miami, Florida, for South America and the Caribbean; by Longman Singapore in Singapore, Malaysia, Thailand, and Korea; by Toppan Co. Ltd. in Japan; by Asia Computerworld in Hong Kong; by Woodslane Pty. Ltd. in Australia and New Zealand; and by Transword Publishers Ltd. in the U.K. and Europe.

For information on where to purchase IDG Books outside the U.S., contact Christina Turner at 415-312-0633.

For information on translations, contact Marc Jeffrey Mikulich, Foreign Rights Manager, at IDG Books Worldwide; FAX NUMBER 415-358-1260.

For sales inquiries and special prices for bulk quantities, write to the address above or call IDG Books Worldwide at 415-312-0650.

Acknowledgments

A book like this could only happen if the most strangest of minds get together at the most unusual of circumstances. The strange minds in this case were Michael McCarthy, former editorial god of IDG Books, and myself. The circumstance was the first annual Waterside Computer Book Publishing Forum in San Diego, March 1991.

Michael presented me with an outrageous idea for a book on DOS, a book with an attitude (summarized by the first paragraph of the Introduction — which are almost his exact words), a book called *DOS For Dummies*. I screamed that I've wanted to do that book for years. I even had an outline ready, which pretty much matched the chapter organization of the book you have in your hands.

The fruition of our insanity has been helped greatly by the fine folks at IDG Books. No other publisher on the planet could have done this book with such success. Chief among the IDG cohort is John Kilcullen. John saw a good thing before it started to happen, and I'm greatly in debt for his attention to the project and massive marketing muscle he's put behind it since.

Other fine souls at IDG books include Jeremy Judson, Mary "the bee" Bednarek, David Solomon, Terrie Solomon, Milissa Koloski, Brandon Nordin, Polly Papsadore, Janna Custer, Megg Bonar, Sandy Blackthorn, Diane Steele, Corbin Collins, Barbara Potter, Tricia Reynolds, Beth Jenkins, Drew Moore, Cindy Phipps, Tony Augsburger, Mary Briedenbach, Valery Bourke, and many others who contribute to this book's success in ways I'm totally clueless about.

Most importantly, I'd like to acknowledge this book's legions of fans. Those hardy souls who advertise this book by word of mouth; who blurt out, "*DOS For Dummies*? That's for me!"; who shyly explain, "This is for my brother-in-law / office / boss / etc."; and who, in thousands of reader response cards, have said "Thank you for writing a computer book just for me." To them, I say you're welcome and thank you for enjoying it.

(The publisher would like to give special thanks to Patrick J. McGovern, without whom this book would not have been possible.)

About IDG Books Worldwide

Welcome to the world of IDG Books Worldwide.

IDG Books Worldwide, Inc., is a division of International Data Group, the world's largest publisher of computer-related information and the leading global provider of information services on information technology. IDG publishes over 194 computer publications in 62 countries. Forty million people read one or more IDG publications each month.

If you use personal computers, IDG Books is committed to publishing quality books that meet your needs. We rely on our extensive network of publications, including such leading periodicals as *Macworld*, *InfoWorld*, *PC World*, *Computerworld*, *Publish*, *Network World*, and *SunWorld*, to help us make informed and timely decisions in creating useful computer books that meet your needs.

Every IDG book strives to bring extra value and skill-building instruction to the reader. Our books are written by experts, with the backing of IDG periodicals, and with careful thought devoted to issues such as audience, interior design, use of icons, and illustrations. Our editorial staff is a careful mix of high-tech journalists and experienced book people. Our close contact with the makers of computer products helps ensure accuracy and thorough coverage. Our heavy use of personal computers at every step in production means we can deliver books in the most timely manner.

We are delivering books of high quality at competitive prices on topics customers want. At IDG, we believe in quality, and we have been delivering quality for over 25 years. You'll find no better book on a subject than an IDG book.

John Kilcullen
President and C.E.O.
IDG Books Worldwide, Inc.

IDG Books Worldwide, Inc. is a division of International Data Group. The officers are Patrick J. McGovern, Founder and Board Chairman; Walter Boyd, President. International Data Group's publications include: **ARGENTINA's** Computerworld Argentina, InfoWorld Argentina; **ASIA's** Computerworld Hong Kong, PC World Hong Kong, Computerworld Southeast Asia, PC World Singapore, Computerworld Malaysia, PC World Malaysia; **AUSTRALIA's** Computerworld Australia, Australian PC World, Australian Macworld, Network World, Reseller, IDG Sources; **AUSTRIA's** Computerwelt Oesterreich, PC Test; **BRAZIL's** Computerworld, Mundo IBM, Mundo Unix, PC World, Publish; **BULGARIA's** Computerworld Bulgaria, Ediworld, PC & Mac World Bulgaria; **CANADA's** Direct Access, Graduate Computerworld, InfoCanada, Network World Canada; **CHILE's** Computerworld, Informatica; **COLUMBIA's** Computerworld Colombia; **CZECH REPUBLIC's** Computerworld, Elektronika, PC World; **DENMARK's** CAD/CAM WORLD, Communications World, Computerworld Danmark, LOTUS World, Macintosh Produktkatalog, Macworld Danmark, PC World Danmark, PC World Produktguide, Windows World; **EQUADOR's** PC World; **EGYPT's** Computerworld (CW) Middle East, PC World Middle East; **FINLAND's** MikroPC, Tietoviikko, Tietoverkko; **FRANCE's** Distributique, GOLDEN MAC, InfoPC, Languages & Systems, Le Guide du Monde Informatique, Le Monde Informatique, Telecoms & Reseaux; **GERMANY's** Computerwoche, Computerwoche Focus, Computerwoche Extra, Computerwoche Karriere, Information Management, Macwelt, Netzwelt, PC Welt, PC Woche, Publish, Unit; **HUNGARY's** Alaplap, Computerworld SZT, PC World, ; **INDIA's** Computers & Communications; **ISRAEL's** Computerworld Israel, PC World Israel; **ITALY's** Computerworld Italia, Lotus Magazine, Macworld Italia, Networking Italia, PC World Italia; **JAPAN's** Computerworld Japan, Macworld Japan, SunWorld Japan, Windows World; **KENYA's** East African Computer News; **KOREA's** Computerworld Korea, Macworld Korea, PC World Korea; **MEXICO's** Compu Edicion, Compu Manufactura, Computacion/Punto de Venta, Computerworld Mexico, MacWorld, Mundo Unix, PC World, Windows; **THE NETHERLAND'S** Computer! Totaal, LAN Magazine, MacWorld; **NEW ZEALAND's** Computer Listings, Computerworld New Zealand, New Zealand PC World; **NIGERIA's** PC World Africa; **NORWAY's** Computerworld Norge, C/World, Lotusworld Norge, Macworld Norge, Networld, PC World Ekspress, PC World Norge, PC World's Product Guide, Publish World, Student Data, Unix World, Windowsworld, IDG Direct Response; **PANAMA's** PC World; **PERU's** Computerworld Peru, PC World; **PEOPLES REPUBLIC OF CHINA's** China Computerworld, PC World China, Electronics International, China Network World; **IDG HIGH TECH BEIJING's** New Product World; **IDG SHENZHEN's** Computer News Digest; **PHILLIPPINES'** Computerworld, PC World; **POLAND's** Computerworld Poland, PC World/Komputer; **PORTUGAL's** Cerebro/PC World, Correio Informatico/Computerworld, MacIn; **ROMANIA's** PC World; **RUSSIA's** Computerworld-Moscow, Mir-PC, Sety; **SLOVENIA's** Monitor Magazine; **SOUTH AFRICA's** Computing S.A.; **SPAIN's** Amiga World, Computerworld Espana, Communicaciones World, Macworld Espana, NeXTWORLD, PC World Espana, Publish, Sunworld; **SWEDEN's** Attack, ComputerSweden, Corporate Computing, Lokala Natverk/LAN, Lotus World, MAC&PC, Macworld, Mikrodatorn, PC World, Publishing & Design (CAP), Datalngenjoren, Maxi Data, Windows World; **SWITZERLAND's** Computerworld Schweiz, Macworld Schweiz, PC & Workstation; **TAIWAN's** Computerworld Taiwan, Global Computer Express, PC World Taiwan; **THAILAND's** Thai Computerworld; **TURKEY's** Computerworld Monitor, Macworld Turkiye, PC World Turkiye; **UNITED KINGDOM's** Lotus Magazine, Macworld, Sunworld; **UNITED STATES'** AmigaWorld, Cable in the Classroom, CD Review, CIO, Computerworld, Desktop Video World, DOS Resource Guide, Electronic News, Federal Computer Week, Federal Integrator, GamePro, IDG Books, InfoWorld, InfoWorld Direct, Laser Event, Macworld, Multimedia World, Network World, NeXTWORLD, PC Games, PC Letter, PC World Publish, Sumeria, SunWorld, SWATPro, Video Event; **VENEZUELA's** Computerworld Venezuela, MicroComputerworld Venezuela; **VIETNAM's** PC World Vietnam

 The text in this book is printed on recycled paper.

About the Author

Dan Gookin got started with computers back in the post slide rule age of computing: 1982. His first intention was to buy a computer to replace his aged and constantly breaking typewriter. Working as slave labor in a restaurant, however, Gookin was unable to afford the full "word processor" setup and settled on a computer that had a monitor, keyboard, and little else. Soon his writing career was underway with several submissions to (and lots of rejections from) fiction magazines.

The big break came in 1984 when he began writing about computers. Applying his flair for fiction with a self-taught knowledge of computers, Gookin was able to demystify the subject and explain technology in a relaxed and understandable voice. He even dared to add humor, which eventually won him a column in a local computer magazine.

Eventually Gookin's talents came to roost as he became a ghost writer at a computer book publishing house. That was followed by an editing position at a San Diego computer magazine, at which time he also regularly participated on a radio talk show about computers. In addition, Gookin kept writing books about computers, some of which became minor bestsellers.

In 1990, Gookin came to IDG Books with a book proposal. From that initial meeting unfolded an idea for an outrageous book: a long overdue and original idea for the computer book for the rest of us. What became *DOS For Dummies* blossomed into an international bestseller with hundreds of thousands of copies in print and many foreign translations.

Today, Gookin still considers himself a writer and computer "guru" whose job it is to remind everyone that computers are not to be taken too seriously. His approach to computers is light and humorous yet very informative. He knows that the complex beasts are important and can help people become productive and successful. Yet Gookin mixes his knowledge of computers with a unique, dry sense of humor that keeps everyone informed — and awake. His favorite quote is, "Computers are a notoriously dull subject, but that doesn't mean I have to write about them that way."

Gookin's titles for IDG Books include the best-selling *DOS For Dummies*, 1st and 2nd Editions; *WordPerfect For Dummies* and *WordPerfect 6 For Dummies*; *PCs For Dummies*; *Word For Windows For Dummies*; and the *Illustrated Computer Dictionary For Dummies*. All told, he's written over 30 books on computers and contributes regularly to *DOS Resource Guide*, *InfoWorld*, and *PC Computing Magazine*. Gookin holds a degree in Communications from the University of California, San Diego, and currently lives with his wife and boys in the as-yet-untamed state of Idaho.

Credits

Publisher
David Solomon

Managing Editor
Mary Bednarek

Acquisitions Editor
Janna Custer

Production Manager
Beth Jenkins

Senior Editors
Sandy Blackthorn
Diane Graves Steele

Production Coordinator
Cindy L. Phipps

Acquisitions Assistant
Megg Bonar

Editorial Assistant
Tricia R. Reynolds

Editors
Corbin Collins
Jeremy Judson
Barbara Potter

Technical Reviewer
Stuart J. Stuple

Production
Tony Augsburger
Valery Bourke
Mary Breidenbach
Sherry Gomoll
Drew R. Moore
Gina Scott

Proofreader
Charles A. Hutchinson

Indexers
Anne Leach
Sherry Massey

Book Design and Production
University Graphics

Say What You Think!

Listen up, all you readers of IDG's international bestsellers: the one — the only — absolutely world-famous ...*For Dummies* books! It's time for you to take advantage of a new, direct pipeline to the authors and editors of IDG Books Worldwide.

In between putting the finishing touches on the next round of ...*For Dummies* books, the authors and editors of IDG Books Worldwide like to sit around and mull over what their readers have to say. And we know that you readers always say what you think.

So here's your chance. We'd really like your input for future printings and editions of this book — and ideas for future ...*For Dummies* titles as well. Tell us what you liked (and didn't like) about this book. How about the chapters you found most useful — or most funny? And since we know you're not a bit shy, what about the chapters you think can be improved?

Just to show you how much we appreciate your input, we'll add you to our Dummies Database/Fan Club and keep you up to date on the latest ...*For Dummies* books, news, cartoons, calendars, and more!

Please send your name, address, and phone number, as well as your comments, questions, and suggestions, to our very own ...*For Dummies* coordinator at the following address:

...For Dummies Coordinator
IDG Books Worldwide
3250 North Post Road, Suite 140
Indianapolis, IN 46226

IDG BOOKS

(Yes, Virginia, there really is a ...*For Dummies* coordinator. We are not making this up.)

Please mention the name of this book in your comments.

Thanks for your input!

Contents at a Glance

Cartoons at a Glance

By Rich Tennant

page 81

page 7

page 60

page 80

page 171

page 319

page 301

page 293

page 327

page 247

More Cartoons at a Glance

By Rich Tennant

page 183

page 5

page 112

page 36

page 207

page 326

page 153

page 320

page 92

Table of Contents

Part VI: DOS Reference for Real People

Introduction

● ●

*W*elcome to *DOS For Dummies,* 2nd Edition, a book with 80 percent less fat than other books on DOS. In fact, the idea here is simple: You're a smart person but a DOS dummy — and you have absolutely no intention of ever becoming a DOS wizard. You don't want to learn anything. You don't want to be bored by technical details or background fodder. All you need to know is that single answer to one tiny question, and then close the book and be on with your life. This is the book you're looking for.

This book covers 100 percent of the things you'll be doing with your computer. All the common activities, the daily chores, and the painful things that go on with a computer; they're all described here — in English — and in a style I believe you'll find engaging, informative, and, at socially correct times, humorous.

About This Book

This book isn't meant to be read from front to back. It's more like a reference. Each chapter is divided into sections, each of which has self-contained information about doing something in DOS. Typical sections include:

Changing Disks

Typing at the Prompt

Deleting a Group of Files

"My Keyboard Beeps at Me!"

Formatting a Disk

Finding a Lost File

"Where Am I?"

You don't have to remember anything in this book. Nothing is worth memorizing. You'll never "learn" anything here. The information here is what you need to know to get by, and nothing more. And if any new terms or technical descriptions are offered, you'll be alerted and told to ignore them.

How to Use This Book

This book works like a reference: You start by looking up the topic that concerns you either in the table of contents or the index. That will refer you to a specific section in the book. In that section you'll read about doing whatever it is you want to do. Some special terms may be defined, but usually you'll be directed elsewhere if you want to learn about the terms.

If you're supposed to type something in, it will appear in the text as follows:

```
C> TYPE IN THIS STUFF
```

Always press Enter after you're told to type something in. In case you're baffled, a description of what you're typing usually follows (with explanations of the more difficult stuff).

Occasionally, you may have to type in something specific to your system. When that happens, you'll be told how to type in the command particular to your situation, usually by replacing the bogus filename in this book with the name of a file on your disk. Nothing is ever harder than that.

If you need more information, you'll be directed to that chapter and section. And if anything goes wrong, you'll be told what to do and how to remedy the situation.

At no time does this book direct you back to the DOS manual (yuck!). However, if you're into learning about DOS, I recommend a good tutorial on the subject. This book will help you after the tutorial is done, but it's not meant as a substitute. (And you definitely don't need to read a tutorial before using this book. Just having to breathe the same air as a computer qualifies you!)

What You're Not to Read

Several sections offer extra information and background explanations. (I just couldn't resist — after writing 20-odd books on using computers, I can't compel myself not to do this.) Those sections are clearly marked and you can quickly skip over them, as you please. Reading them will only increase your knowledge of DOS — and that's definitely not what this book is all about.

Foolish Assumptions

I'm only going to make one assumption about you: You have a PC and you "work" with it somehow. Furthermore, I'll assume that someone else set up your computer and may have even given you a few brief lessons. It's nice to have someone close by (or on the phone) who can help. But you know how unbalanced they can become when you ask too many questions (and don't have enough M&Ms or Doritos handy).

How This Book Is Organized

This book has six major parts, each of which is divided into two or more chapters. Inside each chapter are individual sections that pertain, for the most part, to the chapter subject. Aside from that level of organization, the book is really modular. You can start reading at any section. However, thanks to tradition, I've outlined the entire book below:

PART I: The Absolute Basics

This part of the book contains general background information on using the computer. It's the primary stuff, the things you'll be doing most of the time or have questions about.

PART II: The Non-Nerd's Guide to PC Hardware

Getting into a dissertation on the workings of a microchip is way beyond the scope of this book. However, I do provide a discussion on how to use the hardware — with special emphasis on not dropping it on your foot. There is also a section on how to use a printer, which I find lacking in most other books on DOS.

PART III: The Non-Nerd's Guide to PC Software

Software is what makes your PC go, supposedly. This part of the book contains information about using software and working with disks and files. There is (and I apologize for this) a special section on buying and installing software. Hopefully, you'll have someone else do that for you.

PART IV: Yikes! (Or Help Me Out of This One!)

Good news: Computers don't blow up in your face like they do on 1960s TV shows. Bad news: They still do horrible things that will leave your mouth agape and your soul yearning. The chapters here will soothe your savage nerves.

PART V: The Part of Tens

This part of the book contains several chapters that are lists of ten-somethings: Ten common beginner mistakes; ten things you should avoid; ten things to throw at the computer. You get the idea.

PART VI: DOS Reference for Real People

DOS is nothing more than a mean computer program, plus about 50 or so unusual commands and cryptic utterances. They're all listed here in various categories, with descriptions directly relating to how useful or useless the command is.

Icons used in this book

This alerts you to nerdy technical discussions you may want to skip (or read — for that nerd in all of us).

Any shortcuts or new insights on a topic are marked with this icon.

This lets you know what's new with the latest version of DOS (including DOS 6.2).

A friendly reminder to do something.

A friendly reminder *not* to do something.

Where to Go from Here

Now you're ready to use this book. Look over the table of contents and find something that interests you. Just about everything you can do with DOS is listed here. But primarily you'll be spending your time in what Chairman Mao called "the great struggle with the computer." Do so. Toil, toil, toil. But when you hit a speed bump, look it up here. You'll have the answer and be back to work in a jiffy. Or half a jiffy if you're a quick reader.

Good luck! And keep your fingers crossed (especially if you're ever coerced into using the MSBACKUP program)!

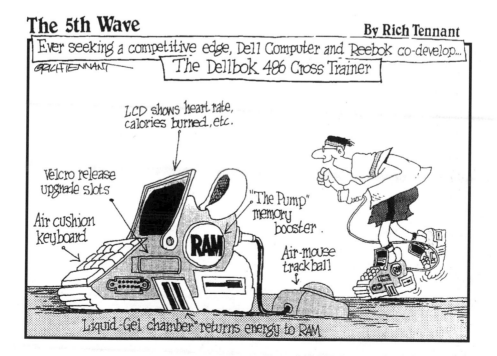

Part I
The Absolute
Basics

"RESPONSE TIME SEEMS A BIT SLOW."

In this part...

Don't you hate those books that have long-winded, stuffy introductions? The wannabe aristocratic author goes on and on about his or her qualifications, rattles off the names of the 400 or so people who helped with this or that, and mentions his or her relatives and loved ones, the entire computer industry, the lone soul who really wrote the book, and so on. These books are usually long on hot air, short on facts, and big on margins. But all you want to do is get to work (and could care less about the author's loftiness).

Well, this book is different.

Chapter 1
Getting On with It

· ·

In This Chapter

▶ Turning the computer on

▶ Examining the screen

▶ Turning the computer off

▶ Leaving a PC on all the time

▶ Resetting the computer

· ·

*T*urning something on or off shouldn't be complicated. The computer is really no exception. You'd think the computer would have several on and off switches to make it tough on you. But no. There's just that one Big Red Switch (which is often neither big nor red) that makes the PC stop or go. Yet that's not such a big deal. What is a big deal is when and how to throw the switch and all the stuff that happens in between. That's what'll make you chew your nails down to the nub or hop on one foot and chant a mantra while clutching your New Age Power Crystal in one hand and flipping the power switch with the other.

Well, fret no more. This chapter covers the basics of turning a computer on, covers what happens just after that, and then doesn't neglect the important stuff about turning the computer off. There's a lot that happens as Mr. PC begins his sun-shiney day. Oh — and this is definitely worth $6 of the cover price — this chapter tells you the lowdown on whether or not you can let your computer run all day and all night without ever turning it off. (Yes, it can be done.)

Turning the Computer On

Turning a computer on is as easy as reaching around the side for the big red switch and flipping that switch to the ON position. Some computers may have their big red switch in front. Still other computers may even paint their big red switch brown or fawn-white.

In keeping with the international flavor of computing, computer companies have done away with the illogical, Western-culture-dominated habit of putting the words *ON* and *OFF* on their on/off switches. To be more politically correct, the PC's switch uses a bar for ON and a circle for OFF (see Figure 1-1). You can remember this by keeping in mind that a circle is an O and the word OFF starts with the letter *O*. (Then again, so does ON. Just don't think about it.) Actually, you can hear the computer when it's on, so if the computer isn't making a noise, flip the power switch in the other direction. The following is a short list of problems (and their solutions) you may experience when starting up:

- ✔ If you can't see the screen, wait awhile. If nothing appears, turn the monitor on.

- ✔ If the computer won't turn on, check to see whether it's plugged in. If it still doesn't come on, refer to Chapter 19, "When It's Time to Toss in the Towel (and Call a DOS Guru)."

- ✔ If the computer does something unexpected, or if you notice that it's being especially unfriendly, first panic. Then turn to Part IV of this book to figure out what went wrong.

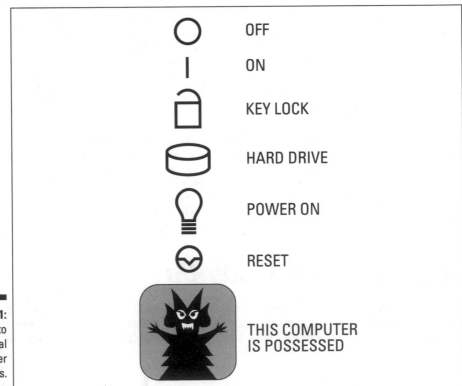

Figure 1-1:
Guide to
international
computer
symbols.

Technical stuff to ignore

Your computer has many plug-inable items attached to it. Each one of them has its own on/off switch. There is no specific order to follow when turning any equipment on or off, though an old adage was, "Turn the computer box on last." Or was it first? I don't know. But one way to save the hassle is to buy a power strip or one of the fancier computer power-control-center devices. You plug everything into it and then turn on the whole shebang with one switch.

Look! Up on the screen!

Is it a burp? Is it a pain? No! It's text. Lots of text. Confusing and bewildering text you see every time you start your PC. Ooops! There, a copyright notice flew by. Yes, it *scrolled* right up the screen and out of view. Sure hope it wasn't important.

Starting the computer with the Big Red Switch is the mechanical part. What you're starting is the computer hardware, which is really nothing but a lot of heavy, cold, and calculating electronic junk that the cat likes to sleep on. Eventually, DOS will come into being, your computer's software part. DOS breathes its breath of life into your PC's nostrils and tosses up text on the screen like the start of a Star Wars movie but without any consequential background information or plot.

You should douse your concerns about all that *start-up* text. Keep in mind that it's just DOS starting and making your PC comfy-cozy for you to work. Computer scientists and the PC Wizards can fret over what it all means. Eventually, the text will stop its maniacal crawl, and you'll be faced with a *command prompt* or some menu system or Windows and can then get on with your work.

✔ The first thing you see before any text will be the words `Starting MS-DOS`. Then there's a reluctant pause as the computer thinks, "Not this again." Then the rest of the text appears. This message does not appear if you're using an older version of DOS.

✔ The nuances of computer hardware and software are covered in Parts II and III of this book.

✔ Working at the command prompt is covered in the next chapter.

✔ Yeah verily, even though the next section is titled "Turning the Computer Off," don't do it just yet. Skip ahead to another chapter in this book and read about what you can do when the computer is on and running.

Turning the Computer Off

Sure, turning the computer off is easy: just flip the big red switch. The power goes DINK, the fan softly warbles away, and the hard drive spins to a low hum and then stops.

Attached to these easy-to-handle instructions is the following armada of rules, listed in order of importance:

- ✔ Never turn off the computer when you're in the middle of something. Always *quit to DOS* first. The only time you can safely turn off your PC is when you're at the DOS prompt. An exception to this is when your computer has gone totally AWOL. When that happens, refer to Part IV of this book.

- ✔ If you're running a program such as DESQview, Windows, or Software Carousel, refer to "Black Box Program Rules" in Chapter 15 for more information about turning off the computer.

- ✔ Don't turn off the computer when any drive light is on. Sometimes you may have quit a program, but the computer is still busily storing away information on the disk. Wait for that DOS prompt and then turn the computer off.

- ✔ Wait at least 30 to 40 seconds before turning the computer on again.

- ✔ If possible, try not to turn off the computer more than three times a day. My advice is to leave the machine on all day and turn it off only at night. However, there is a school of thought that recommends leaving the computer on all the time. If that's your cup of tea, refer to the next section.

I Want to Leave My Computer On All the Time

The great debate rages: should you leave your computer on all the time? Well, anyone who knows anything will tell you "Yes." Leave your computer on all the time, 24 hours a day, seven days a week. The only time you should really turn a system off is when it will be unused for longer than a weekend.

Computers like being on all the time. You leave your refrigerator on all night or when you're away on trips, so why not the PC? It won't raise your electrical bill, either.

The only thing you should be careful about is turning the monitor off when you're away from the computer. Doing so avoids the perils of phosphor burn-in, or what happens when a computer is left on too long and retains an image of

Lotus 1-2-3 (or whatever you use a lot) on the screen — even when the system is off. Turning off the monitor while you're away solves this problem.

- ✔ Screen dimming programs (screen savers) are available to "black out" your monitor after the PC has been idle for a given amount of time.

- ✔ If you do leave your computer on all the time, don't put it under a dust cover. The dust cover will give the computer its very own greenhouse effect and bring the temperatures inside the system way past the sweltering point.

Resetting

Resetting your computer is a way to turn it off and on again without having to actually do that (and it's healthier for the PC than kicking the power cord out of the wall, despite the full feeling that gives you). When you reset, you're restarting the computer while it's on.

There are two ways to reset: If your computer has a reset switch, you can push it. (The universal reset symbol is shown in Figure 1-1). Otherwise, you can press and hold the Ctrl, Alt, and Delete keys at the same time. Release the keys. This procedure is known as the three-finger reset, or Ctrl-Alt-Delete ("control-alt-delete").

TECHNICAL STUFF

The reason for leaving your computer on, if you care to know

There are lots of interesting reasons why you should leave a computer on all the time. One is that the initial process of turning a computer on is a tremendous jolt to the system. It's often said that you subtract one day from the computer's life for each time you switch the system off and then on. But who knows?

The truth is, leaving the computer on all the time keeps the temperature inside the box even. When you turn the system off, the electrical components cool. Turn the PC on again, and the components heat right back up. (The system's fan will keep them from getting too hot.) It's that temperature change from turning the system off and on

that causes the damage. After a time, the solder joints become brittle from the changing temperature and they'll crack. That's when the real problems occur. By leaving your PC on all the time — or just by minimizing the times you turn it off and then on — you can prolong its life.

An opposing school of thought claims that although the preceding is true, leaving the computer on all the time wears down the bearings in your hard drive and causes the cooling fan to poop out prematurely. So be nice to your hard drive's packed bearings and turn the PC off once a day. Ack! You just can't win. (I leave all my computers on all the time, if you care to know.)

Now the question arises: When should you reset? Obviously, at any time you're panicked. Personally, I only reset if the keyboard is totally locked up and the program appears to have gone to the mall for some Mrs. Field's cookies and a soda. (Sometimes Ctrl-Alt-Delete doesn't work in these situations, so if you don't have a big reset button, you have to turn the computer off, wait, and then turn it on again.)

The only other time you really need to reset is just to "start over." For example, I was experimenting with a program that made my keyboard click every time I pressed a key. There was no obvious way to turn off this annoying pestilence, so I reset.

✔ As with turning a computer off, you shouldn't reset while the disk drive light is on or while you are in an application (except when the program has flown south). Above all, do not reset to quit an application. Always quit properly to DOS before you reset or turn off the computer.

✔ Remember to remove any floppy disks from drive A before resetting. If you leave a disk in, the computer will try to start itself from that disk.

✔ A less drastic form of getting out of a tight situation is to use DOS's cancel key combination, Ctrl-C. Refer to "Canceling a DOS Command" in Chapter 3.

✔ If you're running a black box type of program (Windows, DESQview, Software Carousel, etc.), refer to "Black Box Program Rules" in Chapter 15 for information about resetting.

Trivial background fodder

A reset is often called a *warm boot*. This is like a cold boot that has been sitting in front of the furnace all night.

Try Ctrl-Alt-Delete first. If that doesn't work, press your reset button. You only need to press it once. If your system doesn't have a reset button, you'll need to turn off the computer, wait-wait-wait, and then turn it on again.

Chapter 2

The PC Hokey-Pokey
(or That's What It's All About)

In This Chapter

▶ Running a program

▶ Using the DIR command — and why

▶ Looking at a file

▶ Changing disks, drives, and directories

*T*his chapter contains a quick summary of some basic computer stuff and everyday things you do on your beloved PC. These items don't collectively fit into any specific category. These are things you may be doing a lot or topics you have questions about. As with the rest of the book, everything here is cross-referenced.

Running a Program

You get work done on a computer by running a program. If you're lucky, somebody's set up your computer so it automatically runs the program you need. Turn on the PC and *zap!*, there's your program. The only time you've got a problem is when something goes wrong and the program *crashes* or it doesn't turn on like it's supposed to. (Or while you were at lunch, Petey from the mailroom came in and played games, leaving you with a C> on your screen to puzzle over.)

If you're on your own and nothing seems to happen automatically, you need to start a program yourself. Here's how:

First, you need to know the program's name. Then you type that name at the command prompt.

For example, WordPerfect is named WP. To *run* WordPerfect, you type **WP** at the *DOS prompt* and then press Enter:

```
C> WP
```

Table 2-1 lists the names of several popular DOS programs and what you type at the DOS prompt to run them. Note that you don't need to type what's listed in the parentheses; those are extra instructions or information about the program.

- ✔ If your program isn't on the list, you'll either have to read the manual to find out what name you type or ask someone who knows. When you find out what name you type, add it to the list in Table 2-1 (that's what the blank lines are for).

- ✔ If your computer is set up to run some sort of menu system, try typing **MENU** at the DOS prompt to run it.

- ✔ Several of the programs in Table 2-1 enable you to type additional information after the program's name: WordPerfect enables you to type the name of the document you're editing; dBASE can be followed by the name of a database program to run. If you do this, remember to place a space between the program's name and any other information that follows.

- ✔ Yes, Quattro Pro and Quicken both have the same name, Q.

- ✔ Other terms for *running* a program include *loading* a program, *launching* a program, and *starting* a program.

- ✔ DOS prompt? Command prompt? See Chapter 3 for the lowdown.

Background information worth skipping

Programs are also known as applications, though the term *application* is more general: WordPerfect is a word processing application. The program is WordPerfect, and its file is named WP.EXE. You type the name of the file at the DOS prompt. DOS then loads that program into memory and executes the instructions.

Under DOS, all program files are named with either a *COM,* an *EXE,* or a *BAT* ending (called a *filename extension*). Don't bother typing in that part of the name at the DOS prompt — and you don't have to type the period that separates COM, EXE, or BAT from the file's name. Refer to the discussion under "Significant Filenames" in Chapter 18 for more information (worth skipping).

Table 2-1	Popular PC Program Names
Program	*Name to Type/Instructions*
dBASE	DBASE
DESQview	DV (Press the Alt key to run other programs.)
Excel	WIN EXCEL (This program should really be run from Windows.)
GrandView	GV
Harvard Graphics	HG
LapLink	LL
Lotus 1-2-3	123
Magellan	MG
MultiMate	WP
PC Tools	PCSHELL
ProComm Plus	PCPLUS
Prodigy	PRODIGY
Q&A	QA
Quattro Pro	Q
Quicken	Q
SideKick	SK
Ventura Publisher	VP
Windows	WIN
Word	WORD (The non-Windows Word — Word for MS-DOS)
Word for Windows	WIN WINWORD (This program should really be run from Windows.)
WordPerfect	WP
WordStar	WS

The DIR Command

The most popular DOS command is DIR, which displays on the screen a list of files on disk. This is how you can find which programs and data files are located on a disk. DIR is especially helpful if you're missing something; it will help you locate that document or spreadsheet you were recently working on.

To see a list of files, type **DIR** at the DOS prompt and press Enter:

```
C> DIR
```

If the list is too long, you can type the following DIR command:

```
C> DIR /P
```

The /P makes the listing pause after each screenful of files. (Remember, "Wait for the P.")

To see a list of filenames only, type the following DIR command:

```
C> DIR /W
```

The /W means wide, and it gives you a five-column name-only list.

If you want to see the files on a floppy drive, follow the DIR command with the letter of the floppy drive:

```
C> DIR A:
```

Here, DIR is followed by A:, indicating that it should list files on any disk in that drive. (There should be a disk in the drive before you use that command.) If you want to find out which files are on drive B, for example, substitute B: for A:.

- ✔ You can use the DIR command to find files by name, as well as locate files in other *subdirectories* on disk. Refer to Chapter 17 for information on subdirectories.

- ✔ The output of the DIR command shows a list of files on your disk. The list has five columns: the file's name, the file's extension (part of the name), the file's size (in bytes or characters), the date the file was created or last modified, and the time of the last modification.

- ✔ For additional information on hunting down lost files, refer to "Name that File!" in Chapter 18. (You can find even more information on the DIR command in Chapter 18.)

> ✔ In MS-DOS 6.2, large values are displayed complete with handy, chunkifying commas. Older versions of DOS just display big values as one long chunk-o-numbers.

Tech tidbits to skip

The DIR command's output may throw you. When you want to name a specific file, you glue both the file's name and extension together with a period. For example, the following is how a file may look in the DIR command's display:

```
LETTER    DOC    2,560    04-19-94    2:49p
```

However, the name of the file is really:

```
LETTER.DOC
```

The DIR command spaces out the name and extension to line everything up into columns. If you don't want to see files listed in this format, try the following DIR command:

```
C>DIR /B
```

And if the names fly by too fast for you to see, try the following instead:

```
C>DIR /B/P
```

Looking at Files

There are two types of files on a PC: *English* and *Greek.* You can use the TYPE command to display any file's contents. You'll be able to read the ones in English (or *ASCII* — see "Fancy jargon section"). The files in Greek — actually in secret computer code, but it might just as well be Greek — are program files or data files or any other stuff you cannot read.

To look at a file, you must know its name. (If you don't know the name, you can use the DIR command; refer to the preceding section.) You type the file's name after the TYPE command and a space:

```
C> TYPE FILENAME.EXT
```

Press Enter to see the contents of the file, which in the preceding example would be FILENAME.EXT. To see the contents of the LETTER.DOC file, for example, you would enter the following command:

```
C> TYPE LETTER.DOC
```

The file is then displayed on the screen.

- ✔ A really simple way to view—and edit—text files is to use the DOS Editor. Skip merrily up to Chapter 16.

- ✔ If you get a `File not found` error message and you're certain that the file exists, you probably mistyped its name. Reenter the command and check your typing. Or you can use the DIR command to verify that the file exists.

- ✔ Text files usually end with TXT in their filename. The DOC ending is also popular, though DOC doesn't necessarily mean it's a text file. Some common text filenames are READ.ME or README or sometimes README.TXT.

- ✔ If the file still can't be found, refer to "Finding a Lost File" in Chapter 18.

- ✔ You won't be able to see all files, even though your application may display them perfectly. These "Greek" files typically contain special codes and functions for the computer, stuff that the program will eat and then spit back at you as non-Greek information. Unfortunately, the TYPE command just isn't that smart.

Fancy jargon section

Files you can see are referred to as *text* or *ASCII* files. These files contain only regular alphabetical stuff, not computer code, and they're typically formatted in a manner that makes them easily displayed by the TYPE command. ASCII is the name of the coding scheme, and what it stands for is not important, but pronouncing it *ASK-ee* is. (Don't call it *ASK-two*, or you'll be pelted with small rocks.)

An easier yet more advanced way

If the file scrolls by too quickly, you can use the following version of the TYPE command:

```
C> TYPE LETTER.DOC | MORE
```

That's a TYPE command, the name of the file you want to type, a space, and the *bar* character, followed by another space and the word MORE. This command causes the file, LETTER.DOC in the preceding example, to be displayed one screen at a time. Press the spacebar to see the next screen.

The secret to this command is the MORE filter, which is just a special program that reads text and then shows it back to you one screen at a time. The prompt `- More -` is displayed at the bottom of the screen, prompting you to press any key for more text. Another format is

```
C> MORE < LETTER.DOC
```

This command has the same effect as the longer version: the file LETTER.DOC will be displayed one screen at a time. Is that command cryptic looking, or what?

Changing Disks

Steps: Removing a 5¼-inch floppy disk from a drive

Step 1. Make sure that the drive light is not on. You should never remove a disk from the drive when the light is on.

Step 2. Open the drive's latch. The disk may spring out a bit, enabling you to grab it. If the disk doesn't pop out, pinch it and remove it from the drive (just as you would snatch a stubborn piece of toast from the maws of an electric toaster — and don't use a fork either).

Step 3. Put the disk into its paper sleeve. Disks should always be kept in these sleeves when they're not in a drive. If you have a disk caddie or storage locker, put the disk (in its sleeve) there.

Steps: Removing a 3½-inch floppy disk from a drive

Step 1. Make sure that the drive light is not on. You should never remove a disk from the drive when the light is on.

Step 2. Push the button below or to the side of the drive. The disk will spring out from the drive (like the computer is sticking its tongue out at you). Pinch it and slide the disk out all the way.

Step 3. Put the disk into its proper storage place. Unlike 5¼-inch disks, you don't have to keep the rugged 3½-inch jobbies in a sleeve.

Steps: Inserting a 5¼-inch floppy disk into a drive

Step 1. Make sure that a disk is not already in the drive. If there is a disc in the drive, remove it.

Step 2. Make sure that the disk drive's door or latch is open.

Step 3. Insert the disk, label side up and toward you. Slide it in all the way.

Step 4. Close the drive door or latch.

Steps: Inserting a 3½-inch floppy disk into a drive

Step 1. Make sure that a disk is not already in the drive. If there is a disk in the drive, eject it — ptooey!

Step 2. Insert the disk, label side up and toward you. (It only goes in one way.) Slide it in all the way. At some point, the drive will "grab" it and take it in the rest of the way.

   ✔ Only access the floppy drive after you've inserted a disk. If you do otherwise, you'll get a DOS error. Refer to Chapter 22 for dealing with that kind of error.

   ✔ Never change a disk while you're using it. For example, wait until you've completely saved a file before removing the disk.

   ✔ If the drive door latch doesn't close, the disk isn't inserted properly. Try again.

   ✔ Keep your disk drive doors open when there isn't a disk in the drive.

   ✔ Never force a disk into a drive. If it doesn't fit, you're either putting the disk in wrong, there is already a disk in the drive, or what you're sticking the disk into isn't a disk drive. (Many times disks get wedged into the space between two drives; don't be embarrassed; even the "pros" do it. In fact, a former editor-in-chief of mine confessed to me in an unguarded moment that he did it and had to practically disassemble his computer to get the disk out!)

   ✔ OK, because sticking a disk between two drives is an issue, take one of those tiny, sticky write-protect tabs that came with your disks and tape one or more over the space between your floppy drives — or just about any other slot on the front of the computer into which you might someday slip a disk.

   ✔ For more information on disks, refer to Chapter 13.

Changing Drives

The computer can only pay attention to one disk at a time. To switch its attention from one drive to another, type that drive's letter followed by a colon. Press Enter to *log to* that drive. (Whichever drive the computer is currently using is referred to as the *logged drive; using* equals *logged* in computerspeak.)

For example, to change from drive A to drive C, type

```
A> C:
```

To change from drive C to drive B, type

```
C> B:
```

A colon always follows a drive letter in DOS.

- ✔ Drive A is always the first floppy drive; drive C is always the first hard drive. A second floppy drive is drive B. Any additional drives in the system are lettered from D on up through Z.

- ✔ On most systems, the DOS prompt indicates which drive you're currently using, or logged to. If it doesn't, refer to "Prompt Styles of the Rich and Famous" in Chapter 3.

- ✔ Don't change to a floppy drive unless there is a disk in that drive. Refer to the preceding section.

- ✔ If you see the message `Drive not found`, that drive doesn't exist on the system. If you know this to be untrue, refer to Chapter 22.

Technical background and other drivel

Using a drive is the same as being logged to it. Any time you're using your PC, you're logged to one drive or another. This is usually reflected in the DOS prompt.

The *drive designator* is how you tell DOS to log to another drive. It's basically nothing more than the drive letter followed by a colon (not a semicolon). Otherwise, the drive letter by itself could be mistaken for a filename or the name of a program or DOS command. So you must specify a colon whenever you're referring to a disk drive.

Even if you don't have a drive B, you can log to it by typing **B:** and pressing Enter. On single-floppy drive systems, drive B is a *phantom* drive. DOS will prompt you to *switch disks* when you change from drive A to drive B and back again. This is helpful when you are working with more than one floppy disk, but generally speaking it can be a real pain in the elbows. (Maybe someday Andrew Lloyd Webber will write an opera about the Phantom B Drive. Then again, maybe not.)

Changing Directories

Changing drives is no big deal. You can see drive A (or drive B if you have it). And you know that drive C is inside the box somewhere, humming away. But changing directories is another matter. That's done using the CD command, but it also involves a bit of techy-speak because the whole idea of directories (or *subdirectories*) isn't as entrenched in reality as the concept of your A and C drives. Therefore, all the changing directory information is handily stuffed into the following, technical section.

Real boring technical details — but read it anyway because you'll get lost if you don't

DOS is capable of dividing disks up into individual work areas, called *directories*. Each disk has one main directory, the *root directory*. The root directory's symbol is the single backslash (\). All other directories on disk are subdirectories of (under) the root directory.

Directories can have directories of their own, which can have even more directories. That is how a *pathname* is created. If your instructions tell you that your files are to be found in the \SCHOOL\DATA directory, that means that the directory DATA is a subdirectory of SCHOOL, which is a subdirectory of the root directory. Note how the backslash is used to separate items:

\	The root
\SCHOOL	The SCHOOL directory under the root
\SCHOOL\DATA	The DATA directory under the SCHOOL directory under the root

This subject is painfully elaborated on later in this book, primarily all over Chapter 17.

Using the CD command

To change to another directory on a disk, you use the CD command followed by the name of the directory:

```
C> CD \WORD\DATA
```

In this example, the CD command changes directories to the \WORD\DATA subdirectory. Note the space between CD and the directory's pathname.

To change to the root directory of any disk, use the following command:

```
C> CD \
```

✔ Directories and subdirectories are work areas on a disk.

✔ For more information on the root directory, refer to the discussion under "The Root Directory" in Chapter 17; for information on pathnames, refer to "What Is a Pathname?," also in Chapter 17.

✔ A longer version of the CD command is CHDIR. Both do the same thing. I use CD because it's quicker to type.

✔ Directory names contain backslashes (\). This is not the same character as the forward slash (/). Refer to the discussion under "Slash and Backslash" in Chapter 10.

✔ The name of the directory typed after the CD command never ends with a backslash, though it may contain several backslashes. Note that not all directory names you type will start with a backslash. (It depends on "where you are" on the disk, which is elaborated on in "Finding the Current Directory" and "The Tree Structure," both in Chapter 17.)

✔ If you see an `Invalid directory` type of error, you may not be entering the correct directory name. Refer to your sources for the correct pathname. Plan ahead: Ask them for the full pathname and type that in after the CD command.

Changing Diapers

Steps: Changing soiled diapers on a wee li'l baby

Step 1. Open and unfold the new diaper. Lay baby wearing used diaper on top of new diaper.

Step 2. Unfasten used diaper. If it's a boy baby, open just a little bit at first because air tends to make junior want to go right then and there.

Step 3. Gather baby's feet and lift. Remove the dirty diaper, wad it up, and — if it was his or her turn to do this — toss it at your spouse.

Step 4. Clean baby.

Step 5. Gently lower baby onto the new diaper.

Step 6. Fasten diaper on baby. Say something cute, such as "Oogie booga do boo." Baby will smile and prepare to soil diaper again.

Chapter 3
Life at the DOS Prompt

• •

In This Chapter

▶ Determining which version of DOS you're using

▶ Using the DOS prompt

▶ Entering DOS commands

▶ Dealing with two common DOS error messages

▶ Reading manuals and books on entering DOS commands

▶ Using the nifty F3 shortcut key

▶ Canceling a DOS command

▶ Changing the DOS prompt

• •

*P*erhaps one of the most disgusting ways to work with a computer is to type secret codes at a hieroglyphic prompt. But let's be realistic. What's the end result of trying to make something too easy? It becomes boring. The DOS prompt may be cryptic, but it's definitely interesting. (OK, and physical torture can be interesting, but that doesn't mean we volunteer for it in droves.)

This chapter contains information about using the DOS prompt. These are mostly tips, though some of the items here will give you valuable shortcuts and make using the prompt — obscure as it is — a bit easier.

Names and Versions

What this book calls *DOS* is really a computer program created by Microsoft. Its version is called *MS-DOS,* short for Microsoft Disk Operating System. The version Microsoft makes and sells to IBM is called *PC DOS,* short for Personal Computer Disk Operating System. Microsoft sells other versions as well. Various computer hardware manufacturers label DOS using their own names: Compaq DOS, Tandy DOS, Wambooli DOS, etc. It's all DOS.

What's the difference? Very little. MS-DOS is a general DOS for everyone. The brand-name DOSs may have certain special programs included, and those programs may only work on specific computers. But generally speaking, all the flavors of DOS are the same. DOS also has version numbers. There have been six major releases of DOS, numbered 1 through 6. Each major release also has its own minor releases: There was DOS version 1.0, 1.1, 2.0, 2.1, 3.0, 3.1, and so on. The minor release number is separated from the major release by a period or dot. Also, the first minor release is zero, not one.

To find out which name and version of DOS you're using, use the VER command:

```
C> VER
```

Press Enter and DOS displays its name and version number.

✔ Aside from being perhaps the simplest and most stupid DOS command, VER can be used to determine which version of DOS is installed on a computer. If you wind up using an alien computer, type **VER** to see which make and model of DOS is installed. That may explain why some DOS commands function weirdly, or why some commands aren't available.

✔ If the version turns out to be 5.0 or higher, see Chapter 5 on the DOS Shell.

Unimportant background info

The term *OEM* is used to describe an enterprise that puts together a computer. IBM, Tandy, Dell, Gateway 2000, AST, Compaq, Zenith—these are all OEMs, or Original Equipment Manufacturers. Each of them may license its own version of DOS from Microsoft and then repackage and sell that DOS under its own label.

Sometimes you'll see subminor versions, typically from OEM versions of DOS. For example, the first version of Tandy DOS for the first Tandy 1000 computer was 2.11.34. That's the second major version of DOS, the 11th minor version, plus 34 tweaks by Tandy.

Usually, a minor release of DOS (or any software for that matter) warrants the printing of a new manual. To get around this expense, and usually for only very slight modifications, you'll see a tiny minor release, such as DOS 4.01. This kind of release number indicates only minor *bugs* have been fixed or subtle features changed.

If you're curious (and you wouldn't be reading this section otherwise), the OEM versions of DOS usually add programs specific to their machines, including their own custom version of the Basic programming language. If you have PC DOS or Compaq DOS, note that the version of Basic supplied only works on IBM or Compaq computers.

The Prompt, or "What Do You Want?"

The DOS prompt is how DOS tells you it's ready for your input, for you to type something, enter information, or just idly sit back and swear at the computer. In this book, the following prompt is used as an example:

```
C>
```

The prompt on your system may look like this:

```
C:\>
```

- ✔ Sometimes the DOS prompt will be called the *command prompt*. Same thing.

- ✔ The letter in the prompt tells you which disk drive you're currently using (or *logged to*). Refer to the discussion under "Changing Drives" in Chapter 1.

- ✔ The greater-than sign (>) is the all-purpose computer prompt. It means "What do you want?"

- ✔ Other variations of the droll DOS prompt exist. Some contain the name of the current directory, some may show the date and time, and some may look like Bart Simpson. (Refer to "Finding the Current Directory" in Chapter 16 for information on the current directory; refer to the FOX television network for Bart Simpson.)

- ✔ You can change your system prompt using the PROMPT command. Refer to "Prompt Styles of the Rich and Famous" later in this chapter.

- ✔ If you have DOS 5 or 6 and use a mouse, you can use the DOS Shell, you lucky dog, and skip a lot of this stuff most of the time — see Chapter 5.

Prompt Error Messages

Two common error messages are produced at the prompt: `file not found` and `bad command or file name`. `File not found` means that the file you've specified doesn't exist. Don't panic; you may have just typed it in wrong. Check your typing. If that fails, refer to "Finding a Lost File" in Chapter 18.

`Bad command or file name` is similar to `file not found`, though in this case the message is really `program not found`. You may have mistyped the name of a program, added a space, or forgotten something. Refer to "Where Is My Program?" in Chapter 20 for additional information on solving this problem.

✔ Individual programs produce their own unique error messages for file not found. They vary in syntax, but they all mean the same thing.

✔ Other error messages are possible at the prompt, some of which will really burn your buns. Refer to Chapter 22.

Typing at the Prompt

You use the prompt by typing after it. All the text you enter at the keyboard appears on the screen next to the prompt. Of course, what you type are DOS commands, the names of programs, or general insults to the computer.

The information you enter at the DOS prompt is the command line, which is an assortment of words, cryptic and English, that direct the computer to do something. Sending that information to DOS is done by pressing the Enter key. Only by pressing Enter is the information sent, which gives you an opportunity to back up and erase or to change your mind and press Ctrl-C or the Escape (Esc) key to cancel.

✔ As you type, the underline cursor on the screen moves forward. The cursor marks the spot on the screen where all text appears.

✔ If you make a mistake typing at the DOS prompt, press the Backspace key to back up and erase.

✔ If you want to discard the entire command line, press Esc. On some computers, the backslash (\) is displayed and the cursor moves down to the next line on the screen. You can start over from there. (Other computers may just erase the line and let you start over.)

✔ I don't need to mention that the DOS prompt is unfriendly. In fact, DOS is arrogant and only understands certain things. When it doesn't understand something, it spits back an error message (refer to the previous section).

✔ On the bright side, there's really nothing heinous you can do at the DOS prompt. Most of the deadly things you can do involve typing in specific commands and then answering Y (for yes). If you accidentally stumble into one of those situations, type N (for no). Otherwise, there's little you can do at the DOS prompt that will damage your PC.

Beware of Spaces!

There are three bad tendencies beginners have when using the DOS prompt: They don't type in any spaces, they do type in spaces, or they type in periods.

Always keep this in mind: The DOS prompt is not a word processor. You don't need to type formal English; punctuation, capitalization, and spelling are often overlooked. So never end a command with a period. In fact, periods are only used when naming files that have a second part or extension.

Spaces are another sticky point. You must stick a space (and only one space) between two separate items. For example:

```
C> CD \FRIDGE\LEFTOVER
```

Here the CD command is followed by a space. You must put a space after CD or any DOS command.

```
C> WP CHAP02.DOC
```

Here the program WP is run. It's followed by a space and the name of a file.

Just as you shouldn't type in too few spaces, don't type in too many spaces, either. In the preceding example, there is no space in the file named CHAP02.DOC. If you're a touch typist, you may have a tendency to type a space after the period. Don't. Always type in a command exactly as you see it listed in a book, magazine, or computer manual.

- ✔ Some books and magazines may use a funny typeface to indicate *the stuff you type in*. This may make it look like extra spaces are typed in a command, typically around the backslash (\) character. Watch out for this potential pitfall!

- ✔ A few DOS commands may end in a period, but only when that period is part of a filename. For example:

```
C> DIR *.
```

The preceding DIR command lists all files that don't have a second part or filename extension. The *. is a legitimate part of the command. This is about the only instance in which a DOS command ends with a period.

- ✔ If you forget to type a space at the proper place, you'll probably get a bad command or file name error message.

Beware of User Manuals and English Punctuation!

Manuals and instruction books often tell you what to type at the DOS prompt. But there is no established convention for doing this.

This book uses the following method:

```
C> VER
```

The DOS prompt is shown followed by the text you enter in a different typeface than the rest of the text in the book. The prompt is always going to be C> in this book, though it may appear in some other way on your screen.

Some manuals follow what you type with the word Enter, sometimes in a bubble or in some other happy typeface. That means to press the Enter key after you type the command; don't type in the word Enter on the command line.

Some manuals list what you type on a line by itself, without the prompt:

```
VER
```

Some manuals include the command in the text — which is where this can get tricky. For example, they may say:

```
Enter the VER command.
```

Here VER is in uppercase, meaning you type it at the DOS prompt. Sometimes it may appear in lowercase, italics, or boldface. The worst is when they put the command in quotes:

```
Type the "DIR *.*" command.
```

In that example, you can gather that you type the DIR command, followed by a space, an asterisk, a period, and another asterisk. You would not type in the double quotes surrounding the command. In this book, the command would be specified as follows:

```
C> DIR *.*
```

So far so good. But when English punctuation rears its ugly head, you may see one of the following:

```
Type the command "DIR *.*".
```

```
Type the command "DIR *.*."
```

The first example is grammatically incorrect: The period is on the outside of the double quote. Of course, the period ends the sentence — it's not part of the command you should type in. The second example is what most computer book editors do to DOS commands. No, the period is not part of the command, but a period on the inside of a quote is grammatically correct in that circumstance.

If you type in the period as part of the DOS command, you'll see one of DOS's inflammatory error messages.

- DOS commands and program names can be entered in uppercase or lowercase. Most manuals and books, including this one, use uppercase.

- No DOS command ends in a period. There are exceptions, but the point here is that if you see a command ending in a period in a manual or computer book, it's probably a part of English grammar and not something you need to type.

- DOS commands contain spaces. Spaces follow the name of the command, separating filenames and any other options typed after the commands.

- The DIR command outputs filenames with spaces separating the name and the extension. When you type a filename at the DOS prompt, a dot separates the name and extension. Do not use spaces.

- No user manual is 100 percent correct. If you type in the command exactly as it's listed and the computer still produces an error, try it again with a space or without a period.

- General information on using your keyboard is covered in Chapter 10.

The Handy F3 Key

The F3 key provides a handy shortcut whenever you need to retype a DOS command. For example, to list files on the disk in drive A, you type the following command:

```
C> DIR A:
```

If the file you wanted isn't on that disk, remove it and replace it with another disk. Then, instead of retyping the same command, press F3. You'll see the same command displayed:

```
C> DIR A:
```

Press Enter and the command is executed a second time.

If this doesn't work, you may have a *keyboard macro* enhancement program operating. In that case, try pressing the up-arrow cursor key instead.

Canceling a DOS Command

The universal cancel key in DOS is Control-C or Ctrl-C. Pressing this key combination halts most DOS commands. In some cases, it may even halt a DOS operation in progress.

To press Ctrl-C, hold down the Ctrl (Control) key and type a **C**. Release the Ctrl key. You'll see ^C displayed on the screen and then another DOS prompt.

- ✔ Always try Ctrl-Break first. You never want to reset — or worse, turn off — your computer to get yourself out of a jam.

- ✔ Applications programs use their own cancel key, which is usually the Esc key. (There are exceptions, however. WordPerfect, for example, uses the F1 key.)

- ✔ The Ctrl-Break key combination works identically to Ctrl-C. Note that the Break key is usually a shared key; you may find the word *Break* on the front of the key instead of the top.

- ✔ The caret or hat symbol (^) is used to denote *control*. So when you see ^C it means Control-C or the Ctrl-C keystroke. Likewise, ^H means Control-H, ^G means Control-G, and so on. Some of these keys have significant meaning, which there's no need to get into here.

Prompt Styles of the Rich and Famous

The DOS prompt is a flexible thing. It can really look like anything you imagine, contain interesting and useful information, and so on. The secret is to use the PROMPT command.

Other books offer you a tutorial on the PROMPT command and how it works. Rather than bother with that, here are some popular prompts you can create. Just type in the command as listed and you'll have your own excellent DOS prompt.

The standard, boring prompt:

```
C>
```

To create the standard prompt, which contains the current drive letter and a greater-than symbol, type in the following command:

```
C:\> PROMPT
```

The informative drive/directory prompt:

```
C:\>
```

The most common DOS prompt shows the current drive, directory, and the greater-than sign. Type in the following command:

```
C:\> PROMPT $P$G
```

The date and time prompt:

```
Wed 7-31-1994
12:34:25.63
C:\DOS>
```

This prompt contains the current date, time, and then the drive and directory information found in the second example. Note that the date and time information is only current while the new prompt is displayed; it's not constantly updated on your screen. Here's the command you should carefully type to produce this prompt:

```
C:\> PROMPT $D$_$T$_$P$G
```

To make your favorite prompt permanent, you need to edit your AUTOEXEC.BAT file and place the PROMPT command into it. This is covered in Chapter 16.

Additional, worthless information

The prompt can contain any text you like. Simply specify that text after the PROMPT command:

```
C:\> PROMPT Enter command:
```

Or the ever popular:

```
C:\> PROMPT What is thy bidding?
```

You cannot directly specify the following characters in a prompt command: less than (<), greater than (>), and the pipe (|). Instead, use the following: $L for less than (<); $G for greater than (>); and $B for the pipe (|).

Because the dollar sign ($) is used as a special prefix, you'll need to specify two of them ($$) if you want $ as part of your prompt. That's OK; when money's involved, greed is good.

The 5th Wave   By Rich Tennant

"IT WAS AT THIS POINT THAT THERE APPEARED TO BE SOME SORT OF MASS INSANITY."

Chapter 4
File Fitness (Stuff You Do with Files)

● ●

In This Chapter

▶ Duplicating a file

▶ Copying a file

▶ Copying a file to the current directory

▶ Copying a group of files

▶ Deleting and undeleting a file

▶ Deleting a group of files

▶ Deleting a file that refuses to die

▶ Moving a file

▶ Renaming a file

▶ Printing a text file

● ●

A file is basically a collection of stuff on disk, usually stuff you want to keep. One of DOS's main duties (right after confusing the hell out of you) is to work with files. For a filing cabinet, this is obvious. Under DOS, it's not.

This chapter is about working with files — duplicating, copying, deleting, undeleting, moving, and printing them — everything you want to know about files.

Duplicating a File

Duplicating a file is done with the COPY command. You need to know the name of the original file and the new name you want to give the duplicate.

Suppose the file you have is named MUSHY.DOC. You want to make a duplicate file named CRUNCHY.DOC. Here's what you type:

```
C> COPY MUSHY.DOC CRUNCHY.DOC
```

A common reason for doing this is to make a backup file of an original. For example, if you work on CONFIG.SYS and AUTOEXEC.BAT:

```
C> COPY CONFIG.SYS CONFIG.BKD
```

Here the file CONFIG.SYS is duplicated and given the name CONFIG.BKD.

Both the original and the duplicate files will have the same contents but different names. This is because no two files in the same directory can be given the same name.

- ✔ If the operation is successful, DOS responds with the message `1 file(s) copied`. If not, you'll most likely receive a `File not found` error message. That's OK. You probably just mistyped the original filename. Try again.

- ✔ To find out which files are on disk, you use the DIR command. Refer to "The DIR Command" in Chapter 2.

- ✔ For information on naming new files, refer to "Name that File!" in Chapter 18. Generally speaking, files can contain letters and numbers. A filename can be up to eight letters or numbers long; you can specify an optional period and up to three more letters or numbers if you like.

If the duplicate file already exists, DOS overwrites it. This happens without any notice. For example, if the file CRUNCHY.DOC already existed, DOS would copy the original file, MUSHY.DOC, over it. Use the DIR command first to make sure that a file by that name doesn't already exist.

MS-DOS 6.2 brings the dawn of a new day, adding some sympathy to the COPY command's wanton destruction of already existing files. With DOS 6.2, if the duplicate already exists, it tells you so:

```
Overwrite C:CRUNCHY.DOC (Yes/No/All)?
```

This means the file CRUNCHY.DOC already exists. Rather than clobber it without so much as a thought, DOS is asking first. My advice is to type N here — N for "No thanks." (Press Enter after typing N.) Then try the COPY command again and use another name for the duplicate.

Copying a Single File

Copying a file is handled by the COPY command. You need to know the name of the original file and the destination, the place where you want to put the copy.

For example, to copy a file to another drive, specify that drive's letter plus a colon:

```
C> COPY OVERTHAR.DOC A:
```

In the preceding example, the file OVERTHAR.DOC is copied to drive A. On drive A, you'll find an identical copy of the file OVERTHAR.DOC; both files will have the same name and contents. To copy a file to another directory on the same drive, specify that directory's pathname. For example:

```
C> COPY OVERTHAR.DOC \WORK\STUFF
```

Here the file OVERTHAR.DOC is copied to the subdirectory \WORK\STUFF on the same drive.

To copy a file to another directory on another drive, you must specify the full pathname, which includes the drive letter and a colon:

```
C> COPY MENU.EXE B:\MAIN
```

Here the file MENU.EXE is copied to the MAIN directory on drive B.

As with using the COPY command to duplicate a file, if another file with the same name exists, MS-DOS 6.2 will ask the `Overwrite (Yes/No/All)?` question. Type N and press Enter. (Refer to the previous section's checklist for more information.) Other versions of DOS? Don't press your luck.

> ✔ If you want to copy a file to the same directory as the original, you must specify a different name. Refer to the preceding discussion under "Duplicating a File."

> ✔ For more information on pathnames and subdirectories, refer to Chapter 17.

Copying a File to You

A short form of the COPY command can be used to copy a file from another drive or directory to your current directory. In this format of the COPY command, you only specify the original file (which cannot already be in the current directory).

For example, suppose the file DREDGE is located on drive A. To copy that file to drive C (your current drive), you would type

```
C> COPY A:DREDGE
```

To copy the BORING.DOC file from the \WORK\YAWN subdirectory to your current location, you can type

```
C> COPY \WORK\YAWN\BORING.DOC
```

✔ Copying a file in this manner only works when you're not in the directory containing the file. Of course, after the COPY command, the file will be in the current directory.

✔ You cannot duplicate files using this command; you can only copy them from elsewhere to the current directory. If you try this command and the file is in the current directory, you'll get a `File cannot be copied onto itself` error message.

✔ For more information on directories, refer to Chapter 17; information on the *current directory* is offered in the section "Finding the Current Directory" in that chapter.

Copying? Duplicating? What's the diff and why should I care?

True, copying and duplicating a file are the same thing. In both instances, you have two copies of the same file, each containing the same information. The difference is only in the vernacular: A duplicated file is usually on the same drive in the same directory and has a different name. A copied file is usually created on another drive or in another directory.

Note that you can copy a file with a different name, which is like duplicating it. For example:

```
C> COPY SILLY.DOC A:DROLL.DOC
```

Here, SILLY.DOC is copied to drive A — but it's given a new name, DROLL.DOC.

Copying a Group of Files

You can copy more than one file with a single COPY command. This is done by using *wildcards*.

The * wildcard replaces a group of characters in a filename.

The ? wildcard replaces a single character in a filename.

For example, if you want to copy all files with the DOC extension to drive A, you would use the following command:

```
C> COPY *.DOC A:
```

Here the *.DOC matches all files ending in DOC: BABY.DOC, EYE.DOC, EAR.DOC, WHATSUP.DOC, and so on. Note that both the period and the DOC ending are specified after the asterisk. They are copied to drive A, as noted by the A:.

To copy all files, use the *.* (star-dot-star, which is less of a tongue twister than asterisk-period-asterisk) wildcard:

```
C> COPY *.* A:
```

This command is commonly used when you are copying all the files from the floppy drive to your hard drive:

```
C> COPY A:*.*
```

In this example, you're copying the files *to you* from the floppy drive. (Refer to the previous section for the gory details.)

The ? wildcard is used to represent a single character in a filename. For example, assume you had ten chapters in a book, named CHAP01.DOC through CHAP10.DOC. You can copy them to drive A using the following command:

```
C> COPY CHAP??.DOC A:
```

- ✔ For more information on wildcards, refer to the section starting "Wildcards (or Poker Was Never This Much Fun)" in Chapter 18.
- ✔ Refer to Chapter 17 for information on the current directory and pathnames.

Deleting a File

Deleting a file is done with the DEL command. You follow DEL with the name of the file you want to delete:

```
C> DEL SAMPLE.BAK
```

There is no feedback; the DEL command is like the midnight assassin, silent and quick.

If the file you're deleting isn't in the current directory, you must specify a drive letter and colon or a pathname:

```
C> DEL A:MEMO
```

Here the file MEMO is deleted from drive A.

```
C> DEL \WP51\DATA\XMASLIST.93
```

Here the file XMASLIST.93 is deleted from the \WP51\DATA directory.

- ✔ Never delete any file named COMMAND.COM. While you're at it, don't delete any file in your DOS directory. If you're using MS-DOS 6 and DoubleSpace, never ever delete any file that starts with DBLSPACE.

- ✔ Be careful with this command! Delete files you've created, files you know about, and files you've copied. Don't go on a spiteful fit of vengeance and delete files whose purpose you don't know.

- ✔ The ERASE command can also be used to delete files. ERASE and DEL are exactly the same command and do the same things. (I know, it's redundant. But that's what you should expect from DOS.)

- ✔ If the file doesn't exist, you'll see a File not found error message.

- ✔ Information on using pathnames is covered in Chapter 17.

Extra verbiage on why you would want to delete files

Deleting a file with the DEL command seems like a drastic thing to do — especially when you've invested all that time in creating the file. But there are reasons. The first is to clean up space. Some files may contain unnecessary copies of information; some files may be old versions or BAK (backup) duplicates. Deleting them gives you more space.

Zapping extra files is also a part of disk maintenance or "housekeeping." If you've ever created a TEMP, KILL, or JUNK file, you'd use the DEL command to delete them. (Oh, TEMP, KILL, or JUNK may contain information you had to save to disk but now no longer need — stuff like today's bets at the track, the rough draft of your letter to your congressperson, or that second copy of the books before the auditor comes.)

Deleting a Group of Files

To delete more than one file at a time — truly massive, wholesale slaughter — you use the DEL command with wildcards. This can get nasty.

The * wildcard replaces a group of characters in a filename.

The ? wildcard replaces a single character in a filename.

For example, to delete all files with UP as their second part (the extension), you would use the following command:

```
C> DEL *.UP
```

In this example, *.UP matches all files ending in UP, such as FED.UP, SHUT.UP, THROW.UP, and so on. Note how both the period and the UP ending are specified after the asterisk.

As with deleting a single file, the feedback from this command is nil. Yes, even as a mass murderer, DEL makes no noise.

An exception to DEL's silence is when you use the *.* wildcard. Because this deletes all files in the directory, something must be said:

```
C> DEL *.*
```

DOS will heed you with the following message:

```
All files in directory will be deleted! Are you sure (Y/N)?
```

Don't be too quick to press Y here. Ask yourself, "Am I certain I want to ruth-lessly destroy those innocent files?" Then, with a demented "yes" gurgling from your lips, press **Y** and Enter. Boom! The files are gone.

- For more information on wildcards, refer to "Wildcards (or Poker Was Never This Much Fun)" in Chapter 18.

- You can also delete groups of files on other drives and in other directories. Wow! Run amok! But be sure to specify the proper locations for the files, disks, and pathnames as needed.

The File! I Cannot Kill It!

Suppose that one day, when you're feeling rather spiteful, you decide to delete that useless BARNEY.LUV file. You type the following with wicked staccato fingers:

```
C> DEL BARNEY.LUV
```

But upon pressing Enter, you see that DOS tells you `Access denied`. Ha! Will that spoil your mood, or what?

Some background stuff I shouldn't tell you about ATTRIB

The ATTRIB command is used to modify special features of a file that are called *attributes*. One of these attributes is the *read-only* attribute. When a file is marked as read-only, you can only read from the file. Any attempt to modify it, rename it, or delete it will be met with an `Access denied` error message.

To make a file or group of files read-only, the ATTRIB command is used with a +R:

```
C> ATTRIB NOKILL.ME +R
```

In this example, the file NOKILL.ME will be read-only protected. Of course, the protection offered here is minimal: Any dolt can use the ATTRIB command to remove the read-only protection and delete the file. Go figure.

Generally speaking, when you see `Access denied`, it means that someone somewhere doesn't want you to delete the file. There are some very important files on your system. Some may not have names obvious to you. So it's never a good idea to go out stomping on files like a kid through a flower bed. Tsk, tsk, tsk.

Shhh! (Whisper this if you're reading aloud.) If you really want to delete the file, you must first type the following, using the proper filename or wildcard:

```
C> ATTRIB BARNEY.LUV -R
```

That's the ATTRIB command, followed by the name of the file, space, then a minus sign (–), and an R. There cannot be a space between the minus sign and the R.

By pressing Enter, you're removing the "access" protection from the file(s). You can now delete it (or them):

```
C> DEL BARNEY.LUV
```

Need I mention it again? Files are protected for a reason. Only use the ATTRIB and –R when you badly want to delete a file.

Undeleting a File

One of the miracles of DOS 6 — and version 5 as well — is that it enables you to undelete a file you've just — whoops! — deleted. Now I'll be clear about this: Just because you can undelete a file doesn't mean you should be sloppy with the DEL command. But if you ever are sloppy (and who isn't?), you have the UNDELETE command to save you.

Suppose you've just razed the BUBBLE.POP program. Upon realizing this grievous mistake, you type the following:

```
C> UNDELETE BUBBLE.POP
```

Essentially, the UNDELETE command is the opposite of the DEL command. You simply substitute UNDELETE for DEL to snatch the file(s) back.

After pressing Enter, DOS displays some interesting and complex statistics. I have no idea what all that means, but it sure is impressive. (Read it aloud over the phone to a friend, and he or she is certain to think you're a computer genius.)

UNDELETE displays the file's name and whether or not it can be undeleted. If so, you'll be asked if you want to undelete the file. Press **Y**. Furthermore, you will need to supply the first letter of the filename.

You can also use the UNDELETE command with wildcards. For example:

```
C> UNDELETE *.*
```

You'll see the names of all recoverable files in the directory (or those that match the wildcard you've entered). Press **Y** to undelete each as you're prompted. You'll have to specify the first letter of each filename.

✔ If, for some silly reason, UNDELETE doesn't work, then you should try the following variation instead:

```
C> UNDELETE BUBBLE.POP /DOS
```

✔ Retype the UNDELETE command as you did the first time, but add a space, a slash, and then DOS (similar to that shown above). Press Enter, and UNDELETE should work as advertised.

✔ The sooner you undelete a file, the better. This has nothing to do with time; you can turn off your computer, wait a few weeks, power it back on again, and still be able to undelete the file. However, if you create any new files, copy files, or do any other disk activity, your chances of a full file recovery are remote.

✔ If you see a message that reads `The data contained in the first cluster of this directory has been overwritten or corrupted` — don't panic. That's DOS's friendly way of telling you the file cannot be undeleted. Sorry, but it happens.

✔ You cannot undelete a file if you've copied over it with the COPY command.

✔ For more information on wildcards, refer to Chapter 18; for information on directories, refer to Chapter 17, and UNDELETE herself is covered in blazing glory in Chapter 30.

Additional skippable information

A faster way to undelete files is by specifying the /ALL switch. For example:

```
C> UNDELETE *.* /ALL
```

Here the UNDELETE command attempts to rescue all the files (*.*) in the directory. The /ALL switch tells UNDELETE to go ahead and undelete everything — without prompting you Y or N and asking for the first letter of the filename. Instead, each file is given the pound sign character (#) as its first letter. You can later rename each file on its own if you like.

Moving a File

DOS didn't originally have a MOVE command. No, Microsoft must have thought it redundant. After all, you can use COPY to make duplicates of files, then use DEL to obliterate the originals. So why bother with a MOVE command? Well, guilt must have caught up with them. Starting with MS-DOS version 6.0, there's a MOVE command.

Moving a file with MS-DOS 6

To move a file from hither to thither, you use the MOVE command. To move the file BEKINS.VAN to drive A, you type this in:

```
C> MOVE BEKINS.VAN A:
```

DOS takes the file BEKINS.VAN, copies it to drive A, and then deletes the original. After all, that's what a move operation is: copy and then delete.

- ✔ The MOVE command's song goes like this, *Move this file to there.* You type the place you're moving the file — the destination — last. Files can be moved to another disk drive or another subdirectory.

- ✔ If a file with the same name already exists and you have the pleasure of using MS-DOS 6.2, then the MOVE command will display a warning. For example:

```
Overwrite A:BEKINS.VAN (Yes/No/All)?
```

- ✔ This means a file with the name BEKINS.VAN already exists on drive A. Type N and press Enter, and the MOVE command won't stomp it.

- ✔ Remember: The MOVE command deletes the originals. If you want to copy a file, use the COPY command instead.

Moving a file in the pre-DOS 6 caveman days

When you come to think of it, moving a file is simply using COPY to make a duplicate and then using DEL to delete the original. That's basically a *move* (which would be, sort of, like paying the movers to move your furniture to the new house and then having them dynamite the old one).

The first step is to copy the file to the new location:

```
C> COPY BEKINS.VAN A:
```

Above, the file named BEKINS.VAN is copied to drive A. Now delete the original:

```
C> DEL BEKINS.VAN
```

The original file is gone, but the copy still exists on drive A. That's moving.

- ✔ For more information on copying files, refer to "Copying a Single File" earlier in this chapter.

- ✔ For information on deleting files, refer to "Deleting a File" earlier in this same chapter.

- ✔ Renaming a file is like moving a file in the current directory; you make a duplicate with a new name and delete the original. Refer to "Renaming a File" later in this chapter. Oh, I guess it's next.

Renaming a File

DOS enables you to plaster a new name on a file using the REN command. The file's contents and its location on disk stay the same. Only the name is changed (like they used to do on *Dragnet* to protect the innocent).

For example, to rename CHAPTER1.WP to CHAP01.WP, you can use the following:

```
C> REN CHAPTER1.WP CHAP01.WP
```

The old name is specified first, followed by a space, and then the new name. No sweat.

If the file isn't in the current directory, you must specify a drive letter or pathname. However, the new filename doesn't need all that extra info:

```
C> REN B:\STUFF\YONDER THITHER
```

In this example, the file named YONDER is on the disk in drive B, in the STUFF subdirectory. It's given the new name THITHER by the REN command.

Renaming a group of files is possible — but tricky. No, the REN command cannot rename all files (*.*) individually. It can, however, rename a group of files all at once. For example:

```
C> REN *.OLD *.BAK
```

Here all files ending in OLD are renamed. They'll keep their original filenames (the first part), but each will be given the new second name, BAK.

- ✔ REN has a longer version, RENAME. Both are the same command; you can use either, though REN is quicker to type.

- ✔ For information on file-naming rules, refer to "Name that File!" in Chapter 18.

- ✔ You can only use wildcards with the REN command when you're renaming a group of matching files. Generally speaking, the same wildcard must be used for both the original filename and the new name. For more information on wildcards, refer to "Wildcards (or Poker Was Never This Much Fun)" in Chapter 18.

- ✔ Information about accessing other disks and pathnames is covered in Chapter 17.

Only worth reading if you want to rename a subdirectory

The REN command enables you to rename files. But if you want to rename a subdirectory, forget it! DOS is fussy with the REN command and does not enable you to use it to rename subdirectories. So just give up now. That is, give up with the REN command, because it is possible to rename a subdirectoy, but only with the MOVE command — yes, MS-DOS 6's MOVE command. Weird, but what did you expect?

To rename a subdirectory, use the MOVE command just as you would the REN command. For example:

```
C>MOVE WP51 WINWORD
```

The MOVE command is followed by the name of the first directory, WP51. Then comes a space and the directory's new name, WINWORD.

Printing a Text File

DOS has a command named PRINT, but that command is just way too weird to cover in this book. Instead, you can print any text file using the COPY command. Yeah, it sounds odd — but it works. First, a few rules:

1. **Try the TYPE command on the file first.** If you can read it, it will print OK. If you can't read the file (if it looks "Greek"), the same garbage you see on your screen will be sent to your printer. That's probably not what you want.

2. **Before printing the file, make sure your printer is connected, *on-line*, and ready to print.** Refer to "Going On-Line" in Chapter 11 if you need help.

3. **Use the COPY command to copy the file from your disk to the printer:**

```
C> COPY PRINTME PRN
```

PRN is the name of your printer. After pressing Enter, DOS makes a copy of the file PRINTME (our example) on your printer.

4. **If a full page doesn't print, you'll need to eject the page from your printer.** This is done by typing the following command:

```
C> ECHO ^L > PRN
```

That's the ECHO command, followed by a space and then the Ctrl-L character (the eject page command). You produce that character by holding down the Ctrl (control) key and typing an **L** — do not type in ^L (the hat and L characters). Then type a space, the greater-than symbol (>), another space, and then **PRN**. Press Enter, and a sheet of paper magically ejects from your printer. Neat-o.

- ✔ Text files typically have names that end in TXT. The most common text file is named READ.ME or README. Some files ending in DOC are text files, but that's not always the case; type the file first to be sure.

- ✔ It's usually best to print a file using the application that created it. DOS can only print text files.

- ✔ You can also print any text file using the DOS Editor. Jaunt on up to Chapter 16 for information.

- ✔ For more information on the TYPE command and looking at files, refer to "Looking at Files" in Chapter 2.

- ✔ General information about using a printer with your computer is covered in Chapter 11.

Cosmic drivel about ECHO ^L > PRN

The ECHO command is DOS's "display me" command. Anything you type after ECHO is echoed to the screen. This command is primarily used in batch files, which are quasiprograms written by advanced DOS users who think they're really cool.

Ctrl-L is a special control character, actually a single character that you produce by pressing the Ctrl-L key combination. On the screen, this character may look like the ankh symbol, but every computer printer sees this as the direct command to toss out a sheet of paper. For laser printers, that's often the only way you can see your work.

The cryptic (very cryptic) > PRN is what's called *I/O redirection,* and it's leagues beyond what's in this book. Basically, the greater-than sign tells DOS to send its output, the Ctrl-L in this case, to another device, something other than the screen.

The named device is PRN, the printer. In the end, the eject-page command (Ctrl-L) is sent to the printer (> PRN) via the ECHO command. And they all live happily ever after.

Chapter 5
Easier DOS: The DOS Shell

● ●

In This Chapter

▶ Starting and quitting the DOS Shell

▶ Changing the display in the DOS Shell

▶ Moving between different parts of the shell

▶ Copying files in the shell

▶ Deleting files in the shell

▶ Moving files in the shell

▶ Renaming files in the shell

▶ Finding a lost file using the shell

▶ Changing from one drive to another

▶ Changing from one directory to another

▶ Running programs in the shell

● ●

DOS comes with an easy-to-use (yeah, right) *shell program*. The word *shell* means that the program insulates you from cold, prickly DOS, keeping you in a warm, fuzzy graphics environment, supposedly making life easier on you. Inside the shell you can do all of the things you could do outside the shell, though everything's easier thanks to the pretty graphics and fun shell-like ways of doing things. OK, so it may not be that easy, but it's free with DOS, so who's complaining?

Remember that all of these functions are particular to the DOS Shell program, specifically the one that comes with DOS version 5.0 and 6.0 The DOS Shell isn't available with MS-DOS 6.2; it's on the "Supplemental Diskette," which you must order from Microsoft. But, what the heck, anything the DOS Shell does can be done using piddly old DOS all by itself just as well. Refer to the other chapters mentioned here for more information.

Starting the DOS Shell

To start the DOS Shell, you type its name at the DOS prompt:

```
C> DOSSHELL
```

Press Enter, and in a few moments you'll see the DOS Shell program on your screen.

The DOS Shell was installed when your computer was first set up for DOS. If you see a `Bad command or file name` error message, your system was probably set up without the shell. Refer to your system administrator or favorite DOS guru if you would like the DOS Shell installed on your PC.

Do You Have a Mouse?

Let's be serious here: You can get the most from the DOS Shell program only if you have a mouse. Things can be done without a mouse, but the shell was really designed with a mouse in mind.

- ✔ If you don't have a mouse, buy one. If you can't afford one, force someone else to buy a mouse for you.

- ✔ This same flawless logic also holds true for Windows; you need a mouse to run Windows. Refer to Chapter 6 for the luscious details on Windows.

Quitting the DOS Shell

OK, you've seen the DOS Shell. La-di-da. To quit the DOS Shell and return back to plain old command-line DOS, press F3.

You can also press the Alt-F4 key combination to quit the shell.

If you have a mouse (and you should), you can click on the File menu and then select the Exit menu item.

If you don't have a mouse but would like to use the menus, press Alt-F to *drop down* the File menu, and then type an **X** to quit the shell.

✔ The F3 key is compatible with the DOS Shell program offered with DOS Version 4.0 and with an older shell program called the Microsoft Manager. The Alt-F4 key combination is compatible with Microsoft Windows, used there to close a window or to quit the Windows environment.

✔ Refer to Chapter 10, "Keyboard and Mouse (or Where Is the 'Any' Key?)" for more information on using a mouse and mouse terminology.

Changing the Display in the DOS Shell

You can look at the DOS Shell in a number of ways, all depending on the horsepower of your computer's graphics. (Refer to Chapter 9 for more information on graphics and the PC's screen.)

Use the mouse to select the Options menu by clicking on it. Then click on Display. If you don't have a mouse, press Alt-O and then type a **D**. What you see will be the Screen Display Mode dialog box, as shown in Figure 5-1. Use the arrow keys to select one of three types of displays: text, graphics, or the number of lines of information on the screen. Click on the OK button or press Enter to see your new screen (see Figures 5-2 and 5-3).

Another way to change the way the shell looks is to change its layout. This is done with the View menu. You activate the View menu by clicking on it with the mouse pointer, or by pressing Alt-V (see Figure 5-4). Then you can select from five views.

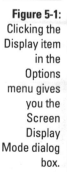

Figure 5-1:
Clicking the
Display item
in the
Options
menu gives
you the
Screen
Display
Mode dialog
box.

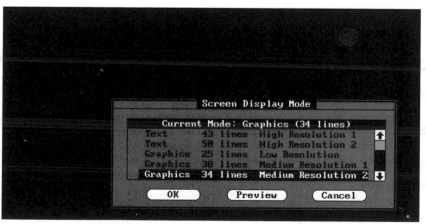

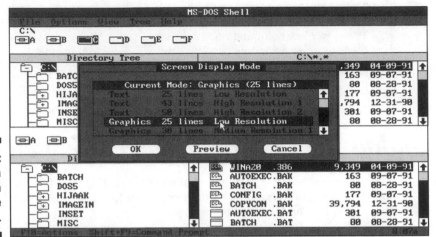

Figure 5-2:
Changing a
screen to a
25-line
display.

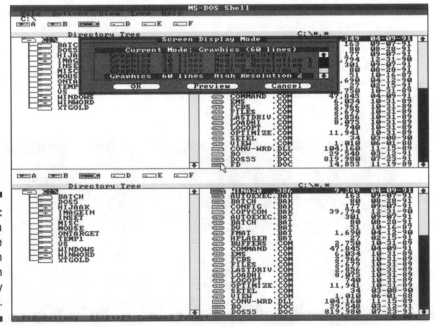

Figure 5-3:
Example of a
60-line
display in
Screen
Display
Mode.

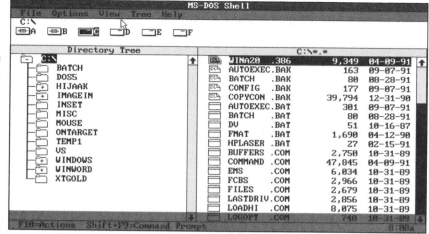

Figure 5-4:
The screen display in Single File List view where only files and directories are displayed.

✔ Single File List: shows only files and directories

✔ Dual File Lists: shows two sets of files and directories (good for copying and comparing information; see Figure 5-5)

✔ All Files: shows only files (good for locating lost files)

✔ Program/File Lists: shows files, directories, and a list of programs to run

✔ Program List: shows only programs to run

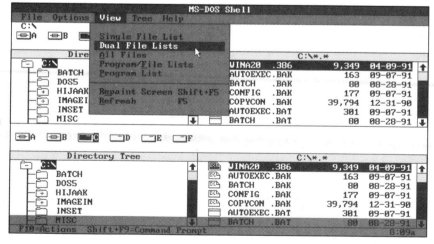

Figure 5-5:
Changing the layout of the shell using the View menu.

Moving between Different Parts of the Shell

You work in only one area of the shell at a time, which can be frustrating because your eyeballs may be trained on one part of the screen, yet the computer is "using" another part. Major pain.

To move between each of the different *panels* in the shell, click the mouse in the appropriate one or press the Tab key until that area's panel is highlighted.

Working with Files

To work with a file using the shell, you must first select the file. This is done by clicking on the file's name using the mouse. That highlights the file's name, letting you know that it's selected.

Copying files

To copy a file using the mouse, first select it by clicking on it. Next, drag the file to the proper subdirectory or disk drive as shown on the screen. A confirmation dialog box appears; click in the Yes button's area.

To copy a file using the keyboard, highlight the file by pressing the spacebar. Press the F8 key to copy the file. The Copy File dialog box appears; enter the subdirectory destination for the file.

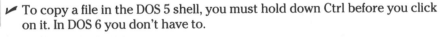

- ✔ Remember that to copy files using the mouse, you must first press the Ctrl (Control) key. If you forget to do this, the file is moved and the original file is deleted.

- ✔ Copying files in DOS is covered in Chapter 4, "File Fitness (Stuff You Do with Files)."

- ✔ To copy a file in the DOS 5 shell, you must hold down Ctrl before you click on it. In DOS 6 you don't have to.

Deleting files

To delete a file, highlight it and then press the Delete key. A dialog box appears, asking if you really want to delete the file. Select the Yes button if you do; otherwise, press Esc.

Deleting files using DOS is covered in Chapter 4, "File Fitness (Stuff You Do with Files)."

Moving files

To move a file, hold down the Alt key and then click on the file. Using the mouse, drag the file to the destination directory or drive on the screen. A confirmation dialog box appears, asking if you want to move the file. Click in the Yes area if you do; otherwise, press Esc to cancel.

If you lack a mouse, then you can copy a file by first selecting it and then pressing the F7 key. Type in a new destination for the file and then press Enter.

> ✔ Moving a file using the DOS command line is covered in Chapter 4, "File Fitness (Stuff You Do with Files)."

> ✔ In DOS 5, you don't have to hold down the Alt key before clicking on the file; just drag it to move.

Renaming a file

To rename a file, highlight it and then select the File menu's Rename item: Click on the File menu using the mouse and then click on the Rename item. Or if you only have a keyboard, press Alt-F and then type **N**.

A dialog box appears, giving you the file's original name plus a cute little box in which to type the new name.

> ✔ Refer to "Name that File!" in Chapter 18 for more information on renaming a file; Chapter 4 has a section titled "Renaming a File" for the basic information on using the REN (rename) command.

> ✔ You can also use the shell to rename a subdirectory — which is something you cannot do at the DOS prompt. Simply highlight the directory name and then choose Rename from the File menu (as just described). Note that the same rules for renaming a file apply to a subdirectory.

Viewing a file's contents

To peek at a file's innards, highlight the file and then press Alt-F to drop down the File menu; type **V** to select View file contents. Alternatively, you can highlight the file's name and press F9. Personally, I find that the F9 key works best.

Note that text files are displayed in a readable format. You can use up- and down-arrow keys, as well as PgUp and PgDn to scroll through the file for your viewing pleasure. (This is much more enjoyable than tangling with the TYPE command. Ick.)

When you're done browsing, press Esc to return to the DOS Shell's main screen.

✔ Unreadable, or "Greek," files are displayed using the horrid — and I hesitate to mention this — *hex dump* format. If this pleases you (or impresses your friends), cool. Otherwise, press Esc and hunt down more readable files.

✔ This feature is only available in the DOS Shell program that comes with DOS 6.

Finding a Lost File

Finding a lost file in the shell is a snap — far easier than any other way of finding a lost file. Here's what you do:

Click on the File menu and then select the Search item. If you don't have a mouse, press Alt-F and then type **H**.

Type in the name of the file you want to find. Press Enter. After a moment, the search results are displayed. The file is listed using its full pathname, which shows you where on the disk it's located. Press Esc to return to the shell.

✔ If the file isn't found, you'll see the message No files match file specifier. Odds are pretty good that the file isn't on that drive. Consider trying another drive; refer to the next discussion, "Changing from One Drive to Another," for details and then try the file search again.

✔ Refer to "Finding a Lost File" in Chapter 18 for methods of locating lost files without using the DOS Shell.

Changing from One Drive to Another

The shell shows you a list of disk drives near the top of the screen. Floppy drive A (and B, if you have it) is listed first, followed by drive C and any other hard drives attached to your PC.

To change, or *log*, from one drive to another, press the Ctrl key plus the letter of that drive. For example, to log to drive D, press Ctrl-D; to log to drive C, press Ctrl-C.

✔ You can also log to another drive by double-clicking on it with the mouse.

✔ Refer to the section "Changing Drives" in Chapter 2 for basic information on logging to another disk drive.

Changing from One Directory to Another

To switch directories, you must make sure that the Directory Tree panel is active. Click in that panel using the mouse or press the Tab key until that area's title is highlighted.

You select a directory by using the cursor keys or by clicking once on a directory's name using the mouse. Any files in that directory are shown in the File panel to the right of the Directory Tree panel.

If the directory has a plus sign by it, it has subdirectories. Click on the directory by using the mouse or press the Plus (+) key to open up the directory and list its subdirectories.

> ✔ Refer to "Changing Directories" in Chapter 2 for some basic information on changing directories; Chapter 17 has lots of information on why and how directories are used.

Running Programs in the Shell

There are three ways to run a program in the DOS Shell. The first is to locate the COM or EXE program file in the list of files, highlight that file, and then press Enter to run the program.

The second way is to select the Run menu item in the File menu. Click on the word File and then select Run using the mouse, or press Alt-F and then type **R** to select the Run item. Then type the name of the program to run in the box provided.

The third way is possible only if someone has configured the shell to show a list of programs at the bottom of the screen in the Main panel. Click in that area using the mouse or press the Tab key until that area is highlighted. Then highlight the name of a program to run and press Enter.

> ✔ You may need someone else to set up the shell to contain a list of programs to run on your computer. This is one of those things beyond the scope of what you need to know, so bug your computer manager or a friend into doing it for you. It really does make running things convenient.

> ✔ Refer to Chapter 15 for some other programs that make life easier for people who hate DOS. Not all of them are free, like the DOS Shell. But many of them are easier to use.

Chapter 6
Breaking into Windows

- -

- -

*N*ext to DOS and its ugly command line, Windows is the most popular way to use a PC. Windows offers a graphical look for your computer and your Windows software. Windows programs are shown as graphics and have menus that enable you to easily see your options and manipulate information using a mouse (computer mouse — no reason to incense the SPCA here). This is a more fun and relaxed way of using a computer than the terse DOS command line (or at least the brochure says so).

I couldn't possibly clue you in to all the facets of Windows in one wee li'l chapter. So to further ease your Windows woes, you can buy a companion book, *Windows For Dummies*, by Andy Rathbone, also from IDG Books.

Starting Windows

Windows should start automatically on your computer. If not, you can start Windows at the DOS prompt by typing **WIN**:

```
C> WIN
```

- Use Windows? Need mouse. Refer to Chapter 10.

- If you want Windows to automatically run each time you start your computer, you need to add the WIN command to the end of your AUTOEXEC.BAT file. Refer to Chapter 16 for details.

- If you get a `Bad command or file name` error when you start Windows, refer to the discussion under "Where Is My Program?" in Chapter 20.

Starting Windows and running a program at the same time

Some programs can only run under Windows. Two of the most popular are Word for Windows (WinWord) and Microsoft's Excel spreadsheet. Normally, you would run these programs inside Windows, which involves hunting down pretty icons and double-clicking with the mouse. However, it's possible to start Windows and load these programs at the same time, saving needless wrist action.

For example, if you want to run Word for Windows at the DOS prompt, type

```
C> WIN WINWORD
```

That's WIN, the command to start Windows, followed by a space and then WINWORD, the program that runs Word for Windows. No mess, no icons, no clicking, no funny after-taste.

To run Excel, type the following:

```
C> WIN EXCEL
```

Again, that's WIN for Windows, a space, and EXCEL to run the Excel spreadsheet.

- Of course, if you're already in Windows, you double-click the proper icon to run the program. These secrets are divulged elsewhere in this chapter.

- Why start Windows this way? If you're only running one program in Windows, this method removes the bother of messing with the Program Manager, the File Manager, and all those goofy games that come with Windows and get in the way from time to time.

Quitting Windows

To quit Windows, first hunt down the Program Manager window — Windows'
main window. After you're there, select the File menu and then choose the Exit
Windows menu item. A small box — a *dialog box* (though it only talks *at* you) —
appears on the screen, proclaiming This will end your Windows session.
Click the OK button to be hurled from the warm, loving Windows environment
back to the hard, cold reality of the DOS prompt.

> ✔ Originally, there was no command to quit Windows. Bill Gates was heard
> saying, "Quit Windows? Why would anyone want to do that?" But eventu-
> ally he relented, and they added the Exit Windows command.

The Beloved Program Manager

DOS has the DOS prompt, and Windows has the *Program Manager.* Like the DOS
prompt, the Program Manager is the point from which you'll start all your
Windows applications and programs. Unlike the DOS prompt, the Program
Manager is a pretty window with lots of fun little icons and other merriment.
The idea here is that fun and merriment make us enjoy using a computer more.
You and I know better, of course.

The Program Manager contains several of its own windows, called *group
windows.* Each group contains similar programs, which are represented by one
or more cute li'l icons (see Figure 6-1).

Q: What's the difference between a DOS program and a Windows application?

A: About $100.

To start a program in the Program Manager, you point the mouse at the proper
icon and then swiftly double-click the mouse button: click-click. Both clicks
have to happen nanoseconds apart, and you shouldn't move the mouse
between them. That runs a program in the Program Manager.

> ✔ Additional information on minimizing icons and working with windows is
> covered in the section "Using a Window's Gizmos" later in this chapter.

> ✔ The icons are tiny and the pictures vague, but you can often tell what
> program the icon represents by reading the name below the icon.

> ✔ The Program Manager's group windows can be minimized to icon size,
> which conveniently shoves them out of the way, preventing *child-window
> overload.* To reopen a minimized group icon, double-click it: zowie! the
> window reappears.

You don't just *run* a program in Windows; you *launch* it. When one of your Windows manuals says to "launch an application," you know that phrase translates into "run this here program." You accomplish this task by double-clicking the appropriate cutesy icon.

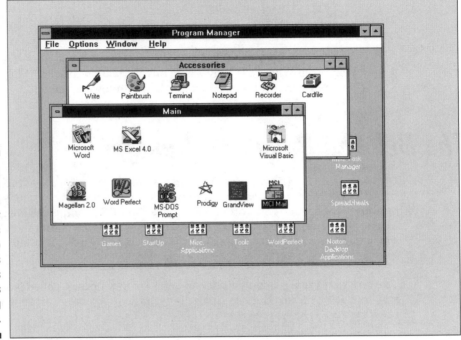

Figure 6-1:
The Program Manager and its group windows and various icons representing applications.

The Treasured File Manager

Unlike with the command prompt, you can't work with files in Windows' Program Manager. To work with files, you need to use the File Manager program, which somewhat resembles the old DOS Shell program that now lies mortally wounded, begging for a bottle of Talking Rain just outside Microsoft's Building 4.

To start the File Manager, look for the File Manager icon in the Program Manager. It looks like a squat, yellow file cabinet stolen from a Dr. Seuss cartoon.

Like the Program Manager, the File Manager contains childish windows. These are *file windows.* You can use more than one file window to see more than one group of files, and you can minimize them into icons at the bottom of the screen (see Figure 6-2).

- Each file window in the File Manager window shows subdirectories on the left side, files on the right, and drive letter icons at the top.

- Refer to the section "Using a Window's Gizmos" later in this chapter for information on controlling a window, closing a window, minimizing, and other graphical gaiety.

- If you install the Windows versions of the special DOS programs, a new menu, the Tools menu, appears in the File Manager.

- For more information on the Windows versions of the special DOS programs, see the section "Special MS-DOS 6 Programs for Windows" later in this chapter.

Changing drives in the File Manager

To look at files on another disk drive, click the letter of the drive you want (at the top of a file window). The subdirectories and files on that drive appear in the window's left and right panels, respectively.

- You can also press the Ctrl key plus a drive letter to see files on that drive. For example, Ctrl-D gives you a peek at drive D.

- If you double-click a drive letter icon, you'll open up a new file window displaying files on that drive. Ta-da, two file windows!

- For more information on changing drives, refer to Chapter 2.

Figure 6-2: The File Manager contains windows with files on the right, subdirectories on the left, and disk drives on the top.

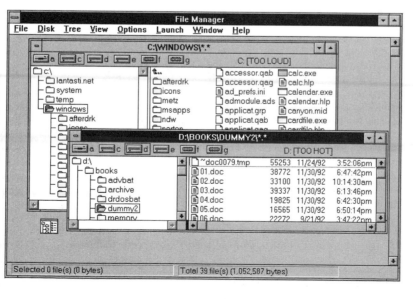

Changing directories

The files displayed on the right side of a file window are all in a particular subdirectory. The subdirectory is highlighted on the left side of the window. To see files in another directory, locate the directory you want in the scrolling list and click it once. The files in that directory are displayed on the right side of the window.

✔ Some directories have subdirectories — directories within directories. To see what they are, select the Tree menu and choose the Indicate Expandable Branches item. That causes little plus signs (+) to appear on the directories that have subdirectories — just like in the DOS Shell.

✔ Directories are marked by a folder icon. If they appear in the file side of the window, they're subdirectories. Double-click them to see what files they contain.

✔ If you double-click a directory with a plus sign, you'll see its subdirectories. Double-click that directory again to *close* it.

✔ To uncoil the subdirectory loop of madness, refer to Chapter 17.

Copying a file

The best way to copy a file in the File Manager is to know where it is and where you want to copy it.

For example, suppose that you want to copy the file 256COLOR.BMP from your C:\WINDOWS directory to a disk in drive A.

Start by opening a file window for drive C and select the WINDOWS directory. In the file side of the window, find the file 256COLOR.BMP. Click that file once with the mouse to select it. The file becomes highlighted. Using the mouse, drag the file's icon to the drive A icon at the top of the window. Release the mouse button when the file is over the icon. Zap! The file is copied.

✔ If you want to copy the file to another directory, drag it to the subdirectory name on the left side of the window.

✔ Another way to copy is to open another file window. For example, you can double-click the drive C icon to open another window and then select a destination directory on the left side of the window. To copy files, drag them from one file window to the other.

✔ Sometimes a window may appear, asking whether you want to copy the file. Click OK.

✔ To copy a group of files, select them all with the mouse: as you click on each new filename, press and hold down the Ctrl key. You can then work with all the files en masse.

Moving a file

Moving a file works just like copying a file. The difference is that you press and hold the Alt key before you drag the file's icon with the mouse. Refer to the preceding section for the lowdown.

> ✔ When moving files, hold down the Alt key before you use the mouse to drag the files.
>
> ✔ Moving a file deletes the original; if you want to duplicate a file, use the file copying methods divulged in the preceding section instead.

Deleting a file

To rub a file out of existence in the File Manager, highlight the offending file's name in a file window. Then squint your eyes and press the Delete key. Unlike DOS, where this action is covert and stealthy, the File Manager pops up a dialog box asking whether you're serious or not. Click OK to delete the file.

> ✔ Wholesale slaughter is possible if you select multiple files at a time: press and hold the Ctrl key as you click each file doomed to extinction.
>
> ✔ You can easily use the Undelete command to reverse the slaughter and restore the deleted files.

Renaming a file

To rename a file, highlight it, select the File menu, and choose the Rename item. Type the new name into the box and click OK.

There are two boxes on the screen for renaming a file. The top one contains the original name; the bottom one is where you type the new name. Remember to type in the bottom box! If you edit the top box, you aren't renaming anything.

Starting a program in the File Manager

You can run programs in the File Manager, which steals a little bit of the Program Manager's pride. Fortunately for the Program Manager, it has all the cutesy icons; the File Manager has terse program names.

To start a program, locate its filename in a file window. In Windows, the program files are all flagged with a rectangular icon that is meant to instill the message "this is a program" in your brain (but fails miserably). After you find the icon, double-click it with the mouse, and the program runs.

✔ Another way to run a program is to select the File menu and choose the Run item. A box appears into which you can type the name of the program you want to run — eerily similar to using the old DOS prompt. (The Program Manager has an identical Run command in its File menu.)

Running a Program in Windows

You have three ways to run a program in Windows. But why bother with the second and third ways when the first is so simple?

Locate a program's icon (little graphical picture) in the Program Manager's window. Double-click that icon. The program runs.

Sadly, this method only works for Windows programs and those applications someone has already installed for you in the Program Manager's window. You're best off if you can browbeat your guru into doing this for you. The following two methods aren't as nice.

The second method is to use the File Manager program, which shows you a list of files on disk. Look for the program names that end in the COM or EXE extension to find the program you want to run and then double-click it. The program starts.

The third method is to type in the program's name, just as you would at the DOS prompt. You do so by selecting the File menu and then Run in either the Program Manager or the File Manager. Type in the full pathname of the program to run it. Hmm, just like DOS.

✔ Note that only Windows-specific programs show up as graphical windows. Everything else looks the same way it does when you run the program under DOS. But don't be fooled: you're still in Windows. (Which also means don't just quit the program and shut off the computer when you're done; return to Windows by typing **EXIT** and quit gracefully from Windows at that point.)

✔ If you're running Windows on a 386 computer, you can press Alt-Enter to make a DOS text program run in a smaller window. (Or maybe it will hang at that point. Give it a try. Take a chance in life.)

Using a Window's Gizmos

Windows is a virtual F.A.O. Schwarz of fun things to play with, stuff to drive you crazy, and interesting toys over which you'll waste colossal amounts of time. There are tiny buttons you *push* with the mouse, graphics that slide and stretch, things to poke, and stuff that drops down. In other words, there are gizmos on the screen, most of which control the way the windows look and how programs in Windows operate.

Changing a window's size

Your windows can be just about any size, from filling the entire screen to too small to be useful, and everything in between.

To make a window fill the entire screen — which is where it's the most useful — click the up-pointing triangle in the window's upper righthand corner. (This changes the up-pointing triangle to a combination up- and down-pointing triangle thingy. Click that button again to restore the window to its original size.)

To turn a window into a doinky little icon at the bottom of the screen, click the lonely only down-pointing arrow button in the upper right corner of a window. This action shoves the window out of the way but isn't the same as quitting. To restore the icon back into a window, double-click it.

When a window isn't full-screen or an icon, you can change its size by "grabbing" an edge with the mouse: Hover the mouse over one side of the window or a corner, press and hold the mouse button and drag the window in or out to a new size, and release the mouse button to snap the window into place.

  ✔ Enlarging a window to full-screen size is called *maximizing.*

  ✔ Shrinking a window down into an icon is called *minimizing.*

  ✔ Positioning a window just so on the screen and then having Windows move it for no reason is called *frustrating.*

Scrolling about

Often, what you're looking at in a window is larger than the window. For example, if a tanned, svelte, and bikini-clad Claudia Schiffer (or Mel Gibson for the ladies) walked by a very tiny window in your wall, you would only be able to see a small part of her or his bronzed form. If you could move the window up and down the wall, you could see more of her or him, but only the same size as the window at a time. This is how *scrolling* works.

To facilitate scrolling a window around, one or two scroll bars are used. The scroll bar is a long skinny thing, with an arrow at either end and an elevator-like box in the middle, as shown in the left margin at the beginning of this section. You use the arrows and elevator to move the window's image up or down or left or right, revealing more of the total picture.

Accessing a menu

Unlike in a DOS program (take WordPerfect — please!), in a Windows application all the commands and whatnot are included on a handy — and always visible — menu bar. It's usually at the top of a window.

Each word on the menu bar — File, Edit, and so on — is a menu title. It represents a pull-down menu, which contains commands related to the title. For example, the File menu contains Save, Open, New, Close, and other commands related to files.

To access these commands, click the menu title. The menu drops down. Then select a menu item or command. If you don't like what you see, click the menu title again to make the menu go away or select another menu.

✔ You can access the menus using your keyboard in two ways: Press the Alt key plus the underlined letter in a menu title. To select a menu item, type the underlined letter. Or you can press and release the Alt key, or just press F10, to access the menus. You can then use the arrow keys to point at the menu item you want.

Closing a window

Closing a program's window is the same thing as quitting the program; you make it disappear. The most common way to close a window is to double-click the long hyphen-thing square in the upper lefthand corner of the window.

Another popular way to close a window is to press Alt-F4. Why Alt-F4? The wind must have been blowing from Utah that day on the Microsoft campus because Alt-F4 sure smells like a WordPerfect command to me.

Another way to close a window — striking because it's obvious — is to select the Exit menu item from the File menu. This also quits the program you're running.

✔ If you close the Program Manager's window, you quit Windows.

Switching Programs

In Windows you can *run* several programs at once. Imagine the productivity boost! Dream of getting two things done at once! Then realize the chaos. Fortunately, you don't really run several programs at once as much as you can switch between two or more at a time without having to stop and restart, stop and restart, over and over.

Although Windows can run more than one program at a time, as a human — and I assume that most of us are — you can only work on the program whose window is up in front or "top o' the pile" or filling the entire screen. To switch to another program, you have several options.

The Quick Way: The quickest way to switch programs is to grab the mouse and click in another program's window, if it's visible. Clicking in a window brings that window to the top of the pile.

Another Quick Way: Shove the current window out of the way, shrinking it down to an icon at the bottom of the screen. This doesn't quit the program; it just *minimizes* it, enabling you to access whatever other windows lie behind it. You accomplish the minimization process by clicking the down-pointing triangle button on the upper right corner of the window.

Nonmousy Ways: If you run out of mouse methods of switching programs, you can try one of three keyboard methods. These are awful to remember, though I'm personally fond of the Alt-Tab key combination approach.

- ✔ **Alt-Tab:** Press the Alt and Tab keys at the same time — but hold down the Alt key and release the Tab key. This displays a little picture box in the center of the screen telling you which program is next. If you don't like that program, keep holding down the Alt key and tap the Tab key again. When you find the program you want, release the Alt key.

- ✔ **Alt-Esc:** Press the Alt and Esc keys at the same time. This switches you to the next program you have active (in the order in which you started the programs). You may have to press Alt-Esc a few times to find the program or window you want.

- ✔ **Ctrl-Esc:** Press the Ctrl and Esc keys at the same time. This summons the Task List window, which shows you a list of the programs currently running. Double-click a program in the list, and you are immediately switched to it. (You can also bring up the Task List by double-clicking the *desktop* or background, away from other windows.)

- ✔ To switch to another window, click it.

- ✔ You can use three key combinations to switch to another window or program: Alt-Esc, Alt-Tab, or Ctrl-Esc.

Minimizing a window by clicking the down-arrow button in the upper righthand corner of the window does not quit that application. Instead, the program is shrunk down to icon size at the bottom of the screen. Double-click that icon if you want to access the program's window.

The General Commands

Windows-specific programs all share common commands. This enables you to easily learn new Windows applications as well as to cut and paste information between two different applications. Ah, yes, more productivity boosting, thanks to Chairman Bill.

Copy

To copy something in Windows, select it with the mouse: Drag the mouse over text or click a picture. This action highlights the text or picture, which means it has been selected and is ready for copying.

After selecting, choose Copy from the Edit menu. The quick-key shortcut for this is Ctrl-C.

- ✔ After your text or picture is copied, it can then be pasted. You can paste into the same program or switch to another program for pasting.

- ✔ When you copy something, it's put into Windows' *clipboard.* You can even look at the clipboard's contents if you start the Clipboard Viewer application in the Program Manager. Unfortunately, the clipboard holds only one thing at a time. Whenever you copy or cut, the new item replaces whatever was already in the clipboard. (Such a clipboard doesn't seem very handy, but Microsoft would like me to remind you here of all the time you're saving in Windows.)

- ✔ Primitive versions of Windows used the memorable Ctrl-Insert key combination as the quick-key shortcut for Copy.

Cut

Cutting something in Windows works just like copying: You select a picture or text and then select Cut from the Edit menu. Unlike with Copy, however, the picture or text you cut is copied to the clipboard and then deleted from your application. The quick-key shortcut for this is Ctrl-X.

✔ You can paste cut text or a picture from the clipboard back into the current application, or you can switch to another application for pasting.

✔ Some old, oddball Windows applications may use the forgettable Shift-Delete key combination as the quick-key shortcut for Cut. (Please don't try to make sense of this.)

Paste

The Paste command is used to take a picture or bit of text stored in the clipboard and insert it into the current application. You can paste a picture into text or text into a picture. Ah, the miracle of Windows.

To paste, select the Edit menu and choose the Paste item. Or you can press Ctrl-V, the Paste key, from the keyboard.

✔ You can paste material cut or copied from any Windows application into another Windows application.

✔ The old, arcane key command for Paste was Shift-Insert — like that means anything.

Undo

The powers at Microsoft have graced us sloppy Windows users with the blessed Undo command. This command undoes whatever stupid thing we just did.

To undo, select the Edit menu and there, the first item on the list, should be the Undo command. How convenient. The key command is Ctrl-Z.

✔ Undo undoes just about anything you can do: unchange edits, replace cut graphics, fix up a bad marriage, and so on.

✔ The old key command equivalent for Undo was Alt-Backspace. This makes no sense to me because the Alt-Shift-Delete-Insert keystroke isn't used by anything, and, heck, let's all go with the Windows programming gang over to Building 16 and have a latté and giggle about end users.

Getting Help

Windows has an incredible help system, and all Windows-specific programs share it. You always activate Help by pressing F1. From there you're shown the *help engine* that enables you to look up topics, search for topics, or see related items of interest, all by properly using your mouse. Here are some hints:

 ✔ You can click green text to see related topics.

 ✔ You can click green underlined text (with a dotted underline) to see a pop-up window defining the term. (Press and hold the mouse button to see the pop-up information.)

 ✔ Browse forward or backward through the help topics to see an index or to look up a specific item.

The *help engine* is its own program. When you're done using help, remember to quit: Double-click on the minus-sign thing in the upper lefthand corner of the window. Also refer to the section "Stopping a Windows Program (Safely)," which is located . . . why, it's next.

Stopping a Windows Program (Safely)

You end a Windows program by choosing Exit from the program's File menu. You can also exit by double-clicking the slot-like doohickey in the upper lefthand corner of the window or by single-clicking said slot-like device and selecting Close from the menu that appears.

Non-Windows programs under Windows must be quit in the same way as you'd quit them under DOS: press F7 for WordPerfect — /, Quit for 1-2-3, and so on.

To exit Windows itself, double-click the minus-like icon thingamabob in the upper lefthand of the Windows Program Manager window. Answer OK to the prompt. (When you're back at the DOS prompt, you can turn off the machine.)

 ✔ Just because you're no longer using a program in Windows doesn't necessarily mean that you've quit it. It's possible to switch between programs without quitting; refer to "Switching Programs" earlier in this chapter.

It's possible to run more than one copy of a program in Windows at a time. For example, you can have several Notepads running, each of which shows you a different text file for editing. Don't let this boggle you. A word of advice: Quit any program you're not using. Doing so removes the confusion, and Windows runs a little faster when it has less to do (which is true of most of us, I suppose).

General Advice

Use your mouse. If you don't have a mouse, you can still use Windows but not as elegantly. Ack, who am I kidding? You *need* a mouse to use Windows!

Have someone organize your Program Manager for you so you can click on any program or file you want to run, and have him or her get rid of all those other programs you don't use that clutter up your screen.

Windows is a *black box* program in that a lot is going on in the background that you might forget about (see Chapter 15). Never reset while you're running Windows. And before you quit Windows itself, make sure that you've properly quit from all the programs you're running under Windows.

Keep in mind that Windows can run several programs at once. Use the Task List (Ctrl-Esc) to see whether a program is already running before starting a second copy. (Yes, you can run several copies of a program under Windows, but you probably only need to run one.)

Be wary of seeing a DOS prompt when you're in Windows. The DOS program may simply be one of Windows' "programs"; seeing it doesn't mean that you've quit Windows, nor is it a sure sign that you can reset or turn the computer off. To be sure, type the EXIT command:

```
C> EXIT
```

If that doesn't return you to Windows, you're not in Windows and it's safe to reset.

If a program crashes under Windows, big deal! Windows is constructed so that one dead program won't topple the whole computer. You simply close that program's window and keep on working — you can even start the program again after it's been properly disposed of. This is one of the neater aspects of Windows. (When it works.)

Special MS-DOS 6.2 Programs for Windows

The following information has been included for those of you who are running the Windows versions of MS-DOS 6's "special programs." These programs include Undelete, Anti-Virus, and the Microsoft Backup program.

These three, special MS-DOS 6 Windows programs were added to Windows'
Program Manager by the DOS Setup program. They'll appear in the group
Microsoft Tools, which may look somewhat like Figure 6-3 if you're lucky.

Figure 6-3:
The
DOS 6
special
programs,
Windows
versions.

✔ Information on the DOS version of Undelete is offered in Chapter 4; Anti-
Virus is covered in Chapter 21; Chapter 17 has information on backing up;
and Chapter 20 has information on restoring from a backup.

✔ *Cogito sumere potum alterum.*

Microsoft Undelete

To get your files back, start the Microsoft Undelete program. You'll see a screen
similar to Figure 6-4, which lists files that have been blown away. The highlighted files show good chances for recovery.

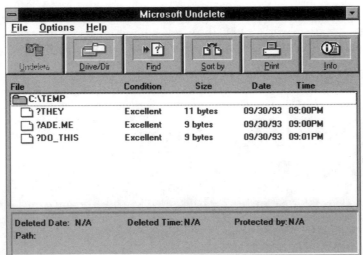

Figure 6-4:
Undelete in
action.

If you're not in the directory that contains the deleted files, click the Drive/Dir button and change to the specific directory or disk drive where the dead files await revival.

To recover a file, click on it with the mouse to highlight it. You can highlight several files by holding down the Ctrl key while clicking.

Click on the big Undelete button to recover the file(s). You'll be asked to type in the file's first letter. Do so. Then press Enter, and the file will be revived.

✔ You can use this version of the Undelete command to actually recover removed subdirectories. This just can't be done with piddly old DOS alone. (So what's with those people, anyway?)

✔ There are actually several "levels" of undelete protection. If you select the Configure Delete Protection command from the Options menu, you can select one of three methods by which DOS will recover files. Delete Sentry is the most efficient, but it's a disk-space hog. Delete Tracker isn't as thorough as Delete Sentry at recovering files, but it's better than Standard protection; Standard protection is what DOS gives you anyway. With Standard protection you'll always have to type in the deleted file's first letter. The other two methods do that for you (since, after all, this is a computer — designed to make life easier, supposedly).

Microsoft Windows Anti-Virus

This one is cinchy: Start Anti-Virus. You'll see a screen with all your disk drives displayed, similar to Figure 6-5. Click on a drive to highlight it, or hold down the Ctrl key and click on several drives to highlight them. Then click on the Detect and Clean button. Anti-Virus will scan for viruses and, if it finds any, will cheerfully remove them.

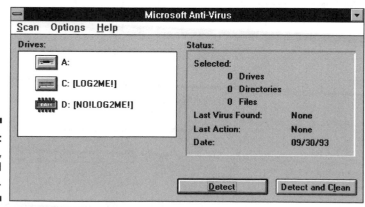

Figure 6-5:
Anti-Virus,
poised and
ready.

✔ The detecting and cleaning part takes a while, but fortunately the screen is interesting to watch.

✔ If a virus is found, Anti-Virus will spaz out appropriately. Read the screen and follow the directions listed for disposal.

✔ Refer to Chapter 20 for more information on Anti-Virus.

Microsoft Windows Backup

The Windows version of Backup is very, very similar to the DOS version. If you've used the DOS version, then you'll find yourself saying "Hey, this looks a lot like the DOS version — and it's almost as annoying!" (See Figure 6-6.)

Because you're so adept at using Windows, you can follow along with the steps outlined in Chapter 17 for "Backing up the whole hard drive, all of it." You'll be in Windows, so you'll need to start the Windows version of Backup instead of typing the command at the DOS prompt. Also, *after* step 3 and *before* step 4, you'll need to type Alt-T to select the Backup To area. From the drop-down list, select a floppy disk to back up to. From that point on, the backup works just the same as it does in DOS, but you'll be in Windows.

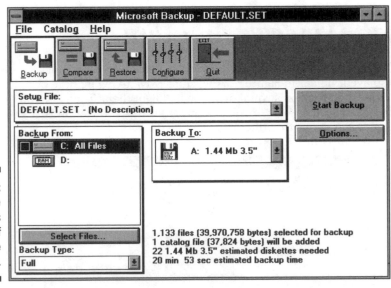

Figure 6-6:
The Windows version of Backup, like déjà vu.

✔ The Windows version of Microsoft Backup starts with a warning about using your floppy drives. Basically, Backup is greedy and wants control of the floppy drives to itself. Heed this warning: Don't use your floppy disks or have another program using a floppy disk while you're backing up.

✔ The diskettes from the Windows version of Backup can be used with the DOS version and vice versa.

✔ I still recommend backing up from the DOS prompt instead of within Windows. Definitely, for restoring a whole hard drive, you'll need to use Backup at the DOS prompt. Refer to Chapter 20 for the gories.

The 5th Wave — By Rich Tennant

"WE NEVER HAD MUCH LUCK BUILDING A DECENT HANDWRITING RECOGNITION SYSTEM, BUT ROY THERE'S DONE REAL GOOD MAKING A FLAT SCREEN NOTEBOOK THAT READS LIPS."

Part II
The Non-Nerd's Guide to PC Hardware

The 5th Wave

By Rich Tennant

ITS NOT THAT IT DOESN'T WORK AS A COMPUTER, IT JUST WORKS BETTER AS A PAPERWEIGHT.

In this part...

This is the kind of hardware you won't find in your True Value store. Nope, it's a world of floppy drives, CPUs, EPROMS, cables, and really nerdy stuff. The sad part is, you just can't use a computer without encountering hardware. And you need to know the terminology so when the manual says, "Plug this into your mouse port," you know not to take it personally.

There's no need ever to go into a technical description of the hardware in your PC. But as a human being, you'll very often have to touch that hardware, frequently at the bequest of some manual or loftier human who knows such things. This part of the book describes the various hardware goodies associated with a PC, the terms you encounter, and how everything fits into the big picture.

As a general definition before getting started, you should know that PC hardware is anything you can touch in a computer system, the physical part. Or, as I like to put it, when you drop hardware on your foot, you will doubtless say "ouch."

Chapter 7
Your Basic Hardware —
What It Is and Why

· ·

In This Chapter

▶ Defining and explaining the various parts of a computer system

▶ Understanding how a microprocessor fits into the big picture

▶ Learning what a math coprocessor is and what it can do for you

▶ Discovering where your disk drives are located and what they're called

▶ Using a port to connect interesting external devices to your PC

▶ Using printer ports and serial ports

▶ Using your PC to keep track of the date and time

· ·

The truth is, you just can't go around calling everything a whatsis. It would be grand, but there comes a point in time when you need a doodad — or a jobbie or a thingamabob. Then, eventually, you've developed your own personalized form of technospeak — a language only you can understand. After all, rumor has it that lawyers started out that way . . . and look where it got them!

This chapter defines a few common things associated with your computer. It describes them using a variety of terms, including geegaw, doojigger, and madoodle. The idea here is to explain your basic PC hardware minus the complex geometric math.

The Nerd's-Eye View

Time for the big picture. Note the items listed in Table 7-1 and their locations. Further, make sure that you can identify each on your PC.

Table 7-1	Basic Computer Hardware Components
Item to Find	*Typical Nerd Description*
Monitor	Video display, or CRT (cathode ray tube)
Keyboard	Manually dexterous input mechanism, or "101 Enhanced"
Computer box	System unit, console, or combative FFC Class B approved anti-EMF regulated shield with titanium white finish
Floppy drive A	Primary disk-based I/O storage device with removable media, or floppy drive A
Floppy drive B	Secondary disk-based I/O storage device with removable media, or floppy drive B (if present)
Hard drive(s) C	Primary fixed disk, nonremovable, high-speed, maximum-capacity, hermetically sealed SCSI 960 Mach 3 whopper
Printer	Dot matrix, thermal, impact, or (preferably) laser

Inside the computer box are various other items: stuff you can't see because, well, it's inside the box. Table 7-2 lists the items you would be able to locate there if, like Superman, you had X-ray vision.

Table 7-2	Internal Computer Components
Item Inside	*Typical Nerd Description*
Memory	RAM, or memory chips or banks, or SIMMs
Main circuitry board	The motherboard, system board
The computer's brain	The microprocessor, or the central processing unit (CPU), or by its number/name
Expansion cards	ISA bus expansion daughter boards
Power supply	210 watt, U/L listed, AC/DC power converter
Other stuff	Other stuff

✔ Generally speaking, the first floppy drive (A) is on top, and drive B is on the bottom. But this isn't always so; some systems may have A on the bottom. My advice is to label each drive using a sticker or one of those letter-puncher devices. Don't just label them A and B, either; label them *Drive A* and *Drive B* or, better still, *A:* and *B:* (with colons, which is how DOS refers to them). You may also want to label their capacity: 360K, 720K, 1.2MB, or 1.4MB.

✔ For more information on computer memory, refer to Chapter 8.

✔ The back of your PC contains lots of connections for various devices and other goodies you can hook up to a PC. For example, both the printer and your monitor hook up to your PC's rump. For information on other things you can plug in back there, refer to "What Are Ports?" later in this chapter.

The Microprocessor

The computer's main microchip is called a *microprocessor.* Like most highways, a computer's microprocessor is named after famous numbers. There are the *8088/8086,* the *80286,* the *80386,* and the *80486.* Generally, the bigger the number, the faster and more powerful your computer (and the more you paid for it).

Telling whether or not you have one microprocessor or another inside your computer box is a job best left up to the gods. The only time this should be a concern of yours is when some piece of software requires one microprocessor and you have another. You'll know this, of course, because the program won't run.

Another issue directly dependent on the type of microprocessor you have is memory — specifically, extra memory in your PC. There are two kinds of extra memory, *extended* and *expanded* memory. Refer to the discussions under "Expanded Memory" and "Extended Memory" in Chapter 8 for more information.

✔ The microprocessor is not "your computer's brain." That's a common metaphor, but it's just not true. A computer with a brain is something scary — like a politician with a brain. No, your computer's microprocessor is more like a calculator. They don't have brains, which I should know because my accountant uses a calculator all the time.

✔ You can buy software programs that will tell you the kind of microprocessor you have in your computer, as well as what kind of video display you have and other information that's not apparent to most people. Such programs include Quarterdeck's Manifest, Norton's SysInfo, PC Tool's SI (System Information) program, and various diagnostic programs, such as CheckIt, WinSleuth, and InfoSpotter. If you have DOS 6 or Windows 3.0 or 3.1, then you can use the Microsoft Diagnostic, MSD, to snoop inside your PC. Refer to Chapter 21.

✔ For all intents and purposes, the i486 systems are identical to the 80386 systems. Any PC software you buy for the 386 won't know the difference if you're using an i486. OK, there may be the rare i486-only software out there, but chances are that it works in such a cryptic way that using it would make your head explode.

✔ Let's see: 80286, 80386, 80486 — the next microprocessor is obviously the 80586 (call it the 586 if you're cool). This is obvious to anyone who's ever stewed over the mathematical series questions on the SAT. Unfortunately, it's wrong. The successor to the i486 is called the *Pentium* by its maker, Intel. Pentium. Does this mean the i686 will be the Sexium?

Pentium jokes

✔ Pentium. Little. Yellow. Different.

✔ The doctor said all that bending is hard on your Pentium.

✔ "And here's another slide of Athens. That's Helen in front of the Pentium."

✔ Thanks to local industry, our fresh water supply is polluted with Pentium (though the fish have gotten a lot smarter).

✔ "Where, pray tell, is Deuterium?" "Why, he's gone with Pentium to the Oracle at Delphi."

✔ You've tried dusting them, you've tried spraying them. Why not try Pentium?

✔ Did you hear about that new dirty magazine in Latin? *Pentium Housium.*

✔ Whole Wheat Corn Goobers cereal now comes with 11 vitamins and minerals, including Iron, Zinc, Paladium, and Pentium.

The differences between a DX, SX, and D2

Microprocessors run around in families. There is the 386 family of microprocessors, which really started it all. The big chip, the one with all the options and extras, is the 80386DX, which can be called just an 80386 or 386. Its little brother is the 80386SX or 386SX (its nickname). The 386SX is a cheaper alternative to the full-on DX chip, offering all the performance but only about half the power (and half the calories) of the bigger chip. It's like the equivalent of a four-cylinder model of a V8 car; it will get you there, but not as fast, and it won't cost as much money.

The i486 family consists of many siblings: The full-on i486DX is the beefy one. Its half-pint brother is the i486SX, which is just as filling but has fewer calories. And then there are the D2 chips, also known as the *clock doublers*. These chips have two speeds, a slower speed that no one advertises and a faster speed that everyone advertises. Pricewise, the D2 chips are cheaper than the full DX chips, and I recommend either over the pokey ol' i486SX.

The Math Coprocessor

A computer's microprocessor is really nothing more than a very fast calculator. For major mathematical calculations, the typical PC microprocessor can be a real slug. A companion chip is available, however, which is the electronic equivalent of giving your microprocessor its own adding machine. The chip is called a *math coprocessor.*

The math coprocessor just does math. Figuratively speaking, software can detect the presence of a math coprocessor and send off all the complex mathematics to that chip, relieving the main microprocessor of the tedious arithmetic tasks. The software still works without the math coprocessor, but it runs much slower.

✔ Math coprocessors have numbers, just like microprocessors. The difference is that while microprocessor numbers typically end in 6, the math coprocessor will be the same number but end in 7. (It's the union that makes up those rules.)

✔ Not every application can use a math coprocessor. Typically, spreadsheets and graphics-design packages are the only kinds of programs that run faster with a coprocessor installed. Refer to your software package to see whether it minds a math coprocessor.

✔ Math coprocessors are expensive, so only buy them if you painfully need them. Then force someone else to install them for you.

✔ The 80486, or i486, chip has a built-in math coprocessor. There is no companion 80487 chip — unless you have an i486SX. In that case, you don't have a built-in coprocessor and would buy an *overdrive* chip that would serve as your math coprocessor (among other things).

Disk Drives

Disk drives are storage devices. There are two kinds: *floppy drives,* which use removable floppy disks for storage, and *hard drives,* which typically store information on nonremovable disks. The files you see with the DIR command (refer to "The DIR Command" in Chapter 2) are what is stored on a disk.

Under DOS, your cherished disk operating system, disk drives are referred to by letters. The first floppy drive on all PCs is called *drive A,* or the A drive. The second floppy drive, whether or not you have one, is *drive B.* The first hard drive in any computer system is almost always *drive C,* with additional drives given letters of the alphabet from D on up through Z.

For the floppy drives, there are two popular sizes. These sizes refer to the dimensions of the disks you slide into the floppy drives: *5¼-inch* for the 5¼-inch square disks and *3½-inch* for the 3½-inch square hard-shelled disks.

Hard drives are internal mechanisms. On most PCs you cannot see the hard drive. If you can see it, it looks like a floppy drive but with tiny air holes instead of a disk slit.

✔ On each disk drive is a *drive light*. The light is on only when the computer is accessing the disk, either reading or writing information. It's important that you do not remove a floppy disk while that light is on.

✔ Refer to "Changing Disks" in Chapter 2 for instructions on removing and ejecting disks from floppy drives.

✔ Most of today's PCs come with both 5¼-inch and 3½-inch size drives. Drive A is typically the 5¼-inch drive, but that's not always the case.

What Are Ports?

The term *port* refers to a "hole" in the back of the computer or a festive dessert wine. You can plug any one of a variety of external devices with which the computer can communicate through a port.

Presently, there are two popular kinds of ports in a PC: the *printer* port and the *serial* port.

✔ Other external devices, such as the keyboard and monitor, are connected via their own special ports. Sometimes external disk drives are added, again via some form of unique port.

✔ A special type of port is available on some PCs. Technically, this port is the *analog-to-digital,* or *A-to-D,* port. A variety of scientific and real-world monitoring devices and such can be plugged into that port. However, most people refer to this port by the device hooked up to it 99 times out of 100: the *joystick* port.

✔ There is no visual clue to determine which port is which. (Well, what did you expect?) Even the experts have to struggle through trial and error sometimes; ports on a PC do look similar. If you ever find out for sure, label them.

The printer port

Mysteriously enough, the printer port is where you plug in your printer. The printer cable has one connector that plugs into the printer and a second that plugs into the computer. Both connectors are different, so it's impossible to plug in a printer backward.

- For more information on printers, refer to Chapter 11.

- Printer ports are also called *parallel* ports or (to old-time nerds) *Centronics* ports. People who refer to ports in this manner should be slapped.

- Other devices can be connected to a printer port, though typically the only one you'll have is the printer. Examples of other devices are voice synthesizers, network connections, external hard drives, extra keyboards, and choo-choo train sets.

The serial port

The serial port is far more flexible than the printer port; it supports a variety of interesting items, which is why it's generically called a serial port instead of a this-or-that port.

You'll often plug the following items into a serial port: a modem, a serial printer, a scanner or other input device, or just about anything that requires two-way communications. Most computers come with two serial ports.

- A serial port can also be called a *modem* port.

- Serial ports are also called *RS-232* ports. No, that's not a Radio Shack part number. Instead, it refers to Recommended Standard 232, which I assume is the 232nd standard The Committee came up with that year. Busy guys.

- You can plug a computer mouse into a serial port. In that case, the mouse is called a *serial mouse*. The mouse can also be plugged into its own port, called — shockingly enough — a *mouse port*. (Refer to your local pet store for more information on mice or turn to Chapter 10.)

Port deciphering hints you may skip

Ports connect to external devices by means of cables. These cables have connectors on both ends that are shaped like the letter D. From this we get the term *D-shell* connectors.

Your typical monitor port has a 15-line D-shell connector, whereas your typical serial port has a 9-line D-shell connector. This isn't worth mentioning, save for the fact that both D-shell connectors are the same size and could be easily confused.

The parallel port uses a 25-line D-shell connector. On some older systems, the serial port uses the same 25-line D-shell connector. This was done purely for spite, and it caused many PC owners countless hours of agony discovering which port was which.

Definitely skip over this stuff

Serial ports are complex in that you must *configure* them. Printer ports are set up to work in a specific manner and require no configuration. But with a serial port, you must configure both the port on your computer as well as the device with which you're communicating.

There are four items you need to configure on a serial port: the speed at which the port operates; the data word format, or the size of the bytes you're sending; the number of stop bits; and the parity. This is only a real hassle when you need to connect a serial printer (refer to "The serial connection" in Chapter 11). To get everything working right, you must occasionally make a full-moon sacrifice to the UNIX god or sing "Zip-A-Dee-Dooo-Dah" while holding your nose and hopping on one foot.

The Date and Time

Most computers come with an internal clock. The clock is battery operated, which enables it to keep track of the time, day or night, whether or not the PC is plugged in.

To check or change the current time, use the TIME command. Type the word **TIME** at the command prompt, and DOS responds with what it thinks is the current time. Here's an example:

```
C> TIME
Current time is 11:13:55.13p
Enter new time:
```

Type in the new time using the hour:minutes format; there's no need to enter seconds or hundredths of a second. (And if you work for the government, there's no need to enter the minutes value either.) If the given time shown is close to correct, just press Enter to keep it. Don't worry — you won't reset the clock to 12:00 a.m. if you don't enter a new time.

You use the DATE command to view or change the current date. It works like the TIME command:

```
C> DATE
Current date is Sat 10-19-1996
Enter new date (mm-dd-yy):
```

Type in the new date using the format indicated.

The date and time you enter is used by DOS when it creates or updates a file. The date and time are then shown in the directory listing along with each file. If you just want to see the current date or time, press Enter when you're asked to enter the new date or time. Pressing Enter doesn't alter the date or time. (Refer to "The DIR Command" in Chapter 2 for more information on the directory listing.)

- ✓ If the computer's clock battery goes dead, you'll need to replace it. For an AT type of computer system, when the clock dies your computer may not start. Before you become incensed, refer to "The Computer Has Lost Track of the Time" in Chapter 19.

- ✓ If you have an earlier 8088/8086 system, it may have a different kind of clock/timer installed. You may need to run a special utility program to permanently change or set the date and time. The DATE and TIME commands won't affect your internal clock.

- ✓ The format for the date and time varies depending on how your computer is set up. DOS uses a date and time format based on your country or region. This book assumes the typical (and I'll agree, backward) U.S.A. method of listing the date.

- ✓ Who cares if the computer knows what day it is? Well, because your files are time — and date — stamped, you can figure things out, like which is a later version of two similar files or two files with the same name on different disks.

Chapter 8
RAM (or Memory, the Way We Were)

- -

In This Chapter

▶ Understanding what memory does and how it fits into your computer system

▶ Determining how much memory you need to run your programs

▶ Learning the terms used to describe various amounts of memory

▶ Using conventional memory

▶ Understanding what the 640K barrier is and why it's so annoying

▶ Understanding upper memory

▶ Understanding expanded memory and extended memory

▶ Managing your memory

▶ Upgrading memory on your PC

- -

In the PC land of Oz, the Scarecrow would be singing, "If I only had some RAM. . . ." Memory, or *random access memory* (RAM), is a storage place in a computer, just like disk space. Unlike disk storage, memory is the only place inside the computer where the real work gets done. Obviously, the more memory you have, the more work you can do. But not only that, having more memory means the computer is capable of grander tasks, such as working with graphics, animation, sound, and music — and your PC remembers everyone it meets without ever having to look twice at his or her name tag.

This chapter is about memory inside your computer — RAM, as it's called in the nerdier circles. Every computer needs memory, but sadly, life just isn't that simple. There are different kinds of memory — different flavors, different fashions for the different seasons. This chapter goes into all that.

Don't Forget Memory

All computers need memory. That's where the work gets done. The microprocessor is capable of storing information inside itself, but only so much. The excess is stored in memory. For example, when you create a document by using your word processor, each character you type is placed into a specific location in memory. Once there, the microprocessor doesn't need to access it again unless you're editing, searching or replacing, or doing something active to the text.

Once something is created in memory — a document, spreadsheet, or graphic — it's *saved* to disk. Your disk drives provide long-term storage for information. Then, when you need to access the information again, you *load* it back into memory from disk. Once it's there, the microprocessor can again work on that information.

The only nasty thing about memory is that it's volatile. When you turn off the power, the contents of memory go poof! This is OK if you've saved to disk, but if you haven't, everything is lost. Even a reset will zap the contents of memory. So always save (if you can) before you reset or turn off your PC.

Common PC Memory Questions

How much memory do I need? The amount of memory you need depends on two things. The first, and most important, is the memory requirement of your software. Some programs, such as spreadsheets and graphics applications, require lots of memory. For example, Borland International's Quattro Pro says — right on the box — that it needs 512K of RAM plus it can use up to 8MB of extra memory, just because!

The second and more limiting factor is cost. Memory costs money. It's not as expensive as it was back in the old stone-tablet days of computing, but it still costs a lot. That 8MB of extra memory that Quattro Pro would like could cost you as much as $400. (That's almost $3,700 in dog dollars!)

Generally speaking, all computers should have at least 640K of *conventional* or *DOS* memory. This memory is the most important.

Any extra memory you have in your computer is a bonus. Extra memory comes in the form of *expanded* or *extended* memory. You may need to buy a special piece of hardware to get this extra memory into your PC.

> ✔ For more information on memory terms, refer to the next section; for information on expanded or extended memory, refer to those sections later in this chapter.

Can I add more memory to my PC? Yes. This is done typically because your applications need more memory. The programs just won't run (or will run sluggishly) without more memory.

> ✓ If a program keeps flashing that red MEM at you, pull out a large caliber sidearm and shoot the computer. Or refer to "Upgrading Memory" in this chapter.

Can I lose computer memory? No. Your computer only has a finite amount of memory, but it cannot be "lost" to anything. Programs use memory when you run them. For example, when you run WordPerfect, it eats up a specific amount of memory. But when you quit WordPerfect, all that memory is made available to the next program. So while a program runs, it "grabs" memory for its own uses. When the program is done, it lets the memory go.

> ✓ Refer to the section "Conventional Memory" for information on running the MEM command to see how much memory your computer has.

What about copying programs? Copying programs uses memory, but don't confuse disk "memory" with computer memory or RAM. You can copy a huge program from one disk to another without worrying about running out of memory. DOS handles the details.

Computer memory can never be "destroyed." Even after a huge program runs or you copy a very large file, your system still has the same amount of RAM in it.

Disk "memory" is just storage space on disk. It's possible to store on your hard drive a program that's huge in size — hundreds of megabytes — more than could possibly fit in memory. How does that work? Some say it's voodoo. Others say it's because DOS only loads a small portion of the file into memory (RAM) at once. Who knows what the truth *really* is?

Memory Terms to Ignore

Many interesting terms orbit the memory planet. The most basic of these terms refers to the quantity of memory (see Table 8-1).

Table 8-1		Memory Quantities	
Term	*Abbr*	*About*	*Actual*
Byte		1 byte	1 byte
Kilobyte	K or KB	1,000 bytes	1,024 bytes
Megabyte	M or MB	1,000,000 bytes	1,048,576 bytes
Gigabyte	G or GB	1,000,000,000 bytes	1,073,741,824 bytes

Memory is measured by the *byte*. Think of a byte as a single character, a letter in the middle of a word. For example, the word "spatula" is seven bytes long.

A whole page of text is about 1,000 bytes. To make this a handy figure to know, computer nerds refer to 1,000 bytes as a *kilobyte,* or one *K* or *KB*. (Actually, 1K is equal to 1,024 bytes, probably because 1,024 is two to the tenth power. Computers love the number two.)

The term *megabyte* refers to 1,000K, or one million bytes. The abbreviation *MB* (or *M*) is used to indicate megabyte, so 8MB means eight megabytes of memory. (Actually, one megabyte is 1,024K, which equals somewhat over one million bytes of information; the actual amount is mind-boggling.)

Further than the megabyte is the *gigabyte*. As you can guess, this is one billion bytes or about 1,000 megabytes. The *terabyte* is one trillion bytes, or enough RAM to bring down the power on your block when you boot the PC.

Just in case you didn't know, RAM stands for *random access memory*. It doesn't mean anything useful.

A specific location in memory is called an *address*.

Bytes are composed of eight *bits*. The word *bit* is a contraction of *binary digit*. Binary is base two, or a counting system where only ones and zeros are used. Computers count in binary and we group their bits into clusters of eight for convenient consumption as bytes.

The term *giga* is actually Greek and it means *giant*.

There is no reason to worry about how much *ROM* (read-only memory) you have in your computer.

Conventional Memory

Normally, any computer would just have "memory." But under DOS, different terms apply to different types of memory. The memory where DOS runs programs is called *conventional memory*. (It may also be called *DOS memory* or *low DOS memory*.)

When a program says it needs 512K or 384K of memory to run, what it refers to is conventional memory.

Your PC can have up to 640K of conventional memory installed. So the maximum amount means you can run almost any program.

Any extra memory — memory beyond the basic 640K of conventional memory — is either extended or expanded memory. Which is which and why you should care is covered later in this chapter.

To see how much memory you have in your computer, you can use the MEM command. After typing MEM at the DOS prompt, you'll see a summary of all the memory in your computer, similar to that shown in Figure 8-1.

```
Memory Type          Total  =  Used  +  Free
-----------          ------    ------   ------
Conventional          640K      37K     603K
Upper                  59K      41K      18K
Reserved              128K     128K       0K
Extended (XMS)*     3,269K   2,533K     736K
-----------          ------    ------   ------
Total memory        4,096K   2,738K   1,358K

Total under 1 MB      699K      78K     622K

Total Expanded (EMS)          3,648K (3,735,552 bytes)
Free Expanded (EMS)*            976K (999,424 bytes)

* EMM386 is using XMS memory to simulate EMS memory as
  needed.
  Free EMS memory may change as free XMS memory changes.

Largest executable program size       603K (617,552 bytes)
Largest free upper memory block        18K  (18,672 bytes)
MS-DOS is resident in the high memory area.
```

Figure 8-1: The MEM command spews forth memory statistics.

The key value to look for appears toward the end of the long and complex output. Look for the line that says *Largest executable program size*. That tells you how much conventional memory you have available (out of 640K). In Figure 8-1, the value is 603K (which is 617,522 bytes to the IRS).

Memory summaries are also displayed for extended (XMS) memory as well as expanded (EMS) memory. Your system may have one, both, or neither.

✔ If your PC has less than 640K of RAM, you can add memory to boost your total. Refer to "Upgrading Memory" later in this chapter.

✔ You'll only see commas in the big numbers with MS-DOS 6.2 (see Figure 8-1). Older versions of DOS display the numbers all chunkilly-wunkilly.

The 640K Barrier

Conventional memory is limited to 640K. That's all the memory DOS has for running programs. Even if you have megabytes of RAM installed in your computer, you have only 640K in which to run programs. Thus, it's called the *640K barrier.*

This is kind of dumb, of course; powerful PCs don't need artificial limitations set on them. I mean, they can tear down the Berlin Wall and eliminate communism, but the smartest engineers in all the land can't pass the 640K conventional memory barrier. Well, actually they did figure out how to pole vault over the 640K barrier. It's complicated and involves installing extra memory.

The solutions for skirting around the 640K barrier involve adding more memory to your system. This is provided in the form of either *extended* or *expanded* memory, both of which are covered in the following sections.

Most programs can work fine in 640K, though for many newer programs it's a tight fit.

> ✔ The reason for the barrier in the first place is how the original IBM PC was designed. Way back in 1982, 640K seemed like plenty. But as the PC has evolved, and as programs become more sophisticated, the 640K limit affects everybody.

Upper Memory

There is a region of memory just above the 640K barrier. This is called *reserved memory,* though starting with DOS Version 5.0, it's become known as *upper memory.*

Upper memory is only used for special advanced computer operations that "load high." If you have an 80386 computer or some kind of third-party memory management software, you can take advantage of upper memory. The secrets of this trick using MS-DOS 6 are divulged later in this chapter, in the section titled "Managing memory."

Expanded Memory

Expanded memory is extra memory in a PC. It's not ordinary, conventional memory beyond the 640K barrier, and you must specifically add expanded memory to your system; no computer comes with it automatically.

What's nice about expanded memory is that lots of DOS programs can use it. Graphics programs like it for storing huge, multimegabyte images. Spreadsheets, such as Quattro Pro, can use up to 8MB of expanded memory to store large spreadsheets.

Because expanded memory isn't a normal part of your computer, it must be added via a special hardware *expansion card*. Furthermore, you'll need to install a special device driver into your CONFIG.SYS file. That device driver provides the link between your software and the expanded memory. (Refer to Chapter 16 for more information on updating CONFIG.SYS.)

- ✔ If you have an 8088/8086 or 80286 AT type of computer, you must add a special expanded memory expansion card to your system. That card contains the expanded memory, and a disk contains software that you can use to add the memory to your computer.

- ✔ If you buy an expanded memory card, make sure it's LIM 4.0 hardware compatible. That gives you up to 32MB of really useful memory on your system, opening the doors to interesting applications and other fun stuff.

- ✔ If you have a 386 or greater system, you can convert that computer's extended memory into expanded memory using special software drivers. The gory details of doing this are best left to the experts. Because it's a dreary day outside, however, I've written about it briefly in the section on "Managing Memory," later in this chapter.

Trivial technical details

Expanded memory adheres to the *Expanded Memory Specification* (EMS) as defined by the *Lotus-Intel-Microsoft* (LIM) standard. If you really want to babble out the acronyms (impress your friends), this is known as the *LIM 4.0 EMS*.

The expanded memory driver that you install into your CONFIG.SYS file is typically named EMM.SYS (EMM stands for expanded memory manager).

Extended Memory

Extended memory is any memory beyond 640K in an 80286, AT, or 386 or later PC. Unlike expanded memory, this memory is simply memory added to those systems; add two megabytes to your AT clone and you have two megabytes of extended memory.

This type of memory is meat on the table for power-mad programs, like Windows and other operating systems such as OS/2 and UNIX, that demand the most from your computer. MS-DOS uses extended memory for some special purposes, but for the most part it is other greedy software that requires this type of memory. And the best part about it is that it's easy to add to your PC: no extra memory cards are required, as with expanded memory.

✔ If you have a 386 computer, it's possible to convert extended memory into expanded memory for those programs that need it. This is covered in the section "Managing Memory," just a few column inches from this very spot.

✔ If you have a 286 system, any extra memory you have in your computer is all extended. Unlike a 386, you cannot convert it directly into expanded memory. Instead, you must buy an expanded memory card and add memory that way. (Sorry, but I didn't make up these rules.)

✔ If your computer runs an operating system other than DOS (which would make it silly for you to buy this book), that operating system may use extended memory. I won't mention the software here since neither IBM nor Novell is paying me any money and, quite honestly, they don't need any freebie plugs.

More trivial extended memory stuff

Extended memory is handled under DOS by using an extended memory manager: XMS. It's a standard, like the EMS is for expanded memory. If you see a line in your CONFIG.SYS file that contains the filename HIMEM.SYS, that's your XMS device driver.

Making more extended memory (no alchemy involved)

Aside from adding more memory to your PC (the best way to get more extended memory), the only other way to give your PC and those extended memory power-hungry programs more of what they need is to cut down on your expanded-memory consumption. Confusing issue. What's really at stake here is a trade-off. Extended memory is typically more beneficial to those programs that need it. Expanded memory can be sacrificed. Consult with your guru on ways to decrease your expanded-memory consumption. Say, "Do something to my EMM386.EXE device driver in CONFIG.SYS. Something about the *noems* option. Here. Have a Dorito." (Third-party memory managers use different device driver names. What are they? Hey, I dunno. I'm not paid to please everybody.)

Managing Memory

Memory management is something unique to DOS. Other operating systems do it automatically. With DOS, you need extra help. Oh, you could do everything just fine without a memory manager. But you'd probably run out of memory quickly in that situation. No, it's best to use a solid PC memory-management product, something like QEMM, 386MAX, Netroom, or the MemMaker program that comes with DOS 6. That way you'll get the most from your memory, and your programs will love you for it.

- ✔ Memory management on a PC is only possible if you have an 80386, 486, or Pentium-type microprocessor. Refer to Chapter 21 to see which type you have.

- ✔ Older PCs, those with 286 or 8080 microprocessors, lack the memory-management abilities of the 386 and later PCs. There are solutions for them, however. I'd plug my book, *Managing Memory with MS-DOS,* here if it weren't for the fact that Microsoft Press publishes it.

The MemMaker solution

Having lots of memory in your PC shouldn't be an antagonizing thing. Never should you have to mess with terms like extended or expanded or upper memory. To prove this, MS-DOS 6 has a nifty utility that will configure, manage, and control all the memory in your PC. It's called MemMaker and it's painless and quick to use. Everyone should follow along with the instructions listed below to get a handle on their PC's memory.

Steps: Optimizing your PC's memory with MemMaker

Step 1. Make sure you're at the command prompt. Quit Windows or your menu program or whatever. Remove any floppy disk you may have sitting in drive A.

Step 2. Run MemMaker. Type the following at the command prompt:

```
C> MEMMAKER /BATCH2
```

That's MEMMAKER, a space, a slash, and then BATCH2.

Step 3. MemMaker is a full-screen program that optimizes your PC's memory. Because you typed the /BATCH2 option when you started MemMaker, it will run all by itself, and you can just sit there and watch (or go to the fridge and get a nice snack). If you do sit and watch, don't be alarmed when MemMaker resets your PC a few times.

Step 4. You'll see a final screen full of statistics. The third column of numbers (under "Change") tells you how much more memory you have now than when you started . . . but — oh! — there it goes, gone from view. Oh, well.

Step 5. You're done.

- ✔ The steps above will set up your PC to use expanded memory (EMS). This is okay for just about any system.

- ✔ MemMaker makes changes to your CONFIG.SYS and AUTOEXEC.BAT files. Do not mess with these changes! (Indeed, it's usually a bad idea to go ripping through either file without knowing what it is you're doing.)

- ✔ If you're currently using another memory manager, MemMaker will ask to disable it before it optimizes your PC's memory. You'll see a message that reads something like `The Bromidic memory manager is running on your computer`. If someone else set up your computer, select the **Exit** option and ask them to ruminate over your old memory manager verses MemMaker. If you're fed up with the old memory manager, select the **Delete** option and plow right ahead.

- ✔ If MemMaker says anything about deleting a "corrupted" MEMMAKER.STS file, press Enter and just keep on going.

- ✔ If you don't start MemMaker with the /BATCH2 switch, you'll have to read all the screens and press Enter about four or five times. Pressing Enter selects the "go-ahead" option in all cases, which is what I recommend. However, by starting MemMaker with the /BATCH2 option, it just goes ahead anyway, saving you all that time and wear and tear on your Enter key.

Other memory management solutions of the third-party variety

Memory management is a relatively new category of computer software. A few years ago only a few products were available. Today, dozens. The one I recommend, though, is Qualitas *386MAX*. It requires the least amount of brain work and does a nice job of keeping your PC's memory house in order. Also, they gave me free munchies during last year's COMDEX computer convention in Las Vegas, so I'm partial to them.

- ✔ The more technically oriented PC user prefers the *QEMM* memory manager from Quarterdeck Office Systems. It's full of bells and whistles and has lots of options and such for concise memory tweaking.

- ✔ An interesting memory manager to consider is *Memory Commander*. I once got a total of 900K free conventional memory with that program. Whammo! It's very unobtrusive.

- ✔ The nice lady who does P.R. for the *Netroom* memory manager says her memory-management package is the best. Just because it says "net" doesn't mean it's for networked PCs only.

- ✔ If you use a third-party memory manager and use MS-DOS's DoubleSpace disk-compression software, be sure to scour the various README text files regarding possible incompatibilities. Refer to Chapter 16 for information on using the DOS Editor to view README files.

How often should I optimize memory?

Memory managers work each time you start your PC. Using various types of magic, DOS obeys the memory manager's instructions and puts memory in order. However, another way to use the memory manager is to *optimize* your memory. This action is done once when you first install the memory manager and can be done again — but only on an as-needed basis. For example, running DOS 6's MemMaker to optimize your memory a second time won't save you more memory.

To get the most from your memory manager, you should only optimize your memory under one of the following circumstances:

- ✔ When you first install the memory manager

- ✔ After you add more memory to your PC (or you remove memory — which is unlikely)

- ✔ After you add a new device driver or TSR (memory-resident program) to your PC

- ✔ After you run a disk-compression program

- ✔ After you edit either your CONFIG.SYS or AUTOEXEC.BAT files

- ✔ When you buy a new computer or one that hasn't had its memory optimized yet (and in that case you'd be running your memory manager for the first time anyway)

Editing CONFIG.SYS and AUTOEXEC.BAT is covered in Chapter 16.

Upgrading Memory

Adding memory to your computer is Lego-block simple. The only problem is that the typical Lego block set, say the cool Space Station or Rescue Helicopter set, costs $27. Your computer, on the other hand, may cost one hundred times that much. This is not something to be taken lightly.

Steps: Upgrading memory involves five complex and boring steps

Step 1. Figure out how much memory you need to add. For example, if you have only 512K in your system, you need another 128K to give yourself the full 640K of conventional memory. If you need expanded memory, you'll need to buy an expanded memory card for your system — plus memory to put on the card. If you have a 386 system, all you need is extra memory.

Step 2. Figure out how much memory you can install. This is a technical step. It involves knowing how memory is added to your computer and in what increments. You should simply tell the shop or your favorite technical guru how much you think you need, and they'll tell you how much you can actually have.

Step 3. Buy something. In this case, you buy the memory chips themselves or you buy the expansion card into which the memory chips are installed.

Step 4. Pay someone else to plug in the chips and do the upgrade. Oh, you can do it yourself, but I'd pay someone else to do it.

Step 5. Gloat. Once you have the memory, brag to your friends about it. Heck, it used to be impressive to say you had the full 640K of RAM. Then came the "I have 4 megabytes of memory in my 386" round of impressiveness. But today? Anything less than eight megabytes and your kids will roll their eyes at you.

✔ The primary reason for upgrading memory is to enable programs to run more efficiently on your system. In light of that, upgrade only when your software requires it or won't otherwise run.

✔ If you want to try it yourself, go ahead. Plenty of easy books on the subject of upgrading memory are available, as well as how-to articles in some of the popular magazines. I'd recommend having someone else do it, however.

✔ Be sure to run your memory manager again after upgrading your memory. Refer to the previous section for scant details.

✔ More information on these memory terms is covered throughout the first part of this chapter.

Chapter 9
The Video Display
(That's the Computer Screen)

*P*erhaps the most important part of any computer is the screen, or what a nerd would call the video display monitor or even a CRT (cathode ray tube). In the old days, the wrong kind of display could really fry your eyeballs. I remember riding down the elevator with bug-eyed people desperately searching for Visine. Today's computer screens are easier to look at and can produce much more stunning displays. Visine sales are down considerably.

This chapter is about the video display, computer screen, monitor, or the thing you look at when you use a computer. There's really not much to do with the display as far as DOS is concerned, but there are some terms you'll encounter that will bug you no end. In fact, there are more acronyms associated with the computer screen than anything else (save the government).

Color and Mono

There are two kinds of computer screens. You can have a *color display,* which is noted for its colorful text and fantastic color graphics, or you can have a *monochrome (mono) display,* which is noted for its text. Yes, like a black-and-white TV set, monochrome computer screens are fairly dull, even when they're orange or green.

A few programs display only text, which makes a monochrome display an inexpensive — and the best — alternative for some systems. Why pay for color? But if your applications require color or offer any color features (such as graphics), a color monitor is an excellent tool.

Whether you have color or mono, you should know that your PC's video system is composed of two different things. There's the *monitor,* which sits on top or alongside of your computer. That's the obvious part. But lurking inside your PC is the second, more important, part. That's the *graphics adapter.* It's the video circuitry that sits inside the computer on an expansion card. That card plugs into your monitor. Together, the monitor and the graphics card make up the complete video system.

- The whole graphics system, both the monitor and the graphics adapter, are referred to collectively, usually by the name of the graphics adapter: *MDA, CGA, EGA, VGA,* or *SVGA.*

- If you have a monochrome system, it's possible to swap it out for a color system. It's also possible to have both a color and monochrome display in the same PC, though few programs take advantage of this, and watching both screens at the same time will make you cross-eyed.

What makes a graphics adapter? (stuff to skip)

What you get when you pay for a major graphics adapter are more colors and higher resolution. Colors simply refer to the number of colors that can be displayed on the screen at once. For example, the VGA display can show up to 256 colors, which makes a very vivid — almost photographic — picture.

Resolution refers to the number of dots, or *pixels,* on the screen. The more pixels, the higher the resolution and the finer the image.

With resolution and color there is a trade-off: You can only have more of one or the other, not both. A high-resolution display gives you few colors. A lot of colors gives you low resolution. This works,

however, because the many colors fool the eye into thinking you have more resolution. (The typical TV has a low resolution but a nearly infinite number of colors.)

For the text screen, resolution is measured by the number of horizontal (columns) and vertical (rows) characters. The typical color display shows 80 characters across by 25 characters down.

The text colors for all the color adapters remain the same: You can have up to 16 foreground text colors and eight background colors. The text on a VGA display is, however, much easier on the eye than the text on an EGA display.

Which Do I Have?

Because this isn't a buyer's guide, there's no reason to babble on about the advantages of color versus monochrome. Your only concern is which you have. Yeah, it's an interesting question, but one that has a definite answer.

The best way to know for certain is to run a PC diagnostics program. If you have DOS 6, you can use the Microsoft Diagnostics program. Type MSD at the DOS prompt and press Enter:

```
C> MSD
```

Look for the spot on the screen labeled Video. It tells you the type of graphics adapter your PC has. For example, one of my PCs says VGA, Tseng SpeedSTAR. This means I have a VGA-type graphics adapter in my PC. The Tseng SpeedSTAR sounds like a Chinese brand racing bicycle, but it's really a Chinese brand computer graphics adapter. My other PC says 8514/A, Tseng, which is another type of PC graphics system. You may see VGA, Unknown, which means you have colorful VGA graphics but MSD is in the dark about the specifics.

Graph-a-Bits Soup

The world of PC graphics involves a lot of TLAs, three-letter acronyms. These TLAs refer to the history and capabilities of the various kinds of video displays you can have lashed to your PC (see Table 9-1). The names actually refer to the graphics adapter located inside your computer. But they're generally used to refer to the complete video system.

Other, future standards may come along. But get this: It takes the software developers literally years to come up with programs that take advantage of a new graphics adapter's features. Sure, there's flash in having a fancy graphics display, but why pay the cash when you won't be using that extra hardware?

- ✔ Each of these color graphics adapters (CGA, EGA, and VGA) is compatible with its predecessors. But these adapters are not compatible with their offspring — you cannot run VGA graphics on your EGA video system, although you can run EGA on VGA.

- ✔ Yes, there are other unconventional adapters out there. Those listed in Table 9-1 are the most popular, but that doesn't rule out some specific stuff or oddball entries.

✔ Some high-resolution graphics systems are only applicable to certain kinds of software. Computer graphics, CAD, and animation and design are all areas where paying top dollar for your display is worth it. If you're only using basic applications, such as a word processor, you don't need top-dollar displays.

Table 9-1	Various Kinds of Video Displays
MDA	MDA stands for *monochrome display adapter*. It's the original monochrome display setup used by the first PCs. This type of display offered no graphics, only text. A clone of the MDA, the Hercules, or monographics adapter, offered graphics. Today, most monochrome systems are Hercules or compatible.
CGA	CGA stands for *color graphics adapter*. When the PC first appeared, the CGA was the only way you could see color text or graphics. But the text quality stank. The CGA could really frost over your contacts, so most people opted for MDA or Hercules.
EGA	EGA stands for *enhanced graphics adapter*. It was a solution that offered crisper text than the CGA plus many more colors. But it was soon overshadowed by the now-popular VGA.
VGA	In its constant effort to keep everyone off their guard, IBM introduced the VGA standard and told the world that it stands for *video graphics array*. (Not video graphics adapter, as some are prone to call it.) VGA offers superior colors, high-resolution graphics, and nice, readable text. A variation on VGA is the SuperVGA, which I recommend as the graphics standard for all DOS computers.
OTGA	OK, OTGA stands for *Other Types of Graphics Adapters*. There's the 8514, which is basically a pricey version of the SuperVGA that has more colors and higher resolution. The XGA standard is yet another Super DuperVGA card. It's mondo expensivo and offers more colors and higher resolutions.

Funky Displays

The standard *resolution* for text on your computer's display is 25 rows of 80 columns of text. That gives you about half a page of written text or, if you're looking at a graphics image, from the top of someone's head to just above his navel.

All color displays are capable of switching between 80 columns and 40 columns. The text gets twice as wide (*fat text*, I call it). To make the text 40 columns wide, you can use this command:

```
C> MODE 40
```

That's 40 as in 40 columns wide. To switch the display back to 80 columns, you use this command:

```
C> MODE 80
```

Again, it's 80, for 80 columns wide. That's about it for the width of your screen under DOS. For the number of rows, you have several choices, depending on the kind of display you have. The best way to determine the number of rows is to try them out.

```
C> MODE CON LINES=43
```

That's the MODE command, a space, CON, a space, and finally the word LINES, an equal sign, and 43 — the number of lines you want to display. Press Enter. Type the DIR command a few times to prove to yourself that you now have 43 lines of text on the screen.

```
C> MODE CON LINES=50
```

This is the same MODE command as the previous example, but the number of lines is increased to 50. This produces a readable display, but the characters are really scrunchy.

Really skippable stuff

If ANSI.SYS is installed, the MODE command can change both the width and the depth of the screen in one swift stroke. The format is

```
MODE CON COLS=x LINES=y
```

For *x* you can specify 40 or 80 for a 40- or 80-column display. The value of *y* is equal to 25, 43, or 50 rows of text on the screen. The following command is the weirdest:

```
C> MODE CON COLS=40 LINES=50
```

Typing in MODE 80 returns the display to normal.

The word *CON:* in the MODE command refers to the *console device,* which is a fancy term for your keyboard and display. In the preceding command, MODE referred to CON:, which means the display. COLS sets the number of columns and LINES sets the rows. But you must specify CON: to make the command apply to the display. (Because MODE also controls the printer and other devices in the same manner, it needs to know which device to reconfigure.)

To return the display to normal, type

```
C> MODE CON LINES=25
```

- ✔ DOS only supports screen modes for 25, 43, and 50 lines.

- ✔ If these screen modes don't work, you may need to install the ANSI.SYS device driver into your CONFIG.SYS file. If you feel the trouble is worth it, have someone else do it, though you can refer to Chapter 16 in this book if you want to take a stab at it yourself.

- ✔ If the screen modes still don't work, you probably don't have a VGA or EGA display in your system.

- ✔ Some programs can take advantage of the smaller, more compact text. WordPerfect supports several of the text modes, as does Lotus 1-2-3. You'll need to refer to your application's manual for the details. (But only if this really intrigues you.)

- ✔ Most graphics adapters come with special programs that offer additional, way-out modes. The adapter in my PC enables a display of 132 columns by 43 rows! Even WordPerfect supports it. But the text is very small and hard to read.

A bothersome explanation of what's going on

The MODE command is used to change the modes of a variety of computer devices. In fact, the MODE command is so confusing it's listed more times than any other command in some books on DOS (eleven times in the old DOS 3.3 manual!).

The MODE 80 command is used to set the color monitor to a width of 80 columns. The number of rows on the screen remains at 25.

The MODE 40 command is used to set a color monitor to a width of 40 columns, which appear twice as fat as they would on the standard display. The number of rows stays at 25.

The MODE mono command is used to activate a monochrome monitor. If you have both a color and a monochrome monitor, this command makes the monochrome one the main screen; typing MODE 80 (or MODE 40) activates the color display. Don't type MODE MONO if you don't have a monochrome display attached to your computer.

Why Doesn't My Game Work?

Of all the graphics-related questions I've ever been asked, this is the most popular: "I tried to run a game on my PC and the screen went blank." The reason is usually that you have a monochrome system. It cannot run color games.

Even if you have a color system, some games are designed specifically for EGA or VGA systems. If you don't have one, the game won't work.

This seems like a trivial subject, but it's really serious. If you want to play games on your computer (and everyone does), you need a color graphics system. Monochrome just doesn't cut it. In the end, you'll probably be happier with your color system anyway.

Other Popular Questions You Don't Have to Read

What are the other questions I'm asked? Here's a list along with my answers.

"Should I buy the newest graphics adapter?" Nope. It takes years for the software to catch up with the new adapter. Chances are, at this stage in the game, any new adapter will only have goodies to offer demanding graphics users. You probably aren't one of them.

"Which graphics adapter is best?" For now, I suggest the SuperVGA. The uppermost resolution of the card is unimportant because few applications support it. However, I recommend buying a card with all the memory installed. Don't save money by planning to upgrade later.

"Can I pick up a used display screen?" Bad idea.

"What about getting a color laptop?" Yeah, they be cool — and expensive. Some are better than others, which means to me that all of them will be getting better in a few years. If you can stand it, wait. Prices will go down, and performance will go up.

The Graphics Looked Great in the Store

They always do, don't they? Graphics sell computers. In the old days, what most people really needed was monochrome. Heck, I had a nice monochrome display on my system for years. But color costs more money and provides a higher sales margin for the computer store. So they push color, and you'll always see a lot of color graphics in any computer store.

Since the late 1980s, more and more applications have taken advantage of color text. Things just looked gross in monochrome! With color text you could get more information on the screen and a prettier display. For the most part, however, nifty graphics like you see in a computer store just don't find themselves in every computer application. Word processors can have pictures in the text, but you can only see the graphics in a special preview mode; spreadsheets have charts and graphs, but, again, only in preview modes. That picture of the gorilla, parrot, or lady you saw in the computer store was only for show.

And, after all, you did buy your computer to do work — didn't you?

The 5th Wave   **By Rich Tennant**

Chapter 10
Keyboard and Mouse
(or Where Is the "Any" Key?)

In This Chapter

▶ Finding special keys on the keyboard

▶ Pressing the "any" key

▶ Using the CapsLock, NumLock, and ScrollLock keys

▶ Determining the difference between the slash and backslash keys

▶ Understanding when to press Enter and when to press Return

▶ Pressing the Alt-S key combination

▶ Pausing a long text display by using the keyboard

▶ Cursing at the WordStar cursor-key diamond

▶ Making the keyboard more (or less) responsive

▶ Dealing with a keyboard that beeps at you

▶ Understanding how a mouse fits into the big picture

▶ Using a mouse

▶ Learning what all the mouse terms mean

▶ Dealing with a mouse that leaves a trail of itself on the screen

I may be weird, but I think a good keyboard can make a good computer. Nothing beats the full responsiveness of a real keyboard, when the keys punch down evenly and are light to the touch. Some keyboards have a built-in click; others may have some pressure point or feel-only click. These features give you the impression that the computer's designers wanted you to feel like you're in control while you use the machine. Who cares if you're typing out mysterious DOS commands when the keyboard feels so good?

This chapter is about the computer keyboard and all the fun things you can do with it. Your keyboard is the direct line of communication between you and the computer. There are subtle ways to use the keyboard and special keys you can type. Knowing how to use them is like making funny or rude noises with your mouth; they may be socially unacceptable, but in the right situations they offer a unique form of payoff.

Oh, and this chapter also describes the most common of computer rodents, the mouse.

Keyboard Layout

The typical keyboard supplied with most of today's computers is referred to as the enhanced 101-key keyboard. Yes, it actually has 101 keys on it. You can count them on your own, and you can examine each key individually. In Figure 10-1 you should note the various areas mapped out on the keyboard. There are four main areas:

1. **The function keys, labeled F1 through F12.** These keys perform various functions depending on the application. (And no two applications use the same function keys for the same function — which you should be expecting by now.)

2. **The typewriter keys.** These keys are laid out like the standard typewriter keyboard. All the alphanumeric keys are there, plus a handful of special computer keys and symbols.

3. **The cursor-control keys.** The *cursor keys,* also called *arrow keys,* are used to move the cursor on the screen. There are four directional keys in an inverted T pattern and six specialized keys above them. These keys are used most often in text editing.

4. **The numeric keypad.** The keypad contains the numbers 0 through 9, plus the period, an Enter key, and various mathematical symbols. The keypad can be used for fast numeric entry, but it also serves a second function as a backup cursor keypad. Refer to the discussion under "The Keys of State" later in this chapter for more information.

   ✔ Some older keyboards lack the F11 and F12 keys, as well as the separate cursor-control keys. They may also have their function keys in two columns to the left of the typewriter keys.

   ✔ Important keys to look for are the Esc (Escape) and backslash (\) keys. These keys are used quite often, and over the history of the PC keyboard, they've been quite migratory. The only reason for pointing this out is that the Esc key used to be next to the Backspace key. Confusing the two was painful; Esc erased the entire line, whereas Backspace erased only one character.

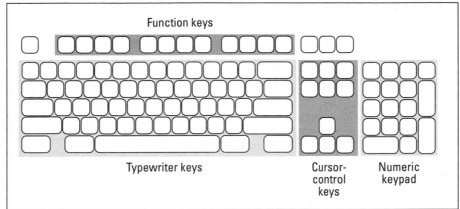

Function keys

Typewriter keys

Cursor-
control
keys

Numeric
keypad

Figure 10-1:
The
enhanced
101-key
keyboard.

✔ Computers use the following symbols for mathematical operations: + is for addition; – is for subtraction; * is for multiplication; and / is for division. The only important special symbol here is the asterisk for multiplication — not the little *x*. This symbol is universal in all areas of computerdom.

So Where Is the "Any" Key?

Nothing is more frustrating than hunting down that elusive *any* key. After all, the screen says, `Press any key to continue`. So where is it?

Any key refers to, literally, any key on your keyboard. But let's be specific: When it says to press the "any" key, press the spacebar. If you can't find the spacebar, or you think it's the place where you order drinks on the Starship Enterprise, try pressing the Enter key. Enter key = any key.

You can press almost any key on the keyboard for the "any" key. The problem is that some keys don't respond and are ill-suited to be "any" keys. These include the Shift keys, CapsLock, Pause, the 5 key on the numeric keypad, and other "dead" keys. You can pound away on them all you like, and the program will never continue.

So why do they say "Press any key" instead of saying "Press spacebar to continue?" I guess it's because they want to make things easy for you by giving you the whole keyboard to choose from. And if that's really the case, why not just break down and say, "Slap your keyboard a few times with your open palms to continue. . ."?

The Keys of State

There are three keys that affect the way the keyboard behaves. I call them the keys of state. They are CapsLock, NumLock, and ScrollLock.

CapsLock works like the ShiftLock key on a typewriter. Press CapsLock once to turn it on. After you do that, all the alphabet keys on the keyboard (26 of them at last count) will produce uppercase letters. Press CapsLock again to turn it off. Note that unlike a typewriter, CapsLock only shifts the letter keys; all the other keys on the keyboard will remain the same.

NumLock controls the numeric keypad. Press NumLock once to turn it on. When it's on, the numeric keypad produces numbers (like you suppose it would). Press NumLock again to turn it off. When NumLock is off, the numeric keypad doubles as a cursor keypad. The arrow keys, Home, PgUp, and so forth, will take precedence. (This is the way most DOS users prefer to use the numeric pad, as a cursor keypad.)

The ScrollLock key is vaguely defined and doesn't do anything under DOS. In some spreadsheets, ScrollLock has the effect of "locking" the cursor keys. So instead of pressing an arrow key to move the cell selector to another cell in the spreadsheet, with ScrollLock on, the whole spreadsheet moves in the direction of the arrow key. Other applications may use the ScrollLock key differently, but under DOS it serves no direct function. (Press it a few times on someone else's computer to irritate a friend.)

The positions of the CapsLock, NumLock, and ScrollLock keys vary. Figure 10-2 shows the locations on an enhanced 101-key keyboard. Other keys that are not keys of state, like the Shift keys, are where you'd expect them to be on any typewriter; two Control keys are on the outside edges of the typewriter area, in lower corners; and the two Alt keys are inside, on either end of the spacebar. Laptop keyboards and older PC keyboards have these keys in different locations, but they're still labeled Shift, Ctrl, and Alt.

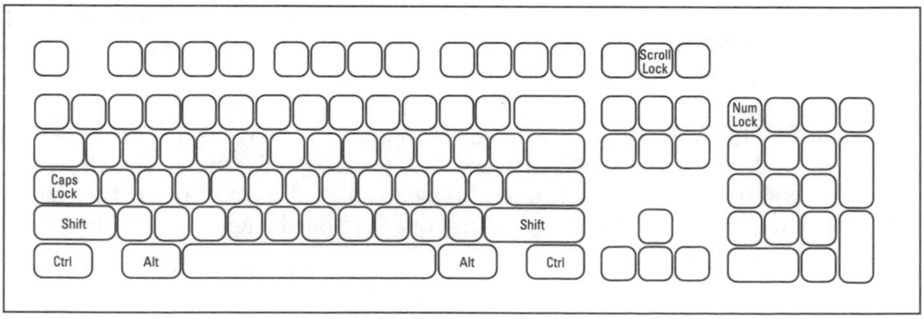

Figure 10-2:
State- and
Shift-key
locations.

 ✔ If your keyboard has a CapsLock, NumLock, or ScrollLock light, it will be on when the corresponding state key is on.

 ✔ If your CapsLock key is backward (sometimes it gets that way), the only way to fix this situation is to reset. For example, if the CapsLock light is on yet you aren't getting uppercase letters, reset to remedy the situation. (Exit your applications first!)

Slash and Backslash

There are two slash keys under DOS. The first is the forward slash (/), the most common of the two. This slash leans forward, like it's falling to the right. On most computers, it's used to denote division, such as 52/13 (52 divided by 13). In English, it's used to divide various words or, most often, as an incorrect replacement for a hyphen.

The backslash is a backward-slanting slash (\) that leans to the left. This character is used in DOS to represent the root directory. It also appears in pathnames to separate the various directory names. For more information on the root directory and directory names, refer to Chapter 17.

Interesting yet skippable information on reverse state keys

When CapsLock is on, the Shift key can be used to reverse the case of a letter. When CapsLock is off, press the Shift key plus a letter to get a capital letter. But with CapsLock on, pressing the Shift key plus a letter produces a lowercase letter.

The same weirdness affects the numeric keypad and the NumLock key. With NumLock on, pressing a key on the numeric keypad produces a number key. Yet pressing the Shift key and a number key produces the corresponding arrow key. For example, pressing Shift-4 on the keypad with NumLock on gives you the left-arrow key. When NumLock is off, pressing Shift plus a key gives you the corresponding number key.

Yeah, this is confusing. If you play around with the keyboard and the CapsLock, NumLock, and Shift keys, you'll see what's going on. But why fill your head with such trivial matters?

Enter or Return?

Nearly all PC computer keyboards have two keys labeled Enter. Both keys work identically, with the second Enter key placed by the numeric keypad to facilitate rapid entry of numbers.

The Enter key is used to end a line of text. After entering the text, press Enter, and the information is *locked in*. After you press Enter at the DOS prompt, the command you typed is sent off to DOS for scrutiny. However, in a word processor you use the Enter key to end a paragraph. (The words *wrap* automatically at the end of a line, meaning you don't have to press Enter to end each line.)

So what is the Return key? Many early computers sported a Return key. Essentially, it's the same thing as the Enter key. In fact, some computers had both an Enter and a Return key.

The difference between Enter and Return is only semantic. Enter has its roots in the electronic calculator industry. You pressed Enter to enter numbers or a formula. Return, on the other hand, comes from the electronic typewriter. Pressing the Return key on a typewriter caused the carriage to return to the left margin. It also advanced the paper one line in the machine.

The Tab key is also used in some applications (mainly databases) to end entry of information into a *field*. Like on a typewriter, pressing Tab moves the cursor over eight spaces or to the next *tab stop*, though on some computers pressing Tab causes the computer to produce a can of a refreshing diet beverage.

You may freely skip over this trivia

When you press the Enter key, the computer generates two different characters. The first is the *carriage return* character. This has the effect of moving the cursor to the leftmost column on the screen, just as a carriage return on a manual typewriter does. (Remember whacking the carriage-return bar?)

The second character produced is the *line feed*. This character moves the cursor down to the next line on the screen. Again, in the ancient days of typewriting, the line feed advanced the paper in the machine. In fact, the carriage return/line feed was usually performed by whacking the same lever.

In computerspeak, you'll often encounter the terms *carriage return/line feed* or the abbreviation CRLF. (Am I the only person who pronounces that "Crullif"?) This simply means that you press the Enter key, or it refers to the two secret characters that end a line of text.

Alt-S Means What?

Alt-S could mean anything, actually. (It's up to each application to assign meanings to certain keys.) The important thing is to know what to do when you see Alt-S, or even Alt+S.

The Alt key works like the Shift key on the keyboard. In fact, there are three kinds of shift keys on the keyboard: Shift, Alt, and Ctrl. This baffles most people because the typewriter only has one shift key, the Shift key.

The positions of the Alt, Ctrl, and Shift keys on the enhanced 101-key keyboard are shown in Figure 10-2.

You use the Alt, Ctrl, and Shift keys similarly: Press and hold Alt, Ctrl, or Shift and then type another key on the keyboard (usually a letter of the alphabet, though function keys are commonly paired with the shift keys).

You produce an uppercase *S* by pressing Shift-S, though no one needs to say "press Shift-S" because most typewriter-using people know that it works that way. But with three shift keys on a computer, you need to specify things. Pressing Alt-S means pressing and holding the Alt key and then typing an **S**. No character appears on the screen; instead, the program may do something, such as save a file to disk.

The Ctrl key works the same way. When you read "press Ctrl-C," press and hold the Ctrl (Control) key, type a **C**, and then release both keys.

- ✔ Even though you may see Ctrl-S or Alt-S with a capital *S*, this doesn't mean you must type Ctrl-Shift-S or Alt-Shift-S. Those are actually separate keystrokes where you press three keys at once. In fact, the Ctrl and Alt keys can be used with or without the Shift key, so most users skip it.

- ✔ The functions of all the Alt and Ctrl keys differ from application to application.

- ✔ Keep in mind that Alt, Ctrl, and Shift can be used with the function keys. In fact, WordPerfect users will recognize 40 function-key combinations using these shift keys plus ten function keys.

- ✔ The Ctrl-key combinations have an abbreviation: The caret or hat character (^) is used to denote Control. When you see ^C, it means the keystroke Ctrl-C or the Control-C character.

Ctrl-S and the Pause Key

In MS-DOS, several Ctrl-key combinations can be used to give you more power over the PC. The two most common are Ctrl-S and Ctrl-C.

Ctrl-C is the universal DOS cancel key combination. It stops any DOS command and cancels just about anything you're typing — a good thing to know. For more information, refer to "Canceling a DOS Command" in Chapter 3.

The Ctrl-S key combination is used to freeze information, suspending it as it's displayed on the screen. This enables you to read rapidly scrolling text by pressing Ctrl-S in a panic-driven frenzy and then . . . the screen stops, dead in its tracks. Press Ctrl-S again (or any key) and the display scrolls again. This all happens until all the information is displayed, or until you press Ctrl-S again to stop.

To test Ctrl-S, you need to display a long document. Typically, you do this with the TYPE command. Here is an example:

```
C> TYPE LONGJOHN
```

As the file LONGJOHN is displayed, it scrolls wildly up the screen. But pressing the Ctrl-S key combination stops it. This enables you to read a bit. When you're ready to see more text, press Ctrl-S, Enter, or the spacebar. To freeze the screen again, press Ctrl-S.

The Pause key on some keyboards has the same effect as Ctrl-S, and it's only one key to press. However, unlike Ctrl-S, you must press any other key but Pause to get things rolling again. For me, I prefer pressing Enter as my "any" key.

- ✔ The Pause key may also be labeled *Hold.*

- ✔ You can always cancel any long display by pressing Ctrl-C.

- ✔ For more information on the TYPE command, refer to "Looking at Files" in Chapter 2.

- ✔ The Ctrl-P key combination switch is another handy DOS control-key function. Refer to "Printing DOS" in Chapter 11.

The WordStar Cursor- and Cursed-At Key Diamond

WordStar was the first popular and most widely used word processor for the personal computer. Not just DOS computers, but the Apple II, a slew of CP/M "boxes," and the old TRS-80 (the "trash-80") could run WordStar. Back then it was the Cadillac of word processors. Sheesh, it even had *block* commands and featured *word wrap*. How could anyone compete? It showed you where the page ended — right there on the screen!

Because most keyboards at the time lacked cursor keypads, the folks who made WordStar came up with an interesting alternative for moving the cursor around. They came up with the WordStar *cursor-key diamond*. This is a set of control-key combinations on the keyboard that represent pressing certain arrow keys, whether or not your computer already has enough arrow keys.

I'm bringing all this up because many popular programs still offer the WordStar cursor-key diamond and control-key commands. Generally, the application also supports the standard cursor-key commands. But if not, Table 10-1 lists all the key commands. Figure 10-3 shows the WordStar cursor-key diamond as mapped out on your keyboard.

✔ There is no need to memorize Table 10-1, though after a while, using these key commands may seem logical to you. (I pray that never happens.)

✔ Different applications use different key commands to do similar things. The only way to be certain is to refer to the manual, although the basic cursor keys plus the control keys listed in Table 10-1 are usually common to all DOS programs.

✔ In the DOS Editor, you use the WordStar cursor key commands to edit a file. Refer to Chapter 16.

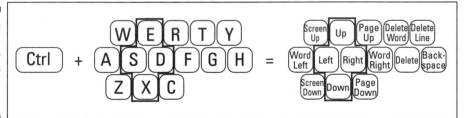

Figure 10-3: The WordStar cursor-key diamond diagram.

Table 10-1	The WordStar Cursor-Key Diamond and Control-Key Commands	
WordStar Command	*Common Key Command*	*Function*
Ctrl-E	Up arrow	Moves the cursor up one line
Ctrl-X	Down arrow	Moves the cursor down one line
Ctrl-S	Left arrow	Moves the cursor left (back) one character
Ctrl-D	Right arrow	Moves the cursor right (forward) one character
Ctrl-R	PgUp	Moves up to the previous page (screen)
Ctrl-C	PgDn	Moves down to the next page (screen)
Ctrl-A	Ctrl-Left	Moves left one word
Ctrl-F	Ctrl-Right	Moves right one word
Ctrl-W	Ctrl-Up	Scrolls the screen up one line
Ctrl-Z	Ctrl-Down	Scrolls the screen down one line
Ctrl-G	Delete	Deletes current character
Ctrl-T	Ctrl-Backspace	Deletes current word (or Ctrl-Delete)
Ctrl-H	Backspace	Deletes previous character

Controlling the Keyboard

You can use the MODE command to control two aspects of the keyboard: how long you have to wait after pressing a key for more characters to appear and how fast those characters repeat.

The PC keyboard sports a feature IBM dubbed the *typematic*. This means that if you press and hold any key, it will repeat. Press and hold the I key and soon you have a dozen or so I's all across the screen. That's the typematic at work.

The initial pause before the key repeats is referred to as *delay*. It can be set to any time interval from ¹/₄ to a full second. The speed at which the key repeats (once it starts repeating) is the *rate*. Keys can repeat at any rate from 2 to 30 characters per second. Both the *rate* and the *delay* are set using the MODE command in the following format:

```
C> MODE CON RATE=20 DELAY=2
```

Here the MODE command sets the computer to the standard typematic repeat and delay: MODE is followed by a space and then CON (which somehow means the keyboard). The word RATE is followed by an equal sign and 20, for a 20-character-per-second repeat rate. The word DELAY is followed by an equal sign and 2, which means it starts to repeat ¾ or ½ second after the key is held down.

Now suppose you're a heavy-handed typist. To avoid having keys repeat on you all the time, you could enter the following:

```
C> MODE CON RATE=20 DELAY=4
```

This command sets the delay to ¾ of a second, or one second even. That should eliminate the repeating keys you see all the time. (You must list both the *rate* and *delay* words after the command.)

If you want your keyboard to be slippery slick, enter this command:

```
C> MODE CON RATE=32 DELAY=1
```

Press Enter and you'll get an idea of how annoying an overly responsive keyboard can be. Enter the first command listed here to restore your computer — or just whack the Reset switch (Ctrl-Alt-Delete) if it severely annoys you.

The MODE command in this capacity only works with certain keyboards. If you have an older PC, you may not be able to change the delay and repeat rates.

My Keyboard Beeps at Me!

On the typical PC, you can type ahead up to 16 characters. A word processor is usually able to eat those characters as fast as you type them. But sometimes, say when you're accessing a disk or the computer is out doing something, you can still type. Apparently, the keyboard remembers up to the last 16 keys you typed, and then . . . it starts beeping at you, once for each key beyond the 16 you've already typed. Those extra keys, typed as you hear the beeps, won't be displayed. Essentially, your keyboard is "full."

There's nothing you can do about this. Some special programs, utilities, or keyboard enhancers may give you more than 16 characters to type ahead. But generally speaking, when the keyboard starts beeping, just stop typing and wait a few moments. Then wait a few minutes more — I had a program that took two full minutes to come back to life!

If the keyboard continues to beep, you've locked it up! The only way to escape this peril is to reset (Ctrl-Alt-Delete), or press the Reset button, or turn the PC off and on again.

Having a Mouse

The computer mouse is a handy pointing device used primarily in graphics programs. It comes in two parts: the mouse-like, hand-held device, usually as big as a fat deck of cards that can fit in the palm of your hand; and the software that tells DOS and all your programs that you have a mouse.

The mouse faces toward you with its tail going back to the computer's rump. There it plugs into either a serial port or a special mouse port. The mouse usually has one or more buttons on top, which you press with your index finger.

The mouse software is installed either in your system configuration file, CONFIG.SYS or your AUTOEXEC.BAT file. You should have someone else do this, preferably at or near the time when he or she attaches the mouse to your computer. (If you want to dabble with editing your CONFIG.SYS or AUTOEXEC.BAT files yourself, refer to Chapter 16.)

The mouse works by being rolled around on the desktop. To use a mouse, you need a relatively wide area of space on your desktop. Look around your desktop. Do you see an open, flat area about 8 inches by 12 inches in size? I didn't think so. To use a mouse, you have to give it some room. On my desk I get by with about a 4-by-4 square for the mouse.

✔ You may want to invest in a mouse pad, a handy device upon which to roll the mouse. It gives the mouse's little ball-foot more traction than your typical Formica pressboard computer desk.

✔ For more information on the serial port, refer to "The serial port" in Chapter 7.

Using a Mouse

The mouse just doesn't become immediately useful; you must have software that takes advantage of it. Fortunately, there is a standard method for using the mouse that makes it a rather painless part of PC computing.

The mouse controls a *pointer* or *mouse cursor* on the screen. This may be the same as the text cursor, the one you see all the time at the DOS prompt, or it may be its own unique cursor, pointer, or square block. Sometimes the mouse cursor is just anyone who barges into the room and starts yelling at the furless little guy.

When you move the mouse around, rolling it on your desktop, the pointer on the screen moves in a similar manner. Roll the mouse left and the pointer moves left; roll it in circles and the pointer mimics that action; drop the mouse off the table and your DOS prompt changes to read "Ouch!" (Just kidding.)

There should be one or more buttons on the mouse. You press them with your index finger while keeping the mouse in the palm of your hand on the desktop. You use the button(s) to manipulate various items on the computer screen. It goes like this: You move the mouse, which moves the cursor on the screen over to something interesting. You click the mouse button, and something even more interesting happens.

What happens, of course, depends on the software you use. And if the mouse has more than one button, each button may perform different functions. It's all up to the application; like many other things in DOS, there are no standards, no rules, no guidelines . . . it's personal computing run amok!

Mouse Terminology

Various mouse terms are associated with using a mouse. These terms are quite simple and, thanks to millions of dollars of research by Apple Computer, they make sense! Only by using your mouse will these terms become obvious to you. It really pays to have a mouse and an application that supports the mouse in order to appreciate these terms. In case you don't, I've defined the terms here anyway.

Button

The button is the device on top of the mouse. Pressing the button is referred to as *clicking,* though clicking has another definition (covered in a later paragraph).

Pointer or cursor

The thing the mouse moves around on the screen is called the *mouse pointer.* I call it the pointer. Some applications call it the *cursor,* which is easily confused with the true cursor God created, the DOS text cursor.

Click

A click is a press of the mouse button. Often you'll read "click the mouse on the NO button." This means there's a graphic something-or-other on the screen with the word NO on it. Using the mouse, you hover the pointer over the word

NO. Then, with your index finger, click the mouse button. This is referred to as *clicking the mouse* on something, usually something on the screen. (Though you could roll the mouse around on your forehead and click it there if you like — just make sure no one's looking.)

Double-click

A *double-click* is like a click-click, two rapid clicks in a row. You do this in many applications to quickly select some item. (The time between clicks varies, but it doesn't have to be *that* quick. Also, don't move the mouse around between the clicks.)

Drag

To drag something with the mouse, you press and hold the mouse button down and then move the mouse around. On the screen this has the effect of grabbing something (pressing the button) and then moving it about on the screen (dragging it). When you release the mouse button, you "let go" of whatever it was you were dragging.

Select

Selecting is the process of highlighting something, making it the target for whatever future plans you have. For example, you select a box by clicking on that box. You select text by dragging the cursor over the text you want; that action *highlights* the text, which is similar to marking a block of text.

Mouse Droppings

As with everything else in a PC, occasionally the mouse screws up. It does so by producing a trail on the screen, commonly called *mouse droppings*. This occurs when you move the mouse around and yet still see the cursor scattered all over the screen, typically more than one cursor that traces the pattern in which you're moving the mouse.

When you see mouse droppings, it usually means one thing: The computer is gaga. Whichever program you were running just forgot to turn the mouse off, and you're faced with the ugly consequences.

There is one solution to mouse droppings: Reset (Ctrl-Alt-Delete). You may consider telling one of the loftier PC users about it. They love to hear about computer bugs.

Chapter 11
The Printer
(Making the Right Impression)

*Y*our PC needs a printer to get that all-important hard copy — a permanent record of your work, output, efforts, what-have-you. Without a printer, you'd have to lug the PC around everywhere and show people your stuff on the monitor. That's tacky.

There are lots of printers out there. The problem is that there are few standards. There is no CGA-EGA-VGA type of compatibility with printers like you have with the computer's monitor. This isn't a problem as long as you stick to the major brands. But when you don't, it's time to rev up that chain saw. . . .

This chapter is about using a printer with your computer. By themselves, printers are harmless enough. But umbilically connect one to the evil PC — nay, the child of Satan himself! — and you're bound for trouble. Here is where you'll learn how to get out of trouble and put your firm thumb of control over the printer.

Getting Connected

Every PC should have at least one printer attached. It's connected via a separate cable: One end of the cable connects to the PC, the other to the printer. It's fairly obvious which end goes where, though on your PC's rump you may confuse the printer port for a serial port.

You can have up to four printers connected to your computer. The number of printers you can connect depends on how many printer ports your PC has. The typical PC has two printer ports, numbered one and two (low-end PCs have only one). If you have only one printer attached, make sure it's connected to port number one, which the dweebs call *LPT1*.

Once the printer is properly connected, you can test it by printing something. There are examples of printing under DOS later in this chapter. But I recommend that you dive into some application and then test printing in there.

- ✔ It's also possible to have a serial printer installed on your computer. This printer connects to the PC via a serial port — not a parallel port. Refer to the next section for more information.

- ✔ If you're plugging in cables on the back of your PC — and this can be any cable from the printer cable to a keyboard cable — make sure your PC is off. Having a PC on while you plug something in can lead to some rather nasty results.

- ✔ If the printer doesn't work, you may have it connected to the wrong port. Try plugging the cable into another, similar connector on the rear of your PC.

- ✔ For more information on ports, refer to "What Are Ports?" in Chapter 7.

DOS's forgettable printer names

DOS refers to everything it controls by a *device name*. The name for the printer is *PRN,* a nice handy three-letter word (without vowels) that means printer. So far so good.

DOS can control up to three printers for each PC. The device name PRN actually refers to only the first printer, the *main* printer. The real, secret names for the three possible printers are *LPT1, LPT2,* and *LPT3. LPT* stands for *line printer.* It's probably one of those massive, 1940s-type computer devices.

I bring this up because, well, I'm a nerd. Beyond that, you may occasionally see these names used and confused. For example, you may be asked, `Is your laser printer connected to LPT1?` As far as I can translate this, it means "Is your printer hooked up to the first printer port?" Beware of such deceptive terms that weave their way into computer manuals and books.

The Serial Connection

Out of the 1,700 or so printer makes and models available for the PC, you'll find a handful that operate out of a serial port — not the almost-sane printer port, which you would expect. These are usually older printers, or printers designed for use on non-IBM-type computers.

Nothing is bad about owning a serial printer. They work just fine, and connecting them to your computer is as easy as plugging in the special serial printer cable. That's the easy part. The hard part comes with setting up the computer and telling DOS about it.

The first part is to set up the printer to a specific speed or *baud* and a *data word format*. This is done by holding the manual in one hand and setting these minute switches on the printer with the other. I really have no idea how your particular printer does it, but what you want to do is set it to either:

```
9600, 8, N, 1
```

(that's the fast setting) or:

```
2400, 8, N, 1
```

(that's a slower setting). Refer to the manual for the proper settings, or something that looks similar to the examples.

On the DOS side, before you can use the serial printer you must give DOS the following two commands. The first is used to set up the serial port in the exact same manner as you've set up the printer:

```
C> MODE COM1:9600,N,8,1
```

Here the MODE command is followed by a space. Then comes COM1 and a colon, which represents your first serial port. That's followed by the speed, 9600 in our example, and then N, 8, and 1 to match the 8, N, and 1 you set your printer to. If you specified a different speed (say 2400), substitute it for 9600 here.

The second step is to tell DOS that its printer device, called PRN, is now on the serial port instead of the printer port. That's done with the following command:

```
C> MODE LPT1=COM1
```

Ugh. Real Greek, no less. Basically, this is the MODE command, a space, the hieroglyph LPT1 (meaning DOS's primary printer) and then COM1 (which means the first serial port to which your printer is attached).

After entering those two commands, you can use your printer under DOS — even in applications — as you would a parallel printer.

These commands are confusing. Trust me on this: No one I know has memorized them. Even I had to look them up to write them down here. You're forgiven if you repeatedly have to refer to this section to start your computer each day.

✔ If these commands are something you'll be typing every day when you start your computer, why not make them a part of your AUTOEXEC.BAT automatic startup file? Refer to Chapter 16 for the details.

✔ Note that the serial printer cable is a special kind of cable, usually labeled as a "serial printer cable." You cannot use the same serial cable as you would, say, to connect a modem; it won't work.

✔ For more information on parallel and serial ports, refer to "What Are Ports?" in Chapter 7; for information on setting up a serial port, refer to "The serial port," also in Chapter 7.

Going On-Line

Before a printer can print, three things must happen: The printer must be connected to the computer; you must have paper in the printer; and the printer must be *on-line* or *selected*.

Somewhere on your printer is a button. That button may be labeled *on-line* or *select*. Pressing it puts the printer into the "ready" mode, making it ready to print. If the printer is off-line or deselected, it's still on but not ready to print. Usually you take a printer off-line to advance paper, change a font, or unjam it. But you can only print again by putting the printer back on-line or selecting it.

✔ Most on-line, select, or ready buttons have a corresponding light. When the light is on, the printer is ready to print.

✔ If the printer lacks an on-line, select, or ready button, it's probably ready for printing all the time.

Form Feeding

The act of ejecting a sheet of paper from the printer is referred to as a *form feed*. There's a button for this purpose on most printers. It's called, remarkably enough, "Form feed," though sometimes the label "Eject" is used. To eject a page of paper from the printer, you first take the printer off-line by pressing the on-line or select button and then you press the form-feed or eject button. Zwoop! Out flies a sheet of paper.

This button seems rather silly . . . until you need a full sheet of paper to shoot out of the printer. Even more important, a laser printer won't spit out a sheet of paper until it has printed the whole thing. So if you want to see what you've printed and you haven't printed a full page, you must take the printer off-line and press the form-feed or eject button. Press select or on-line to turn off the little light.

✔ For more information about the on-line or select buttons, refer to the previous section.

✔ Most nonlaser printers also have a *line-feed* button. This button simply advances the paper one line of text each time you press it. As with form feed, you must have the printer off-line or deselected to use the line-feed button.

Force a page out

There is a special character called the *form feed*. It's the Ctrl-L character, often shown as ^L. When this character is sent to the printer — any printer — it's an immediate instruction to the printer to eject a page. But although typing Ctrl-L produces the form-feed character, sending it to the printer isn't obvious.

To send the Ctrl-L keystroke to the printer, type the following DOS command:

```
C> ECHO ^L > PRN
```

That's the ECHO command, a space, and then the form-feed character produced by pressing Ctrl-L. (That's not the caret and L characters.) This is followed by a space, the greater-than symbol (>), another space, and then the letters PRN (for printer). Press Enter and the printer spits up a page.

The Page Didn't Come Out of My Laser Printer!

Laser printers are unlike their more primitive dot-matrix cousins. With a *dot-matrix printer,* aside from getting mediocre text quality, you get to see what you print as it's printed (even hear it, too!). Laser printers are quiet. But they don't print until one of two situations occur:

1. The laser printer will print if you've printed a whole page full of text, not before. Unlike the dot-matrix printer, nothing is really put down on paper until you fill up a sheet.

2. You can always force a laser printer to print what's been sent to it so far by giving it a form feed. You can do this by pressing a special button on the printer or by using a secret DOS command. Both of these are covered in the previous section, "Force a page out."

In a Jam?

Paper flows through your printer like film through a projector; each sheet is magically ejected from a laser printer like the wind blowing leaves on an autumn day. Poppycock! Paper likes to weave its way through the inner guts of your printer like a four-year-old poking his fingers into your VCR. When this happens, your printer can become jammed.

For dot-matrix printers, you can unjam most paper by rewinding the knob. But turn off the printer first! This disengages the advancing mechanism's death grip on the paper platen, which means it makes it easier to back out the jammed paper. If the paper is really in there tight, you may need to remove the platen. When that happens, you need to take the printer apart to get at the problem; call someone else for help unless you want to take it apart yourself.

For laser printers, a light flashes on the printer when the paper gets jammed. If the printer has a message read-out, you may see the message "Paper jam" displayed in any of a variety of languages and subtongues. Make your first attempt at unjamming by removing the paper tray. If you see the end of the paper sticking out, grab it and firmly pull toward you. The paper should slip right out. If you can't see the paper, pop open the printer's lid and look for the jammed sheet. Carefully pull it out either forward or backward. You don't have to turn the printer off first, but watch out for hot parts.

Sometimes printers jam because the paper you're using is too thick. If that's the case, removing the paper and trying it again probably won't help; use thinner paper. Otherwise, paper jams for a number of reasons, so just try again and it will work.

Printing on One Line or Massive Double Spacing

Two common printer flubs are the "Everything is printing on one line!" expression of panic and the "Why the heck is everything double-spaced all the time?" annoying interrogation. Both problems are related, though solving them doesn't involve lying on a couch and talking about your mother.

Somewhere on your printer is a series of tiny switches. The computer weenies call them *DIP switches*. Flipping one of those tiny switches will solve your problem, whether everything is printing on one line or you're seeing all your text double-spaced. (They're both actually the same problem, which is covered in the information that follows, which you can ignore.)

The switch will be identified in your manual. It has the name "Add linefeed" or "Automatic linefeed" or "LF after CR" or something along those lines. To fix your problem, flip the switch. It's a tiny switch, so you may have to mutilate a paper clip to reach in and flip it (turn off the printer first).

- ✔ If flipping this switch is something you don't feel like doing, have someone else do it.

- ✔ If you cannot locate the switch on the back of your printer, it may be inside, under the printing mechanism. If so, turn the printer off when you're in there fumbling around.

- ✔ If this doesn't fix the problem right away, turn the printer off, wait, and then turn it back on again.

Printing problems explained, which you can ignore

Each line sent to the printer ends in two special codes: the *carriage return* and *line feed*. The carriage return tells the printer to start printing on column one again — on the left side of the page. The line feed, following the carriage return, tells the printer to print down on the next line on the page. Simple enough.

The problem is that not every computer sends the printer a carriage return/line feed combination. Some computers only send a carriage return. When that happens, no line feed takes place and all your text is printed on one ugly, ink-stained line.

To solve the problem of printing on one line, the printer can be told (via a switch) to supply its own line feed automatically after each carriage return received. That way, if your computer is dumb enough to send only the carriage return to end a line, the printer supplies the line feed and everything prints as you've intended.

The problem of double spacing happens when that same add-a-line-feed switch is on and the computer is already sending a carriage return/line feed combo. In that case, at the end of the line the printer adds its own line feed, giving a double-spaced effect. Turning the tiny switch off fixes that problem.

Printing the Screen

There is a special button on your keyboard — a feature — that causes all the text you see on the screen to be printed. It's called the Print Screen key, though that particular key may be labeled "Print Scrn" or "Prt Scn" or something even more cryptic.

The technical term for printing the screen is a *screen dump*. Normally, I wouldn't mention that here, but I personally find it hilarious: "Excuse me, dear, I've got to take a screen dump." Riotous stuff!

To practice, make sure your printer is on-line and ready to print. Then press the Print Screen key. Zip-zip-zip. A few minutes later, you'll see a copy of your screen on the printer. (If you have a laser printer, you'll have to eject the page; refer to the discussion under "Form Feeding" earlier in this chapter.)

✔ For more information about the keyboard, refer to Chapter 10.

✔ If the printer isn't on and you hit Print Screen, one of two things may happen. The first, and hopefully what happens all the time when you accidentally press Print Screen, is that nothing happens. Whew! The second thing that may happen is that the computer waits for the printer so it can print your screen. And it waits. And waits. Turn the printer on and watch it print; there's no way to cancel out of this with Ctrl-C.

Print Screen woes

The Print Screen key isn't the miracle most people suppose it is. For example, if your screen shows lines and boxes along with text, you may not see those characters displayed. In fact, you may see lots of *m*'s or colons or other odd characters or even italic text.

The reason for the Print Screen garbage is that your printer isn't capable of printing the IBM *graphics set*. If your printer can somehow wiggle itself into an IBM-compatible mode, you'll see the characters just fine. Otherwise, you'll have to live with all the *m*'s and whatnot.

Another Print Screen woe is that the *screen dump* only copies text. If you're using a graphics program and are looking at a picture of the latest screen god or goddess seductively biting his or her lower lip — and, by God, you want a hard copy of this to tape up by your pillow — then pressing the Print Screen key won't help you. Unfortunately, Print Screen only copies text and any attempt to *dump* a graphics image (no matter how badly you crave it) results in garbled output — and emotional disappointment.

> ✔ If you're running Windows, pressing the Print Screen key *captures* the current screen or window. That image is stored in the Clipboard, and you can paste it elsewhere for editing, printing, or salivating.

> ✔ Some programs are available that replace DOS's lame Print Screen key with a smarter program, one that prints graphics. Refer to your local software-o-rama for the particulars.

> ✔ If you hit Print Screen and your printer is turned off (or disconnected), the computer sits there and waits for the printer to do something — forever if need be. Turn the printer on — or reboot.

Printing DOS

The normal way you use DOS is to type in a command and expect (hopefully) that DOS will display something that pleases you on the screen. In fact, all of your interaction with DOS is shown on the screen which, I'll admit, comes in handy. Even more handy is to sometimes have a *hard copy* of all DOS's output — a transcript of your DOS session, but without sending the $2 to "Transcripts," at some P.O. box in Jersey. This is done using the *DOS print switch,* which is actually a keyboard command.

If your printer is on and ready to print, you can press Ctrl-P to activate DOS's printing function. After pressing Ctrl-P, DOS sends all output to both the screen and the printer. Everything is output, even embarrassing errors. But more important, you'll see vital information such as file listings, displays, and other trivia.

To turn off DOS's printing function, press Ctrl-P again.

- ✔ If you just want to print a single file, refer to "Printing a Text File" in Chapter 4.

- ✔ If you just want to print a directory listing (the output of the DIR command), refer to "Printing a Directory" in the next section.

- ✔ Laser printers won't print anything until a full page is generated. To see what you've printed before then, refer to the discussion under "Form Feeding" earlier in this chapter.

- ✔ The only way to be sure you've turned off DOS's printing function is to press Enter a few times. If the DOS prompt doesn't appear on your printer, the printing is off. If it does, try Ctrl-P again.

- ✔ Ctrl-P is what computer wizards call a *toggle*. A toggle is a single command that turns something both on and off, going either way each time you use the command.

Printing a Directory

The handiest thing to print is a list of files on disk. Under DOS, you see a list of files using the DIR command. But that only spits out the file information to the screen. To send the information to a printer, first make sure the printer is on and ready to print, and then type the following command:

```
C> DIR > PRN
```

That's the DIR command, followed by a space, the greater-than symbol (>), another space, and then PRN (which means *Printer* in the Land of No Vowels).

- ✔ If you want to use any of the DIR command's options, sandwich them between DIR and the greater-than symbol (>). Note that the /P (pause) option would be rather silly at this point.

- ✔ If you print a directory to a laser printer, you may need to eject the paper from the printer to see the output; refer to the discussion under "Form Feeding" earlier in this chapter.

- ✔ You won't see the directory on the screen when you use this command. If you want to see the directory on the screen, use the DOS printing function, as discussed in the previous section.

Why Does It Look Funny?

Printing anything from DOS has its consequences: If your printer cannot display the IBM graphics characters, they'll appear as other, odd characters on your hard copy. Seriously, the best place to print anything is from an application. But even then, you may not get what you want from your printer.

The answer lies in a piece of software called a *printer driver*. Like a slave driver, the printer driver utterly controls the printer, telling it to do exactly what the application wants. Why can't the application do this itself? Because there is no standard DOS printer. There are hundreds of printers, any one of which you may have attached to your PC. To tell your application which printer you have, you must set up the printer by directing the application to talk to it via a printer driver.

Installing a printer driver is usually done when you first set up an application (which is covered in Chapter 14). You select your printer's name and model number from a list and then your application and your printer can work in sweet harmony. But this isn't always the case.

Sometimes, someone (maybe you) will select the wrong printer driver. Or worse, the application may not support your printer. As an example, WordPerfect has printer drivers for more than 1,000 different printers. My mailing-label program (which I won't name because I'm sorry I bought it) only supports five printers — and I don't have any of them. Needless to say, the output from that program looks terrible (but, what-the-hey, only the post office has to read the labels).

Each application enables you to set up your printer differently, so it is impossible to mention all the possibilities here. If you cannot find the proper driver or locate your printer by name, you can always opt for the *Dumb printer* option. This is where the program controls your printer in a text-only mode. It may not be the miracle of computers you dreamed of, but it works.

Those Funny Characters at the Top of the First Page

Occasionally, you may see some odd characters at the top of every page or just the first page you print. For example, you may see a ^ or &0 or E@, or any of a number of ugly-looking characters that you didn't want there and that don't show up on your screen. It requires a major "Hmmm."

Hmmm.

Those characters are actually secret printer-control codes. Normally, the characters are swallowed by the printer as it prepares itself to print. The problem is that the software on the computer is sending your printer the wrong codes. Since your printer doesn't understand the codes, it just prints them as is. Hence, you see ugly characters.

The solution is to select the proper printer driver for your software. You want a printer driver that knows your printer and how to send it the proper codes. This is stuff that's best done by the person who (supposedly) installed your software on the computer. It can be changed in most cases. But better make someone else do that for you.

Chapter 12
More on Modems

*F*air warning: Telecommunications is not simple, and nothing I can do in writing will make it simple. Why? Because the modem and communications vendors have come up with fifty jillion different ways to do things and some of the most arcane jargon this side of quantum physics to describe it. Which *port* is your modem plugged in to? What is its *speed*? What *duplex* mode, *start and stop bits*, *transmission protocol*, and other gobbledygook make using a modem a nightmare?

The best possible way to use your modem is to get somebody else to set you up from soup to nuts, including preparing a *dialing directory* and walking you through the basics for the kinds of things you need to get done. In this chapter I'll just review the basics, in case it helps.

What Does a Modem Do?

A modem is a device that takes the digital information from your computer and translates it into audio signals that can be sent over common phone lines (see Figure 12-1). In a way, the computer sends painful bits and bytes to the modem, which then converts them into sounds and "sings" them over the phone line (and I'm not talking operatic here). Using the modem, you can send information to another computer by calling its modem on the phone.

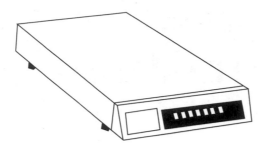

You control a modem, and therefore talk with another computer, by using *communications software,* also called *telecom software.* It controls the modem, dials up other computers, sends information, and does just about everything in a complex and confusing manner. (Seriously, communications software is perhaps the most consistently cryptic of any application.)

✔ The most common device to plug in to a serial port is a modem. In fact, the serial port is often referred to as a *modem port.* Refer to Chapter 7 for the lowdown on ports.

✔ Modem is a contraction of the words *modulator-demodulator.* But instead of calling it a *lator-lator,* they chose *mo-dem.* Also, there are more modem jokes in the computer world than anything else, typically "How many modem do you want?"

✔ Modems are judged by their speed — how fast they can talk to each other. Your computer can chat with the modem at blistering speeds, but the modem is limited (by design and price) as to how fast it can talk. The speed value is measured by *bits per second,* or *bps.* Refer to the section "Communications Terminology Explicated," later in this chapter.

Hooking up your modem

There are two kinds of modems: internal and external. The internal modems sit inside your computer, snugly wedged into an expansion slot. External modems sit outside the computer and must be connected to a serial port via a modem cable.

Internal modems have several advantages. The most obvious is that they're hidden from view, tucked inside the PC. This means they don't eat up desk space or a power socket on the wall. It may also mean that the modem came with software, which removes another computer decision process.

To plug in your internal modem, locate someone whose fear level about such things is lower than yours and bribe them heavily. Although you can do it yourself, I recommend the safe approach of having someone else do it.

External modems have several advantages. The most obvious is that you can see them and their pretty little lights, which tell you whether the modem is still breathing or has passed on to a higher plane of existence. You can also turn off an external modem if the need arises, and you can easily adjust its speaker volume.

Anyone can install an external modem: Take it out of the box and peel back the Styrofoam and wrapping. Set it on your desktop. Plug the power cord into the wall. Plug the phone cord into the wall (and optionally plug the phone that was plugged into the wall into the modem). Plug one end of a modem cable into the modem. Plug the other end into your PC. *Plug, plug, plug your modem, gently into the wall; merrily, merrily, merrily, merrily, comm is such a ball!*

Personally, I prefer external modems. The reason is portability. I bought my current modem in 1985 and have used it on a TRS-80 computer, an Apple II, a Macintosh, a NeXT, and a PC. An internal modem would have been useful only on a PC it can plug into.

Now all that's left is wrestling with communications software.

The Horror of Communications Software

A communications program is software that controls the connection between your computer and some other remote computer system, such as an on-line service (like CompuServe, GEnie, or MCI Mail) or a local BBS (like the other services but cheaper — and free — and run by some kid in your neighborhood).

Communications software does a great deal, which is probably why it's so darn cryptic. Basically, it has to coordinate several elements:

- ✔ Your computer's serial port
- ✔ The modem itself
- ✔ Setting things up to call another computer
- ✔ Talking with the other modem that answers the phone
- ✔ Doing interesting things while you're talking to the other computer
- ✔ Odd terminology

The nice part is that once you've set the various options, using the communications software and your modem is a cinch (which is why I recommend having someone else configure your *dialing directory*).

✔ Some on-line services, such as Prodigy or America OnLine, require special software rather than a general-purpose program like Procomm or Crosstalk.

✔ What you're doing with communications software is calling another computer. That computer's modem answers the phone, talks to your modem, and then the two computers start sending information back and forth to each other. But while you're connected, you're essentially running a program on that other computer. This is the weird part of communications that makes some people sit in their chairs for hours without moving.

Calling Another Computer

Before you call another computer, your communications software must tell your modem certain things about the computer system you're about to dial up. This must be done for each other computer you call, since each computer that answers the phone is different (and that's probably due to some arcane law passed during the Bush administration).

Assuming that your modem is hooked up right and your communications software works (more or less), you need to know the following basic (yeah, right) information about the other system — the one you're about to phone:

✔ The speed (for example, 1200 bps or 2400 bps)

✔ The number of data bits (7 or 8)

✔ The parity (Odd, Even, or None)

✔ The number of stop bits (usually 1)

Both your modem and the other modem must agree on these items if any communications is to take place. Modems are stubborn. If any one of these items doesn't match up, the other modem may answer, but it won't understand what your modem is saying — it's like when a lawyer calls you unexpectedly. This is why you must make your modem match the other modem.

The following is the most typical setting:

2400 bps for the speed, 8, N, 1

This example translates into a modem that talks at 2400 bps, uses 8 data bits, no parity, and one stop bit. That's called a *data word format* of 8, N, 1. The other popular data word format for PC communications is 7, E, 1:

2400 bps for the speed, 7, E, 1

Chances are, most systems you dial up will use 8, N, 1. If not, 7, E, 1 should be your selection.

✔ These settings must be made before you call the other computer. You cannot change them once the call has been made.

✔ How you control these settings depends on your communications software. Thanks to the rule that no two PC programs should be alike, each telecom package does things differently.

✔ Common values for a modem's speed are 300, 1200, 2400, and 9600 bps. Faster values also appear. The idea is to match your modem's speed with the speed of the other modem. If a variety of speeds is listed, use the fastest speed your modem has that's compatible with the answering modem.

✔ There are other, truly weird settings for the data word format. With a PC, you can get by nearly all the time with 8, N, 1.

Dialing the modem

Modems work just like phones: They dial a number. Another modem should answer, in which case both modems start singing to each other, and the connection is made (providing you've properly set up the gobbledygook in the previous section).

Ah, but before you call, you need to know the other computer's number. Once you find that out, you use your communications software to dial that number.

For example, press Alt-D to bring up a dialing command. Then enter the phone number, say **1-555-234-5678**. Press Enter (or whatever your communications program dictates), and the modem dials that number.

After one or more rings, the modem you're calling should answer the phone and send its distinctive warble. The pitch of the warble will vary as the two modems compare notes, and then it will fall abruptly silent, and (if all goes well) you will see the word CONNECT on your screen. Wait a second or two and then follow the instructions of the service you're calling.

✔ If you don't see anything right away, press Enter. This might wake up the other computer.

✔ If you don't get a response at all, or if you get a long stream of garbage characters across the screen, hang up. Use the *hang-up* or *disconnect* command in your communications package. You can try calling again, which sometimes works. (Hey, modems are moody.) Or consider changing the data word format from 8, N, 1 to 7, E, 1 or vice versa. Or just toss up your arms and call your guru.

✔ One of four things can happen when you call up another computer: The other computer answers — which is great and what you want; or it's busy, which happens a lot; or there's no answer, in which case you can call back right away or later; or a human answers. If a human answers, do them a favor and don't call back using your modem. The places that publish modem (or *BBS*) numbers frequently make mistakes. Don't bug poor Mrs. Henderson by redialing her phone every 30 seconds from midnight to 2 a.m.; she probably hates computers more than you do.

✔ Assuming you aren't calling Mrs. Henderson's house, many communications programs have automatic redial features. That way you can redial a busy computer over and over until it answers. (However, this is a poor excuse to sit and stare at a computer for an hour, so I recommend calling back once every 10 minutes since most people spend about that long on-line anyway.)

✔ Calling with a modem is just like using the phone. The phone company (at present) does not charge any more for modems making phone calls than for people. Long distance and toll charges still apply.

✔ When you're using your modem, no one else can call you. I know, this sounds dumb, but few people realize they're using the phone because it's not immediately in their ear. Incidentally, if you pick up the phone while the modem is working, you'll hear a horrid high-pitched squeal — the modem in action. If you talk, you'll see random characters on your screen, or you may break the connection. (Other people in the house will do this more often than you.) Because of this, I recommend getting a second phone line for your modem.

Logging in

When the modem you're calling answers, it says "Hey, wake up!" to its computer. That computer then runs special software. What you're doing on-line is using that software remotely, from your own computer. You can send messages to others who use the system, read your mail, join a conference, play on-line games, send files to the system, or have the system send you files. Oh, it can all be so much fun. But everything starts with logging in.

```
LOGIN:
```

You need to tell the other computer who you are. This is done by typing your full name or nickname at a login prompt. Sometimes the prompt says LOGIN; other times it just may ask for your full name or first and then last names. If you've never called the system before, read the instructions on the screen to see how you can become a member and get your own account.

Calling another human by using your modem

Suppose you and that crazy Earl both went down and bought modems at the same time. You hook them up and then Earl calls and suggests that you phone each other up so you can "chat" electronically. This is a fun thing to do when you first get your modem (but old timers seriously roll their eyes over the thought).

To make it happen, you both should agree on your modems' speed and data word format. Let me help: Set your communications programs and modems to 2400 bps, 8, N, 1. Sure, your modem may be able to go faster, but you can barely type at 300 bps, so 2400 bps is more than fast enough.

The next thing you need to decide is who gets to call whom. One of you needs to be the calling computer, and the other must direct your com-munications package to answer the phone. Then the caller must dial up the answerer. This is a lot more complex than it sounds, though. If you're just sitting there and you see RING on the screen, type **ATA** and press Enter, and your modem will answer the phone. (Don't ask me how that works.)

Once you're connected, start typing at each other! You won't see what you type unless you activate the local echo command. Or check to see if your communications package has a special chat mode and use it. Keep in mind that if you have anything important to say, you can always pick up the phone and talk verbally. This is definitely much quicker than watching Earl always back up and correct his typing mistakes.

After you enter your login ID, you'll be prompted for a password. This is a secret word used to ensure that you are who you logged in as. Once that's entered and verified, you continue to use the on-line system.

- ✔ Many systems have interesting ways to log in. Some just come up right away; others require you to press Enter first. For example, CompuServe has you press Ctrl-C to get a prompt asking for your ID and password. Whatever the case, be sure to read any instructions on the screen, which should tell you what you can do next.

- ✔ If you're just calling another person who's expecting you, just type something and see if you get a typed response from that person.

- ✔ If, when you type, you see double letters or no letters at all, you need to switch your *duplex*. This is also called *local echo* in most communications programs (and it's usually the Alt-E key combination that controls it).

Doin' the On-Line Thing

On-line means something is connected. Your printer is on-line when it's actively paying attention to your computer and printing whatever the computer tells it to print. With a modem, you're on-line when you're actively conversing with another computer.

Most of what you do on-line is dictated by the other computer. You can read messages, peruse your mail, chat, and so on. This is all handled by the remote computer, so you just sit there and type. But there are times when you need to tell your computer to do something. There are three big issues I can think of:

Capturing a file. This is where you direct your communications program to start recording what you're receiving from the other computer. You can send the information to a file on disk or to your printer.

Uploading. This is where you send a file to the other computer. First, you tell the computer that you're sending it a file. You explain what type of file you're sending, give it a name, and answer whatever other questions you're asked. Then you send the computer that file. This involves selecting a mode for sending, such as XMODEM, ZMODEM, and so on.

For example, suppose you're sending REPORT.XLS to the office's computer. You dial up the office computer, log in, and then weave your way to the place where you upload the file. You tell the office computer that you're sending it REPORT.XLS. It asks which protocol you'll be using and provides a list:

```
1. ASCII
2. XMODEM
3. YMODEM
4. ZMODEM
```

Your communications software supports all these, so you pick ZMODEM. The office system says Start uploading your file. On your end, you tell your communications software to send a file using ZMODEM, and then you enter the filename.

You'll be alerted when the file is sent, at which time you continue using the office computer as you did before.

Downloading. This is the opposite of uploading. Here you're telling the other computer to send you a file. It works the same way uploading works, but because more people download than upload, here are the steps in brief outline form:

Steps: Downloading a file

Step 1. Locate the file you want to download. The other computer will have a command that displays a list of files. Examine the list carefully or use a Search or somesuch command to locate the file(s) you want.

Step 2. Tell the other computer that you want to download. Select the Download option. The exact name varies, depending on which computer you're calling.

The next two steps may be reversed on some systems:

Step 3. The other computer will ask you for the name of the file you want it to send you. Type in the filename. Sometimes it will ask for a number, so you'll type in the number instead.

Step 4. The other computer will ask how you want the file sent. This is the *protocol* question. Select a protocol (XMODEM, YMODEM, ZMODEM, Kermit) based on what your communications software can handle. XMODEM is the most common; ZMODEM is the best.

You've told the other computer what to send and how to send it. Now you need to tell your communications software to receive a file.

Step 5. Type your communications program's Download or Receive File command. In most cases, that's the PgDn key.

Step 6. Select the protocol. This must match what you told the other computer: XMODEM, YMODEM, and so on.

Step 7. Type in the filename.

Step 8. Go for it!

The other computer will send the file, and your computer should receive it 100-percent okay. That's why there are "protocols" — to ensure that the file you get is the file that the other computer sent.

Your communications software will let you know once the file is fully received. Mine beeps at me, which I find annoying, but it's handy since I can hear it in the other room and don't have to sit and watch a 15-minute download.

✔ As you can guess, there is a massive opportunity for screwing up here. Downloading is one of the most complex aspects of using already complex communications software. My advice is to try it first by using the preceding eight steps. Then, if you're still in the dark, refer back to your horrid communications manual. At least you'll have a bit of experience when you look in there, and maybe it will help you decipher what they're trying to say.

✔ In the Windows Terminal communications program, the *Binary* protocol is the same thing as XMODEM elsewhere.

On-Line Attitude

On-line telecommunications is a new and exciting way to communicate. Just as with learning a foreign language, however, there are some rules about on-line communications you should be aware of before you take the plunge. Don't get me wrong; this can be fun. I do it all the time and have made quite a few enemies of my friends.

✔ Happy people go modeming.

✔ You can't "see" anyone you "meet" on-line, so don't assume anything about them. Modem people are old, young, and come from diverse backgrounds, though studies show they're typically male, upper income, and Republican. Still, don't hold that against them.

✔ Please don't type in ALL CAPS. Type your letters and comments in mixed case — like you do when writing a letter. To most on-line people, all caps reads LIKE YOU'RE SHOUTING AT THEM!

✔ Don't "beg" for people to send you e-mail. Participate in discussions or just be obnoxious, and you'll always have a full mailbox.

✔ The art of written communication is lost on the TV generation. People use the phone to communicate where you hear inflection and gather extra meaning. Unfortunately, an on-line message lacks such nuances. And since we don't all have the written vocabularies we should, a joke, side remark, or kid can easily be taken seriously (way too seriously). Remember to keep it light. Adding "ha, ha" occasionally lets people know you're having fun instead of being an on-line jerk. Speaking of which . . .

✔ There are many on-line jerks (ha, ha). The best policy to take with them is to ignore them. No matter how much they steam you, no matter how ludicrous their ideas or remarks — golly, even if they're a Libertarian — don't get into a "flame thrower" war with them.

✔ In an on-line debate, ignore anyone who quotes "the dictionary" as a source. I hate to break it to you, but there is no National Institute of English that defines what words mean. Dictionaries are written by people as ignorant as you and I. Heck, I could write and publish a dictionary if I wanted to and make up entirely new definitions for words. Nope, the dictionary is not a source to be quoted.

✔ An on-line debate isn't over until someone compares someone else to Adolph Hitler. Calling the person a Nazi or the generic "fascist" also counts.

✔ Never criticize someone over spelling. English is a beautiful and rich language, utterly lacking in logic or spelling rules. Phonics, ha! *It* starts with a P for Pete's sake! There's no sense in drilling people on their spelling (unless it's truly awful, in which case you're probably dealing with a 12-year-old).

Saying Bye-Bye

When you're done using the remote computer, you should tell it good-bye — which is only polite. Use whichever command it has to hang up the phone. Always let the other computer hang up first. This enables it to properly clear your call, stop charging you on-line access fees, and so on.

✔ Sometimes the good-bye command is on a menu. It may be H for hang-up, G for Good-bye, O for Off, or E for Exit. If you have a command prompt, you may have to type in the command. For example, on CompuServe you must type in **BYE** and press Enter. On MCI Mail, you type **EXIT** and press Enter. Other variations include **LOGOFF**, **LOGOUT**, and **QUIT**. When in doubt, type **HELP**.

✔ Only if the other computer appears dead or just totally confused should you hang up on your end: Tell your communications software to hang up the phone.

The Most Common Sources of Problems

Once you get going, telecommunications can be easy. Yeah, and I've heard some weirdos can rip out their toenails without any sensation of pain. You may encounter some problems from time to time. Chances are they'll probably be one of the following:

✔ Not having the right cable between your computer and your modem. It needs to be a standard RS-232 serial cable or *modem cable*. You cannot use a serial printer cable or a *null modem cable*.

✔ Not having the modem connected to the correct port on your computer. Most PCs have two serial ports, COM1 and COM2. Most communications programs assume you use COM1. If not, tell your software you're different and are using COM2.

✔ Using a modem that is not fully Hayes compatible. Your communications software assumes your modem to be Hayes compatible. If it's not, you'll need to select a proper modem driver or just sit in a pile of ash and weep bitterly because some bozo sold you an incompatible modem.

Unzipping the ZIP File Mystery

Occasionally you may download a strange type of file with the extension ZIP. You may be all proud and happy that you actually got everything to work and then find yourself crushed because that cool painting program you downloaded is named PAINT.ZIP, and — Lord only knows why — it doesn't run. Boo-hoo. Sniff, sniff.

Any file ending in ZIP is called an *archive*. It's actually a collection of several files, all of which have been compressed and compacted into one handy ZIP file. This is the way most downloads are stored on BBSs and other on-line systems. Rather than have you toil with downloading dozens of files one after the other, the files are all stored in a single ZIP file. And because the files are compressed, they take up less space on disk and take even less time to download. The only problem is getting the files out of the ZIP file — unzipping them, so to speak.

To unzip a ZIP file you need a special program, a *utility* called PKUNZIP. It's part of a group of programs available from PKWare, the company that makes PKUNZIP and its companion program, PKZIP. These are the number one PC file-archiving programs available for DOS and the source of all those ZIP files you may encounter while modeming.

Using PKUNZIP is easy. Just type **PKUNZIP**, a space, and then the name of the ZIP file you want to decompress (or "explode"):

```
C> PKUNZIP PAINT.ZIP
```

Above, PKUNZIP is followed by PAINT.ZIP, the name of a file you downloaded. After pressing Enter, you'll see PKUNZIP go to work, extracting all the files sitting tight in the ZIP file archive and saving each one to disk. In a few moments, the operation will be complete, and you'll be able to play with your downloaded program(s).

✔ The easiest way to get PKZIP is to download the file from a BBS or national on-line service. The program is named PKZIP*xxx*.EXE. The *xxx* part of the filename is replaced by numbers, indicating PKZIP's version number. After downloading, type PKZIP*xxx* (the name of the file you downloaded), and it will "explode" into the various PKZIP and PKUNZIP utilities. COPY or MOVE those files to your PC's UTILITY subdirectory or store them in a special place where you'll always have access to them (refer to Chapter 18).

✔ The honest way to get PKZIP is to order it from PKWare directly. It advertises in national computer magazines and it changes its address and phone number too often for me to justify putting it down here.

✔ Even if you don't order PKZIP from PKWare, you're expected to pay for it. This type of software is not "free" just because you downloaded it. Pony up. Check the file named ORDER.DOC for ordering information.

- PKZIP comes with a manual "on disk." Check the file named MANUAL.DOC for more information.

- ZIP files need not contain dozens of files. Sometimes they only contain one file, though because the file is in an archive, it takes up less space on disk and is quicker to download than had it not been compressed.

- No, ZIP files have nothing to do with disk compression and programs such as Stacker and MS-DOS's DoubleSpace. The idea is the same, but only one file is compressed, not a whole disk.

- There are other archiving programs similar to PKZIP, though not as popular. Each has its own unzipping utility, and each has its own filename extension: ZOO, LZH, ARC, PAK, and so on. Since this opens a whole can of worms — and a compressed can at that — I'll give you permission to bug the on-line system's operator or on-line guru for help with those types of archives.

Communications Terminology Explicated

I'm not trying to mentally agitate you with terminology, but computer communications is full of it (so to speak). The following are specific terms related to on-line communications. I've tried to describe them in as sane a manner as possible.

Baud. A modem's speed is often referred to as *baud,* though that term is technically incorrect. The speed is really measured in bits per second, or bps, which is defined below. There's no reason to bring this up other than I'm granting you license to correct anyone who refers to bps as a "baud rate."

BBS. An acronym for an electronic bulletin board system. This is a local, typically hobbyist-run on-line computer system. BBSs have more of a neighborhood or community flavor than the big, impersonal national systems.

bps (speeds). An acronym for bits per second, the speed at which a modem can communicate. A speed of 2400 bps roughly translates into 240 characters per second, which is almost 2,400 words per minute that can be sent between two computers.

Carrier. This refers to the tone the two modems sing to each other. You'll hear it used most often when someone says they've "dropped the carrier." While an impressive mental image of the *U.S.S. Nimitz* splashing down into the Caribbean appears, think of it instead as hanging up the phone.

Chat. To type at someone else while you're on-line. This can be a lot of fun. It can also be boring to sit and watch some of the slowest typists in the world — and then experience the agony as they backspace over the whole line of text to correct a spelling mistake.

Communications settings. This refers to the modem's speed and data word format, which must be tailored to each BBS you call.

Data word format. There are three elements to the data word format: the word length (8 or 7), the parity (Odd, Even, or None), and the number of stop bits (1 or 0). The most common data word format in PC communications is 8, N, 1. The second most common is 7, E, 1. These settings must match those of the computer you're dialing.

Download. To copy a file or program from the computer you're calling to your own computer.

Duplex. This refers to how characters appear on the screen. *Full duplex* means you send characters to the other computer, and everything you see on the screen comes from the other computer. This is also known as *no echo*. *Half duplex* means the characters you type appear on your screen directly. This is also known as *local echo*. This term can be freely ignored. Only when you can't see what you're typing should you go into local echo mode.

E-mail. This is electronic mail — personal, private messages you can send to other people who dial into the same computer you do. This is perhaps the most rewarding part about on-line communications, getting lots of mail. (But please don't beg for others to send mail to you; participate and you'll get mail.) By the way, the post office is thinking of starting an e-mail delivery system. The problem is they can't figure out how to slow it down.

Host. Another term for the computer you're calling, the one answering the phone.

Log in. To identify yourself to the host computer. You log in by entering your name or a special nickname or ID number.

On-line. To be connected and chatting with another computer.

Speed. See bps.

Upload. To send a file from your computer to the host computer.

XMODEM, YMODEM, ZMODEM, and so on. These are file transfer protocols. Programs and files are typically sent from one computer to another by using XMODEM, YMODEM, ZMODEM, or a number of other methods for sending files without errors.

The 5th Wave

By Rich Tennant

"IT HAPPENED AROUND THE TIME WE SUBSCRIBED TO AN ON-LINE SERVICE."

Chapter 13
All You (Don't) Want to Know about Disks

∙ ∙

In This Chapter

▶ Understanding why disks are really *hardware*

▶ Buying disks

▶ Preparing a disk for use by DOS (formatting)

▶ Formatting different size disks

▶ Learning what not to do with disks — the no-no's

▶ Determining which type of disk is which

▶ Changing a volume label

▶ Write-protecting a disk

▶ Reformatting an already formatted disk

▶ Duplicating disks

∙ ∙

*B*oth computers and humans have two kinds of long-term storage. The internal storage in a human is provided by a wet slimy thing called a brain. It's fast on the uptake and can store volumes of information but is sluggish on the retrieval. Inside a computer, the hard drive provides fast but limited storage and retrieves quickly.

Humans supplement their brain-storage device with storage media, such as scraps of paper with things written down on them. Computers use floppy disks, on which information can be written and removed from the computer, taken elsewhere, or just stored. Both systems have their pluses and minuses.

This chapter is about using *floppy disks*, the removable long-term storage devices used by computers. You use floppy disks to make safety copies of your important files, move files between computers, back up information from the hard disk, or play a limited-distance version of Frisbee. Floppies can be frustrating or fun, but above all they must be formatted (see "Formatting a Disk" in this chapter).

Why Are Disks Hardware?

A common misconception among computer users is that a floppy disk is actually software. This is not so. Floppy disks are hardware. Keep in mind that hardware is something you can touch or drop on your foot. (Though a floppy disk doesn't hurt as much as a monitor that's been dropped on your foot, it is still hardware.) See Figure 13-1 for a peek at what these floppy disks look like.

The confusion comes about because floppy disks store software. The software is on the disk, magnetically encoded. So just as you wouldn't call a compact disc "music," don't confuse the floppy disk with the software that's recorded on it.

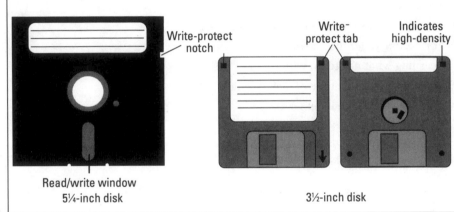

Figure 13-1: The two sizes of floppy disks

Write-protect notch

Read/write window
5¼-inch disk

Write-protect tab

Indicates high-density

3½-inch disk

Buying Disks

You should always buy disks that match the size and capacity of your floppy drives. Buying high-capacity disks may be expensive, but the cost works itself out over the long run because they store more data per disk. And forget about buying cheap low-capacity disks and trying to format them to high-capacity — it just doesn't work.

There are two sizes of disks: 5¼-inch and 3½-inch. These values refer to the length of the disk's edge (because all disks are square).

The capacity of the disk refers to how much information it can hold. There are two capacities: low-capacity and high-capacity. For 3½-inch disks, a very high or *extended* capacity also exists.

The object is to buy disks to match the size and capacity of your floppy drive. See Table 13-1 for details on what disks to buy.

✔ If you have a high-capacity 1.2MB 5¼-inch drive, or the 1.4MB or 2.8MB 3½-inch drive, you buy the corresponding disks. You can, if you like, buy the low-capacity disks, but you can only format them at their lower capacity. Refer to "Formatting a Low-Capacity Disk in a High-Capacity Drive" later in this chapter.

✔ If you only have a low-capacity drive, buy the low-capacity, DS/DD disks. You cannot use the high-capacity disks, and you shouldn't even buy them.

✔ There is nothing wrong with buying discount disks in bulk. I do this all the time, though I prefer to buy brand name and guaranteed disks for backups and serious work.

✔ Do not buy so-called *quad-density* disks. These disks are for an older PC disk format that no longer exists.

✔ Do not format high-capacity disks to a low-capacity. Refer to "Formatting a Low-Capacity Disk in a High-Capacity Drive" in this chapter for more information.

✔ If you're thinking about buying a low-capacity disk and magically making it into a high-capacity disk, *don't!* Refer to "Why Can't I 'Notch' a Disk to Make It High-Capacity?" later in this chapter.

Table 13-1	Floppy Disk Sizes and Capacities
Floppy Drive Size and Capacity	*Buy These Disks*
5¼-inch, Low	Low-capacity, 360K, or DS/DD
5¼-inch, High	High-capacity, high-density, 1.2MB, or DS/HD
3½-inch, Low	Low-capacity, 720K, or DS/DD
3½-inch, High	High-capacity, high-density (HD), 1.4MB, or DS/HD
3½-inch, Extended	Extended-capacity, 2.8MB, or DS/ED

Formatting a Disk

Before you can use a disk, it must be formatted. All disks come "naked" out of the box. (A few are preformatted, and you pay extra for it.) This is because you can use floppy disks on a variety of computers — not always DOS computers. For DOS to use the disk and store information on it, you must format that disk the way DOS likes. You do this with the FORMAT command.

To format a disk, first place it label side up and toward you and insert it into drive A. Close the drive's door latch after inserting a 5¼-inch disk. Type the following:

```
C> FORMAT A:
```

After pressing Enter, you'll be asked to insert the disk. That's already done, so press Enter again and the disk begins formatting.

After formatting is complete, you'll be asked to enter a *volume label* for the disk. Press Enter (unless you want to type a label name; it's optional). If you want to format another disk, press **Y** when it asks you and then remove the first disk and replace it with another.

You can also format disks in drive B. Here is the command you use:

```
C> FORMAT B:
```

Follow the same steps as listed for drive A.

- ✔ Never format any drive other than A or B; you should always use the two FORMAT commands listed here when formatting disks.

- ✔ The disk you format must be the same size and capacity of the drive you're using: High-capacity disks for high-capacity drives; low-capacity disks for low-capacity drives.

- ✔ If you see the message Track 0 bad or Disk unusable, refer to Chapter 22.

- ✔ You can format a low-capacity disk in a high-capacity drive; refer to the next section.

Formatting a Low-Capacity Disk in a High-Capacity Drive

It's possible to format a disk of lower capacity in a high-capacity drive. You would do this to be compatible with computers that have only the lower capacity drives or if you're using cheaper, low-density disks. If that's never your situation, there's no need to do this.

To format a low-capacity disk in a high-capacity drive, you must first get the low-capacity disk. Never format a high-capacity disk to a lower format. (It renders the disk useless.)

Insert the low-capacity disk into your high-capacity drive, label up and toward you. For a 5¼-inch drive, latch the drive's door shut after you've inserted the disk.

If you're formatting a low-capacity (360K) disk in a high-capacity 5¼-inch drive, type the following FORMAT command:

```
C> FORMAT A: /F:360
```

That's FORMAT, followed by a space, A and a colon (meaning drive A), a space, /F and a colon, and then the number 360. Press Enter and follow the instructions on the screen. Keep in mind that if you answer Y when asked to Format another?, you will still be formatting the low-capacity disks.

If you're formatting a low-capacity (720K) disk in a high-capacity 3½-inch drive, type this FORMAT command:

```
C> FORMAT A: /F:720
```

This is the same FORMAT command as listed in the preceding example, save for typing the number 720 instead of 360. Follow the same instructions listed under the first FORMAT command. Remember that any additional disks you format by answering Y will be formatted at 720K.

If you have an extended-density (2.8MB) drive, you can use the preceding FORMAT command to format a 720K disk, or you can use the following FORMAT command to format a 1.4MB high-capacity disk:

```
C> FORMAT A: /F:1440
```

Follow the instructions on the screen. (Technically, this is formatting a high-capacity disk in a higher capacity drive. Silly? Yeah, I know.)

- ✔ If you want to format the low-capacity disk in drive B, substitute B: for A: in either of the preceding commands.

- ✔ If the FORMAT command refuses to format the disk for any reason, you can force it to format by adding the /U option. Here are the modified commands:

```
C> FORMAT A: /F:360 /U
C> FORMAT A: /F:720 /U
C> FORMAT A: /F:1440 /U
```

Again, *do not* use these commands to force-format a high-capacity disk to a lower capacity. Always use low-capacity disks when you're formatting low-capacity.

Why Can't I "Notch" a Disk to Make It High-Capacity?

One of the worst tricks you can pull with disks is to format a low-capacity disk to a higher capacity. It sounds simple, and it even works for a time. But will you trust your valuable data to it, especially when you're only saving a few cents on the dollar?

It goes like this: When the high-capacity 3¹/₂-inch disks came out, most people noticed that the disks were identical in every way to the low-capacity disks, save for two things. First, the high-capacity disks had an extra hole in them. And second, the high-capacity disks cost more than the low capacities. This led many misguided souls to believe that you could magically make a low-capacity disk into a high-capacity one simply by punching a hole in it. They even justified this by saying that both the disks "looked alike." This is as silly as it sounds.

True, if you mutilate a low-capacity disk, you can format the disk at the higher capacity. You can even use the disk for a time with no ill effects. This is how the charlatans were able to dupe so many people; their demonstration disks worked flawlessly back at the store. But once you tried to use those disks two or three times, they became riddled with errors.

Eventually, the modified disks became worthless. Forget about getting your data back! In fact, you couldn't even reformat the disks to a lower capacity. By punching a hole in a 3¹/₂-inch disk, you're taking a losing gamble. Don't do it no matter what you hear.

How low-density disks are different from high-density disks

Though all disks look alike, the magnetic recording material on the disk has differences the eye cannot see. I like to make the comparison between a disk's surface and a sandbox (minus the kids and Tonka trucks).

A low-density disk is like a sandbox filled with coarse sand. Using a rake, you can draw lines in that sand. This works because the lines the rake makes are fairly far apart. If they aren't, the sand will fall back in on itself; it won't hold the grooves made by the rake because the sand is so coarse.

If the sandbox is filled with fine sand, you can use a finer rake and make many more grooves in it. Because of the fine sand, the grooves hold their pattern. This is essentially the difference between a low-capacity and high-capacity disk. A high-capacity disk has "finer" magnetic material and can hold many more *tracks* (where information on the disk is stored) than a low-capacity disk.

When you format a low-capacity disk to a high-capacity, typically by fooling it with a hole punch, it's like making fine grooves in coarse sand. This may hold for a while. But because the sand isn't fine, eventually the grooves (tracks on a disk) disappear. The same thing happens on the disk. Because the information you write to the disk clings to these tracks, when they go, so does your data.

Which Disk Is This?

Ever pick up a disk and wonder silently to yourself, "Where the heck did this disk come from?" If you do that a lot, I have one maxim for you:

Label your disks!

Every box of disks — even the cheapies — comes with several sticky labels. Here's how you use them:

1. Write information on the sticky label using a pen. Describe the disk's contents or give it a general name: *Files for home* or *Backup stuff* or *Emergency disk* or . . . you get the idea.

2. Peel the label off and gently apply it to the disk.

There. That's easy. With all your disks labeled, you'll never worry about wondering what's on them. And you'll be able to find commonly used disks more quickly.

✔ If you don't label a disk, you can use the DIR command to find out what's on it. Refer to "The DIR Command" in Chapter 2.

✔ As a suggestion, label disks right after you format them. That way, all formatted disks will have labels. If you find a disk without a label, that tells you it's probably unformatted. (But check it with the DIR command first to be certain.)

✔ You may also want to write the capacity of the disk, say 1.2MB or 360K, on the label. This will help out in situations where you have many computers with different kinds of drives in them.

✔ You can write on the labels after they're on the disk. Use a felt tip pen and don't press too hard. If you use a ballpoint pen or pencil, you may dimple the disk inside and ruin any data there.

✔ You can peel and remove a label from a disk if you want to change it.

✔ Don't write on the disk's sleeve instead of the label. Disks can change sleeves.

✔ Programs are available that enable you to create custom labels for your disks, even putting filenames and the disk's contents on a nifty little sticky label.

✔ Don't confuse the sticky label with the *volume label*. The volume label is an electronic name you attach to a disk when it's formatted. Refer to "Changing the Volume Label" later in this chapter.

✔ Don't use Post-its as disk labels. They fall off when you're not looking and can sometimes get stuck inside your disk drives.

What Kind of Disk Is This?

Even if a disk is labeled, sometimes it's hard to tell if it's a low-capacity or high-capacity model. The following tips should clue you in to which disk is which:

If the disk is a 360K 5¼-inch floppy:

It may have a label that contains one of the following: DS/DD; double sided/double density; 40 TPI or 40 Tracks Per Inch.

As a visual clue, if you remove the disk and look at its center hole, you'll see a reinforcing *hub ring*. The 1.2MB disks typically lack this feature.

If the disk is a 1.2MB 5¼-inch floppy:

One of the following clues may be written on the label: the letters HD or the term High-density; double sided/high-density; Double Track; 96 TPI or 96 Tracks Per Inch.

The visual clue is the absence of a reinforcing hub ring typically found on most 360K floppies.

If the disk is a 720K 3½-inch floppy:

It may have one of the following clues written on its label: DS/DD; double sided/double density; DD; Double Track; 135 TPI or 135 Tracks Per Inch.

The primary visual clue is that the disk is missing a hole in the lower righthand corner. (This hole is opposite from the write-protect hole.)

Skippable background info on DS/DD

Often when you buy a box of disks you'll see DS/DD (it stands for double sided/double density). This is an ancient relic from the days when floppy drives were less capable and mankind had dozens of confusing disk formats to choose from.

The first kind of disk drive only wrote on one side of the disk. This was referred to as the single-sided floppy drive — like a record player. (Actually, it was just a disk drive because double-sided drives didn't yet exist.)

Through the miracle of technology, the wizards were able to store more information on this single-sided floppy. This type of storage was called *double density* because it put almost twice as much information on the disk. So there were two different kinds of disks you could buy: SS/DD, for single sided/double density; and SS/SD, for single sided/single density.

When mankind figured out how to write information on both sides of a disk in a single drive, the *double-sided* disks emerged. Two new flavors of disks could be bought: DS/DD, for double sided/double density; and DS/SD, for double sided/single density. Madness ensued.

For a while there was also a *quad-density* format. Then came the *high-density* or *high-capacity* format. Today, there are four basic disk formats and four types of disks you should buy. They are all listed in Table 13-1.

The newest format is the *extended-density* disk, which stores eight times as much as a double-density disk. This brings to light the utter silliness of referring to a disk by its density. (Actually, they're called *Ed disks,* after the famous talking horse.) So what will the next density be? Maybe "super density." And then what's next? The "super dooper density" disk.

If the disk is a 1.4MB 3½-inch floppy:

The 1.4MB disk may have one of the following clues on its label: DS/HD; double sided/high-density; the interesting graphic (double line) letters HD. (The HD is usually your best clue; all the manufacturers use it.)

The key visual clue is the extra, see-through hole in the lower-right corner of the disk. The lower capacity disks lack this hole.

If the disk is a 2.8MB 3½-inch floppy:

Extended density 2.8MB disks have one of the following clues on their label: DS/ED; double sided/extended density; or the best clue, a large graphic "ED" on the disk.

The key visual clue is the extra, see-through hole on the corner of the disk, which the 720K disks lack. Note that this hole is not even (horizontally) with the write-protect hole; it's a bit lower, which is how you can tell the difference between a 2.8MB disk and a 1.4MB disk.

Using the CHKDSK Command to Check a Disk's Size

If a disk is formatted, you can use the CHKDSK command to determine its size. The CHKDSK command is known as *check disk,* which is kind of what CHKDSK looks like without all the superfluous vowels. Basically, this command reports information about your disk, most of it technical.

To see how much information you can store on a floppy disk, and therefore see its size or capacity, type **CHKDSK** at the DOS prompt, followed by **A:**, indicating the drive currently holding your floppy disk. Press Enter, and prepare to be overwhelmed:

```
C> CHKDSK A:
```

After pressing Enter above, you'll see something like this:

```
Volume DOS HAPPY    created 09-05-1993 8:16p
Volume Serial Number is 0D1B-0FF8

   1,457,664 bytes total disk space
     832,000 bytes in 38 user files
     625,664 bytes available on disk

         512 bytes in each allocation unit
       2,847 total allocation units on disk
       1,222 available allocation units on disk

     655,360 total bytes memory
     617,552 bytes free
```

There are four chunks of information here, most of it trivia. The most important is the first number value, which tells you the size of your disk. Above, it says there are 1,457,664 bytes of *total disk space.* That means this disk is a 1.4MB, formatted floppy disks. Other values are divulged in the following table.

Floppy Disk Size	Long, Involved Number Displayed
360K	365,056
1.2MB	1,228,800
720K	730,112
1.4MB	1,457,664
2.8MB	2,915,328

> ✔ To check the capacity of a disk in drive B, substitute B: for A: in the above CHKDSK command.

> ✔ The value `bytes available on disk` tells you how much space is left on the disk for storing files.

> ✔ The commas appear in CHKDSK's output only with MS-DOS version 6.2. Earlier versions of DOS don't have the handy commas. Also, MS-DOS 6.2's CHKDSK command is riddled with information about running the ScanDisk program instead. Refer to Chapter 17 for information on Scandisk.

> ✔ Refer to Chapter 17 for information on how to deal with any errors CHKDSK may report.

Changing the Volume Label

When you format a disk, the FORMAT command asks you to enter a *volume label*. This is an electronic name encoded on the disk — not the sticky label you should apply later. Giving your disk a volume label can be a good idea, especially if your sticky label falls off the disk. In that case, you could find out the name of your disk electronically using the DIR command. The volume label appears at the top of the DIR command's output, and you can use the handy VOL command to find a disk's volume label. Type

```
C> VOL A:
```

or

```
C> VOL B:
```

The VOL command reports back the disk's volume label, or it may tell you that the disk has no label.

After you've formatted a disk, you can change the volume label using the LABEL command. Type **LABEL** and then follow the instructions on the screen:

```
C> LABEL
```

After pressing Enter, you'll see the current label for the drive, as well as the cryptic volume serial number. DOS asks you to enter a new label up to 11 characters long. The label can contain letters and numbers. If you want a new label, type it in. If you don't want to change the label, don't *type* anything, but *do* press Enter.

If you enter a new label, DOS changes it on the disk. You can use the VOL command again to verify the new label.

If you just pressed Enter and your disk already had a label, DOS will ask if you want to delete the old label. If so, press **Y**. Otherwise, press **N** and you'll keep the original label.

To change the label on a disk in any drive, follow the LABEL command with that drive letter and a colon. Here's an example:

```
C> LABEL A:
```

Here, the label is examined/changed for drive A. Substitute B: for A: in our example to replace the label on drive B.

✔ The VOL command can be followed by any drive letter and colon. You use this to see the volume label for any other disk in your system.

✔ Remember to insert a floppy disk in drive A or B before using the LABEL or VOL command on those drives.

Write-Protecting Disks

You can protect floppy disks in such a way as to prevent yourself or anyone else from modifying or deleting anything on the disk.

To write-protect a 5¼-inch disk, go grab one of those tiny, Velamint-size tabs that came with the disk in the box. Peel the tab and place it over the notch in the disk, which should be on the lower-left side as you insert the disk into the drive (see Figure 13-1). With that notch covered, the disk is write-protected.

To write-protect a 3½-inch disk, locate the little sliding tile on the lower-left side of the disk as you slide it into the drive. If the tile covers the hole, the disk can be written to. If you slide the tile off the hole (so you can see through it), the disk is write-protected (see Figure 13-1).

When a disk is write-protected, you cannot alter, modify, change, or delete anything on that disk. And you cannot accidentally reformat it. You can read from the disk and copy files from it. But changing the disk — forget it!

To un-write-protect a 5¼-inch disk, peel off the little tab. This renders the disk sticky, but it's a livable problem. You can un-write-protect 3½-inch disks by sliding the tile over the hole.

Reformatting Disks

Disks must be formatted before DOS can use them. But once formatted, you can reformat them. This can be done under two circumstances: when you want to totally erase the disk and all its data, or accidentally.

Obviously, you shouldn't erase a disk that you don't want to erase. All the data on the disk goes bye-bye. The only way to avoid this is to be careful: Check the disk with the DIR command first. Make sure that it's a disk you want to reformat.

Personally, I erase disks all the time. I have stacks of old disks that I can reformat and use. The data on them is old or duplicated elsewhere. So reusing the disk is no problem. Here's the FORMAT command you want to use:

```
C> FORMAT A: /Q
```

That's the FORMAT command, a space, and then A and a colon, which directs the FORMAT command to format a disk in drive A. That's followed by another space and a slash-Q. That tells DOS to *Quickformat* the disk. It's very fast.

If DOS refuses to Quickformat the disk, try the following FORMAT command:

```
C> FORMAT A: /U
```

This is the same command as the last one but with a slash-U instead of a slash-Q. This command tells DOS to *unconditionally* format the disk. It takes longer than the Quickformat, but it generally works.

About the ol' "Insufficient space for the MIRROR image file" message

Sometimes you may try to reformat a diskette and end up with the following message:

```
Drive X error. Insufficient space
for the MIRROR image file.

There was an error creating the
format recovery file.

This disk cannot be unformatted

Proceed with format (Y/N)
```

What DOS is trying to tell you here is that the magic it does to allow a disk to be unformatted can't happen. The disk you're reformatting is very full. Therefore, you must be double sure you want to format it because it can never be unformatted. My advice is to press Y here if you're certain. Otherwise, use another disk.

✔ If you want to reformat a disk in drive B, substitute B: for A: in these examples.

✔ Note that you cannot Quickformat a disk to a different size. In fact, you shouldn't be reformatting disks to a different size anyway. But if you must, use the /U option as shown here.

✔ Only Quickformat newer disks. If a disk has been sitting around a while, use the FORMAT command without the /Q. That takes longer, but the FORMAT command will do a better job to ensure that the disk is still usable.

✔ After formatting a disk, you'll see a list of statistics. If one of the statistics mentioned is *xxxx* bytes in bad sectors, you have a bum disk on your hands. My advice: Toss the sucker. If you still have the receipt, and the store said they were "fully guaranteed," you can try to get your money back. Good luck!

✔ You can recover accidentally reformatted disks by using MS-DOS 6.2. Refer to "I Just Reformatted My Disk!" in Chapter 20.

Duplicating Disks (the DISKCOPY Command)

To make a duplicate of a file on disk, you use the COPY command. (Refer to "Duplicating a File" in Chapter 4.) To make a duplicate of a floppy disk, you use the DISKCOPY command. DISKCOPY takes one floppy and makes an exact duplicate of it, even formatting a new disk if it was previously unformatted.

There are two things you cannot do with the DISKCOPY command:

1. You cannot DISKCOPY two disks of different size or capacity.

2. You cannot use DISKCOPY with a hard disk or a *RAM drive*. (If you don't know what a RAM drive is, go to the refrigerator and reward yourself with a cool, carbonated beverage.)

When you copy disks, DOS refers to the original disk as the *SOURCE*. The disk to which you're copying is the *TARGET*.

To make a copy of a disk, first write-protect the original, the source. (Refer to the section "Write-Protecting Disks" earlier in this chapter.) Put your write-protected original into drive A. Close the drive's door latch for a 5¼-inch disk.

Type the following command at the DOS prompt:

```
C> DISKCOPY A: A:
```

That's DISKCOPY, a space, and then A: twice (meaning drive A mentioned twice and separated by a space). Press Enter and DOS examines the disk, spews out some technical mumbo-jumbo, and then:

```
Reading from source diskette . . .
```

The drive churns away for a few moments. Then you're asked to insert the target:

```
Insert TARGET diskette in drive A:
Press any key to continue
```

Remove the source disk and insert your duplicate disk. Close the door latch if you have a 5¼-inch disk. Press Enter.

```
Writing to target diskette . . .
```

Take a few seconds to put the original (the "source") back in a safe place. When the operation is complete, you can use the duplicate instead of the original.

 ✔ When the operation is complete, DOS asks whether you want to do another DISKCOPY. Press Y if you do, N if you don't.

 ✔ In MS-DOS 6.2, after the copy is complete, you'll be asked if you want to make another duplicate of the same disk — another TARGET. Press Y if you do, N if you don't. Then you're asked whether you want to copy another disk (another SOURCE). Press Y if you do, N if you don't.

✔ You can do a DISKCOPY in your B drive by substituting B: for A: in the preceding command.

✔ You can use the following DISKCOPY command if and *only* if your drives A and B are of the same size and capacity:

```
C> DISKCOPY A: B:
```

This command is faster because you don't have to swap disks.

✔ If the target disk is unformatted, DISKCOPY formats it. If it's already formatted, DISKCOPY replaces the original contents with the copy.

✔ The DISKCOPY command is the only accurate way to duplicate a disk. Even the COPY command cannot always make a full copy of all the files on a disk.

✔ You may be asked to swap the SOURCE and TARGET diskettes a few times. This can be maddening. If it bothers you, consider updating to MS-DOS 6.2 where they (finally) stopped the DISKCOPY disk-swapping madness.

✔ Only use DISKCOPY to copy disks for your use, not for friends — it's illegal to copy licensed programs for others.

Part III
The Non-Nerd's
Guide to PC Software

The 5th Wave   By Rich Tennant

In this part...

Essentially, software is what makes the hardware go; the computer is the orchestra and software is the music. (Software is to the computer nerd what sheet music is to the conductor.)

Software is the reason you bought your computer. Forget brand names and speed and power and pretty cases. What makes a computer work is software, and software is what makes your work on the computer productive.

Chapter 14
Basic
Software Setup

• •

In This Chapter

▶ Locating software that works on your computer

▶ Installing software (generally speaking)

▶ Operating a new program and performing basic functions

▶ Learning a new program (the best way)

▶ Updating software

▶ Reading a command format

• •

*I*f you play your cards right, you'll never have to install any software on your PC. Someone else, someone who loves to do such things, will install the software for you. To install a program, you have to learn steps that are required only once. So making someone else do it for you can be a blessing.

This chapter is about using software for the first time. It also includes information on selecting and installing a program, which can be pretty involved. There is also a strategy covered here on learning and using software for the first time — not that you'd want to become an expert or anything.

Finding Compatible Software

The proud new computer owner — and enthusiast — finds it hard not to gravitate to the local software store. They come, they drool, they buy. For everyone else, the software store is like the fourth ring of hell — or an eight-mile-square auto parts store with 10,000 guys named "Bud" who won't help you. But armed with the proper knowledge, you may be able to find what you want, or at least find someone for help.

Steps: Finding the software that's right for you

Step 1. Know what you want to get done. Software does the work, so finding software means you need to first know what kind of work you need to do. For example, will you be writing? Then you need a tool to help you write, a *word processor*. There are dozens of them out there — an overwhelming number. But at least you've taken the first step by narrowing down what you need. (Even if you think it's a category that doesn't exist, ask someone. There may be a software package just for you.)

Step 2. Find compatible software. At this point, you know you have a DOS computer. Therefore, you can only buy DOS software. There are lots of technical details about software that may limit which computer it runs on. For example, some software requires fancy graphics hardware; some requires a lot of memory. If you know these details, you can compare what your computer has to the software's requirements, which are usually listed on the side of the box.

If you don't know what you have, ask the salesperson. Tell him or her that you're not sure what system you have and that you don't want to buy something that requires too much horsepower. (Besides, that stuff is expensive.)

Step 3. Try that software. Pick a few different packages to try out. Most software stores let you try before you buy. Let the salesperson set you up. Then play. Because you know what you want to do, this step shows you how easy some of the software is and how difficult it can be. Check for the level of so-called help offered in each package. Maybe one out there is just for you.

You should also find out what kind of support is available for the software. Does the company have a support line? Is it toll free? These are vital questions, and the answers may help you choose one package over another. You should also check the software store's return policy.

Step 4. Maybe shop around. If you don't like one store, go to another. If there's something in particular you don't like, be sure to be nasty and tell the store's manager. Also tell them where you're headed. You can price shop if you want, but most software stores offer great discounts anyway. However, if you find a store where the salesperson really knows the package you're interested in, it may be a good idea to buy it there. Nothing beats someone to call on the phone for help.

Step 5. Buy it. Slap down your VISA card and buy the software! But don't buy too much at once. A common mistake is to overwhelm yourself with too much software. Often some packages will gather dust while you concentrate on others. So work on the issue at hand, solve one problem at a time, and don't overdo it.

Installation

No one really likes to install software. Well, I do (but I'm a nerd). I love the smell of a new software package. And, like everyone else I know who owns a computer, I take pride in trying to set the thing up without first reading the manuals. Of course, I don't think you're this crazy.

Installation means copying the program you've just bought from floppy disks to your computer's hard drive. It also means more, typically configuring or setting up the program to work with your particular PC, printer, and the rest of that stuff. That is why installation is best left up to your local computer guru. If not, you can follow the outline given here. Because each computer program installs itself differently, this material is covered in a broad sense. But it gives you a general idea of the task you're about to undertake.

Read me first!

Computer manuals and those national sweepstakes with you-know-who's picture on the envelope both have something in common: There are lots of little pieces of paper and instructions for the interesting things you must do. But computer manuals are easier to deal with. Seriously. There's no need to hunt through everything, fill out various forms, or paste Uncle Ed's picture in the TV set. Just look for a sheet of paper somewhere that says *Read me first!* Read it and you're on your way.

The installation program

You install a program by sticking Disk 1 into your PC's first floppy drive (drive A) and then running the installation program. If the disk doesn't fit into drive A, stick the disk into drive B and substitute B for A in the following instructions. The name of the installation program is usually *install,* though *setup* is also popular. There are two steps here. The first is *logging to drive A.* This is covered in the section "Changing Drives" in Chapter 2. Basically, after sticking Disk 1 into floppy drive A (and closing the drive door latch for a 5¼-inch disk), you type in the following:

```
C> A:
```

Typing A and a colon logs you to drive A. Press Enter.

Next, you enter the name of the installation program. This name is probably listed in the manual, on the disk label, or on the *Read me first!* sheet of paper, or that paper will tell you where to find these instructions. Be wary! Even though installing the program is the first thing you'll ever do with it, it's rarely the first chapter in the manual. (I've always wondered why that's the case.)

For example, if the name of the installation program is INSTALL, you type

```
A> INSTALL
```

Press Enter.

Sometimes the installation program is called SETUP. If so, you type this:

```
A> SETUP
```

Press Enter here too.

Don't forget to *read the information on the screen!* It's important, especially so for an installation program. In fact, many "experts" usually screw up software installation by not reading the screens. Follow the instructions closely.

The location

The first thing the installation program asks you is "Where do you want to put me?" Dumb question. You want to put the program in your computer.

The application needs its own workspace on your hard drive. This is referred to as a *subdirectory*. Only advanced users may have some special scheme or plan in this instance. You should accept whatever suggestion the installation program makes — it's probably a good one.

Configuring a computer application

Configuration is the stupidest part of setting up a computer application. This is where the program asks you information about your own computer: "What kind of printer do you have? What kind of display or monitor is attached? How much memory do you have? Do you have a mouse?" These questions are ridiculous! After all, the computer program is asking you those questions, and it's already inside the computer where it can look around more easily than you can.

Still, you may have to tell the computer what it has (which, again, is like asking other people how old you are at your next birthday party). These questions can be difficult. If you don't know the answers, grab someone who does. Otherwise, guess. The *default* or *automatic selection* options tell the program to guess on its own, so if they're available, select them.

An important item to select is a *printer driver,* which is a fancy way of telling the application which printer you have manacled to your PC. Look for your printer's name and model number listed. If it's not there, select *Dumb* or *Line* printer (and then go to your dealer and beat up the guy who sold you the printer).

The READ.ME file

Finally, there are last-minute instructions or information offered in a special file on disk. It's given the name *README, READ.ME, README.TXT,* or *README.DOC.* Good installation programs ask you if you want to view this file. Say yes. Look through the file for any information that applies to your situation.

A utility is usually offered with a program to provide automatic viewing of the READ.ME file. If not, you can view it using the following DOS command:

```
C> MORE < READ.ME
```

That's the MORE command, a space, a less-than sign (<), another space, and the name of the READ.ME file. If the file is named just README, type it in without a period in the middle.

- ✔ For information on pathnames and directories, refer to Chapter 17.

- ✔ For information on using the TYPE command for viewing files, refer to "Looking at Files" in Chapter 2.

- ✔ A great way to view a README file is using the DOS Editor, which is covered in Chapter 16.

Using Your New Software

After you run the install or setup program, you get to use new software. As a suggestion, after installing any new software, reset your computer. Press Ctrl-Alt-Delete or punch your Reset button. (Some installation programs may do this automatically.)

To use the new program, type its name at the DOS prompt. A list of popular program names is provided in Chapter 2. If your program isn't on the list, type the name mentioned in the manual. (If nothing happens, refer to "Where Is My Program?" in Chapter 20.)

You're doing this step just to make sure that the program works as advertised. If something doesn't work, don't be too quick to blame yourself. Programs have bugs. Keep in mind that the features of a new program aren't immediately obvious.

If anything out of the ordinary happens, do the following: Check with your computer supervisor or local computer guru. Check with the software developer (its help number should be listed somewhere in the manual or in the material that came with it). Finally, you can check with your dealer. Dealers try to be helpful, but it would be impossible for them to know the details of every piece of software they sell. They can, however, replace defective disks for you.

- ✔ For information on resetting, refer to "Resetting" in Chapter 1.

- ✔ Running programs (in a general sense) is covered in "Running a Program" in Chapter 2.

Learning and Using Software

Using software to get work done is why, unfortunately, we need computers. But using software involves learning its quirks. That takes time. So my first suggestion for learning any new software is to give yourself plenty of time.

Sadly, in today's rush-rush way of doing everything, time isn't that easy to come by. It's a big pain when the boss sends you down to the software store expecting you to come back and create something wonderful before the end of the day. In the real world, that's just not possible (not even if you're an "expert").

Most software comes with a workbook or a tutorial for you to follow. This is a series of self-guided lessons on how to use the product. It also tells you about the program's basic features and how they work.

I highly recommend going through the tutorials. Follow the directions on the screen. If you notice anything interesting, write it down in the tutorial booklet and flag that page.

Some tutorials are really dumb, granted. Don't hesitate to bail out of one if you're bored or confused. You can also take classes on using software, though they may bore you as well. Most people do, however, understand the program much better after the tutorial.

After doing the tutorial, play with the software. Make something. Try saving something to disk. Try printing. Then quit. Those are the basic few steps you should take when using any software program. Get to know it and then expand your knowledge from there as required.

If you feel bold, you can take a look at the manual. Who am I fooling? Computer manuals are awful. Sometimes they'll help, especially if the manual is a reference, enabling you to quickly thumb to what you want, read it, and then get right back out (like this book). But never read the manual all the way through.

✔ Some businesses may have their own training classes that show you the basics of using the in-house software. Take copious notes. Keep a little book for yourself with instructions for how to do what. Take notes whenever someone shows you something. Don't try to learn anything, just note what's done so you won't have to make a call should the situation arise again.

✔ If your computer is set up using a menu system, your program will probably be added into the menu. Furthermore, there may be additional automation offered in the form of *macros* or *templates*. These simplify the operation of the program and make your life a heck of a lot easier (see "Black Box Program Rules," in Chapter 15).

Updating Your Software

Occasionally, your computer or your software may be updated. For computer updates, you may have to make modifications to your program, telling it about the new hardware just installed.

For example, if Those In Charge change printers, add a network or new monitor, give you a mouse, or change anything else on your computer, you should ask your favorite computer wizard if any of your software needs to be alerted to the modifications. Then let the computer wizard make those changes.

Computer software is also updated on a frequent basis. New *versions* come out all the time. If you fill in your registration card, you'll be alerted to the new version and what it has to offer. Then, for a nominal or outrageous fee, you can order the new version. My advice: Only order the update if it has features or makes modifications you desperately need. Otherwise, if the current version is doing the job, don't bother.

- If you notice nothing different after changing hardware (all your programs run), there's no need to update anything. Just keep on (ugh) working.

- If you don't bother updating your software for several years, you may miss out on something. After a time, software developers stop supporting older versions of their programs, books on the subject go out of print, and it gets harder to find help. When that happens, you'll need to buy the new version.

What about updating DOS?

Yeah, DOS is software, just like other programs on your computer. And DOS gets updated every so often. It goes like this: This cigar-chomping bigwig at Microsoft looks out the window and says, "Hey, let's do a new version of DOS and make *even more* money!" Then someone comments, "Why? Isn't everyone happy with the current version of DOS?" But, suddenly, he's fired. And they do an update anyway.

Updating DOS is tricky. Often the newer version of DOS has many more features than the older version. Do you need those features? If not, don't bother with the update. But unlike regular software, everything else uses DOS. Everything! Even Windows. (Shameful, but it's true.) The problem is that those other software packages may soon come to roost on the newest version of DOS, meaning you may get left out in the long run.

My advice is this: Don't bother updating DOS until at least six months after the newest version is out. By then, it should have all the bugs worked out. And you can still put off that decision for a good year or so before other software starts relying on the new features in DOS.

About the Darn Command Formats

Whenever you see a DOS command listed in a book or manual, you'll often see its *command format*. This is perhaps the most cryptic part about using DOS. The command format tells you what to type, what's optional, what's either/or-ish, and what everything does. If street signs were like this, people would ignore them.

The command format has three parts, though they're not separate:

- ✔ Requirements
- ✔ Options
- ✔ Switches

The *requirements* are items that you must type at the command line. Take the FORMAT command. Here is what its command format may look like:

```
FORMAT drive:
```

FORMAT is the name of the command. It's required. *Drive* (and a colon) is also required, but it's in italics. This means that you must type something there — something that means "drive" — but what you type is up to you. Here, *drive* means to put a drive letter (and a colon) there. This would be explained in the command's description: *Drive* is required and indicates a disk drive letter. For *drive* you would substitute A: or B:.

The following command contains an *option:*

```
VOL [drive:]
```

The VOL command is required. But anytime you see square brackets, it means that what comes between them is optional. In the preceding example, *drive* (and a colon) appears in brackets, meaning that a drive letter (and a colon) is optional after the VOL command. Again, this would be explained in the definition that follows the command format. It will also explain what happens if you don't specify the option.

Note that you do not specify the brackets when you type the command at the DOS prompt. Brackets are only a visual clue in the command format. Here's an example:

```
VOL B:
```

Here the volume label of the disk in drive B will be displayed. B: is the optional [*drive*:] part of the command, as specified in the preceding example (and without the brackets).

Here is a command format for the DEL command, which deletes files:

```
DEL filename [/P]
```

Here DEL and *filename* are both required. *Filename* indicates the name of the file you want to delete, which can be any file on your disk. The /P (slash-P) is a *switch,* and it's optional, appearing in brackets. What /P does and why you would want to list it would be listed in the instructions.

All switches start with either a slash or a dash, and most of them are optional. The typical switch is a single letter, and it can be either upper- or lowercase. Some switches are more than one letter, and some have options. Here's an example:

```
[/D=drive:]
```

That whole whatchamacallit is optional. The switch (/D) is followed by an equal sign and *drive,* which indicates that you must specify a disk drive letter (and a colon) in that spot. So /D is optional, but if you use it you have to fill in a disk drive letter.

Finally, there are optional either/or situations. These are options where you must specify either one switch or the other. This is written as follows:

```
[ON|OFF]
```

In this example, the item is optional because it's in brackets. If you specify it, you must either use ON or OFF, not both. The vertical bar or pipe character (|) tells you to pick one or the other if you want this option.

✔ These command formats are used in the official DOS manual, as well as in DOS 6's on-line "help." For more information on the on-line help, refer to Chapter 21.

✔ When a command requires a filename, it's often written in the following format:

```
[drive:][path]filename
```

The filename part is required, but specifying a drive letter (the drive-colon) or a path or both is optional. The drive allows you to specify on which drive the file lives; the path is used to identify the file's subdirectory. More information about paths can be found in Chapter 17.

The 5th Wave — By Rich Tennant

"I THINK 'FUZZY LOGIC' IS AN IMPORTANT TECHNOLOGY TOO. I'M JUST NOT SURE WE SHOULD FEATURE IT AS PART OF OUR TAX PREPARATION SOFTWARE."

Chapter 15
Software Mystery Grab Bag

● ●

In This Chapter

▶ Learning black box program rules

▶ Using a menu system

▶ Dealing with dBASE

● ●

*L*et's face it, there are two kinds of people in the world: computer enthusiasts and the rest of us. The computer enthusiasts use many different programs and love learning new ones. The rest of us have one, maybe two programs we use often enough to feel comfortable with, and we sincerely hope we never have to learn a third.

If you ever do end up using a third (or fourth, or . . . gulp), you should probably consider using some type of computer shell or a menu system. That's a special program that takes care of running your computer. Like a seashell protects a soft, gooey underwater creature from being eaten by larger, predatory creatures, the computer shell protects you from DOS. No DOS prompt. No commands to memorize. Just press A for WordPerfect, and you're on your way.

This chapter discusses using DOS menu systems and shells. It also covers black box programs, which are things you use on your computer that someone else has set up for you (macros, menu systems, dBASE, batch files, and so on). In case of disaster, always consult your guru first. Otherwise, turn here for help.

Black Box Program Rules

Before I begin with the popular programs, I need to explain what a black box program is.

A *black box program* is a program that runs itself so that you, the user, don't have to know how it works. The details are concealed inside a "black box."

For example, dBASE is a program that can run other programs for you, such as order entry, a customer list, or any number of database programs. Such programs usually prompt you through the things you're to do. Microsoft Windows is a single program that can run a number of other programs. And there are lesser kinds of programs, usually called *menu systems,* that run all the programs on your computer from one handy menu. These are all black box programs, doing the DOS dirty work for you while you sit back and get work done.

What follows are rules for using a black box program, particularly those that supersede rules I've already pounded into your head elsewhere in this book. These are general rules you can use on any black box program to get out of trouble.

Basic black box information

Fill in this information if you're using a black box program on your PC. If you don't know the answers, get the answers; force them out of your PC guru at gun point if necessary (I'm not one to advocate the use of violence to get what's rightly yours, but it's always worked for me). Why get this information? Because when things go wrong, it helps you save yourself, maybe by looking in this book rather than having to wait for the guru to return from lunch or vacation.

The formal name of your black box program: _____

How that name is pronounced: _____

The command you type to start your black box program: _____

Its drive and directory: _____

(Use this information to locate the program if you ever "lose" it; refer to "Where Is My Program?" in Chapter 20 for your hunting license.)

Files associated with the black box program that you should never delete:

Filename:	**In English:**
_____	_____
_____	_____
_____	_____
_____	_____
_____	_____

Your guru's phone number: _____

Times when it's OK to call: _____

(Just ask your guru that last question to be nice; feel free to call whenever you need him or her. Bring along a sack of Doritos, Pizza Rolls, or White Chocolate Almonds as a bribe.)

Note the names of programs you run. For example, if you're in dBASE, you'll probably be running several "do" files. Write down their names here. If you're in Windows, you're running some programs that have *icons* (little pictures on the screen). Write down their names and what they do. The same holds true for whichever black box program you're running.

Program Name (do file):   **What It Does:**

_____   _____

_____   _____

_____   _____

_____   _____

_____   _____

_____   _____

Exit from the black box program before turning off or resetting your computer. In a black box program, you can be at a DOS prompt that makes it look all right to reset or turn off your PC. However, that DOS prompt may just be part of the black box program — not a *real* DOS prompt.

If you find yourself at a DOS prompt in a black box program, type the EXIT command:

```
C> EXIT
```

This should return you to the black box program. From there, you should quit the black box program and return to the real DOS prompt. At that point it's OK to reset or shut off your computer.

Using a Menu System

A menu system is a nifty little program that does away with the DOS prompt. (Well, as far as you're concerned it's gone.) Provided that someone nice has set things up, this kind of black box program comes up right when you start your PC. You'll see a menu of choices, each of which represents something you'll do on your PC:

A. Word processing

B. Lotus

C. Backup files

D. Crash the network

To select an item, press the proper letter or number key. It's that simple. You don't have to mess with DOS or remember commands. You do still have to know how to use your software.

✔ If you find yourself suddenly at the DOS prompt, try these two things to get back to your menu. First type **EXIT** and press Enter:

```
C> EXIT
```

This should return you to your menu program or to your word processor or other application. If not, try typing **MENU** and pressing Enter:

```
C> MENU
```

If this doesn't work, then — and only as a last resort — reset your PC with Ctrl-Alt-Delete. And if that doesn't work, call your guru. Chop some onions first so you'll get more sympathy.

✔ There are many popular menu programs. If you don't have one and find the notion intriguing, I suggest the product Direct Access from Fifth Generation Systems. It's the DOS menu system everyone else tries to copy. (No, I don't get a kickback here; it's just worth recommending.)

✔ Even stolid old Windows is a menu system of sorts. Actually, Windows is more of a shell because it doesn't really make things easier, just different.

Batch file menu systems

DOS has its own programming language — actually two of them. First comes the *QBASIC programming language,* which you don't want to mess with. Then there's the *batch file programming language,* which you may be curious about.

Batch files are nothing more than text files that contain DOS commands. DOS runs all the commands in the file one after the other, just as if you typed each line at the DOS prompt. The difference is that it all happens automatically. Also, you can use special DOS commands in the batch file, which makes it sort of programlike.

One of the advantages of the batch file program is that it's possible to create a home-brew menu system using these batch files, plus a few magical flips of the wrist by a guru or other loving, yet knowledgeable, DOS user.

These are the DOS batch file commands: CALL, CHOICE, ECHO, FOR, GOTO, IF, PAUSE, REM, and SHIFT. I wrote a book on batch file programming for another publisher and I highly recommend it. Here is the title, just in case the jealous IDG editor didn't cut it out: *Advanced MS-DOS Batch File Programming,* Windcrest/McGraw-Hill.

dBASE — So Popular It's Scary

Often you will be working on an application program that someone else has written in dBASE. Now don't start chomping at your fingernails. dBASE, and other database programs similar to and better than it, is used to create PC software. That's its purpose — to provide a way to access information in a database. In fact, you may be using a program right now that was written in dBASE and not even know it.

If you're using a dBASE-like product, turn to this section when something goes wrong and you find yourself out of the prepared application, wishing you knew how to get back in. On the other hand, you may need to use dBASE directly to look at your data or generate simple reports. I give you a few basic tips here.

(This covers dBASE IV; if you can't find the Command Center and stuff like that, you probably have an older version, maybe dBASE III or even II. Most of the parts that don't refer to the Command Center will work equally well in earlier versions, though. And if you ask your programmer nicely, he or she can probably write in the equivalents in those earlier versions for you.)

Starting dBASE and running dBASE applications

If you're using an application (a program written in dBASE for you), the developer may have set it up to start automatically when you turn the computer on in the morning, or he or she may have given you explicit instructions for starting the program. If not, or if you somehow ended up at the DOS prompt (C>) and want to start dBASE, here's how.

You start dBASE by typing at the DOS prompt:

```
C> DBASE
```

✔ If you're missing dBASE, it's usually found in the \DBASE subdirectory on drive C. Type the following:

```
C> C:
```

Then:

```
C> CD \DBASE
```

If you know the name of the prepared application, you can load it at the same time that you load dBASE; for example, to load a dBASE application called INVOICE, type this:

```
C> DBASE INVOICE
```

A logo screen and ominous sounding licensing message is displayed as the program loads, demanding that you press Enter to accept the license. If you're using dBASE IV and you didn't specify the name of an application, you should next see the dBASE IV Control Center screen. If all you see is a blank screen with one line at the bottom and a single dot . . . don't panic. To get into the Control Center, type

```
ASSIST
```

To run an application from the dBASE IV Control Center, move the highlight to the application name in the Applications column and press Enter. When the prompt appears asking if you would like to modify or run the application, choose Run.

What's the darn dot supposed to mean?

If you unexpectedly exit a dBASE application, you may find yourself not at the DOS prompt but at the *dBASE dot prompt,* perhaps the most horrid of any prompt in all of computerdom. To wit:

```
.
```

Yikes! That's just a period at the left of the screen with the blinking cursor next to it. No fun.

To run a prepared application for which you know the name (you made your programmer write it down for you earlier in this chapter, remember?), do this (let's say the application name is INVOICE):

```
. DO INVOICE
```

The application loads and you're back home.

Loading a dBASE IV database catalog

dBASE IV data and associated reports and applications are grouped into what is known as a *catalog.* When you start the Command Center, it opens the catalog that was in use the last time the program was run. To change catalogs, press Alt-C to activate the Catalog menu at the top of the screen. Choose the Use a Different Catalog option.

You can access the various data files, reports, and forms in the catalog by using the arrow keys to move the highlight to the item you're interested in and pressing Enter.

Canceling a command

The dBASE cancel key is Esc, which cancels almost any changes you make. The Esc key also backs you out of all menus and operations like browsing files or creating forms.

Undoing commands

When editing data in a form, you can undo changes to the data by selecting the Undo command from the Record menu, as long as you do this before moving to the next record. If you've already moved, you're out of luck . . . the changes are permanent.

The other thing you can undo in dBASE is record deletion. When you choose to delete a record, it's still there — the program just flags the data to signify that it's really not supposed to be there. Depending on how your copy of dBASE is set up, these marked records may disappear from your view of the data completely or they may show but indicate *Del* in the status line. Either way, you can undelete them with the Clear Deletion Mark option on the Record menu.

Getting help

On-line help in dBASE is accessed by pressing the F1 key. The help screen gives information on the particular operation you're working on at the time. You can use the window options to view related topics or a table of contents. When viewing the help table of contents, F3 will take you to a more generalized list, while F4 displays a narrower group of topics.

General advice

The only thing you want to really be careful not to do in dBASE is something called *packing the database*. This shows up as a menu option to Erase Marked Records at various places in the system. Do not *ever* choose this option unless you actually know what you're doing. This process really erases the records that are only pretending to be erased when marked for deletion. Once you do this, they are gone forever.

If you ever press the Esc key one too many times and find yourself back at the blank screen with the dot, remember to type **ASSIST** to get back to the dBASE IV Control Center. If you get to this point and really just want to get out of the program completely, type **QUIT**. *Never never never* exit dBASE by pressing Ctrl-Alt-Delete. dBASE files almost always get corrupted when you do this.

Chapter 16
Playing with the Editor

● ●

In This Chapter

▶ Using the DOS Editor

▶ Editing a file already on disk

▶ Printing a file

▶ Editing your CONFIG.SYS and AUTOEXEC.BAT files

● ●

*O*ne of the most useful tools available with DOS Versions 5.0 and later is the Editor, which is called EDIT (because the word "Ed" was trademarked long ago by the Mr. Ed people). This program works like a word processor, enabling you to create and edit text files on disk. Although it lacks the full blown power of a major word processor, the Editor does contain some nice features and can be used in a variety of situations when a word processor is just too clunky. For example, rumor has it that Elvis answers all his fan mail using the DOS EDIT program.

This chapter covers using the DOS Editor program. It also contains information on editing your CONFIG.SYS and AUTOEXEC.BAT files. *What* these two files do is important, yet *how* they do it isn't crucial knowledge. How to edit the files, specifically the instructions for inserting special text, is described here in a — yes, I'll admit it — tutorial fashion. You don't need to know why you're doing this; you don't even need to know what you're doing. But when DOS tells you to edit your CONFIG.SYS or AUTOEXEC.BAT file, these are the instructions you need.

Using the DOS Editor

DOS comes with a program called EDIT. You use this program to create and edit *text files* on disk.

EDIT works like a word processor, but it lacks many of the fancier features — like the capability to print, apply fancy formatting, spellcheck, create graphics, and so on. However, for just writing text — plain ol' English — EDIT is a fine and dandy thing to have. And you'll find yourself using it often in your DOS travels.

- ✔ A *text file* is a file that contains only text — no fancy information, no Greek or any other unorthodox or unreadable stuff. For example, files you can see by using the TYPE command are text files (see "Looking at files" in Chapter 2).

- ✔ The name of the DOS Editor program is EDIT. However, for EDIT to run you need the QBasic program (QBASIC.EXE) that also comes with DOS. This is because EDIT isn't really a program at all! No, it's just a super secret "mode" of the QBasic program. Baffling, heh? The point here is that you need both the QBasic program *and* EDIT to use the DOS Editor. If you delete QBASIC.EXE, you can't use the Editor.

Starting the Editor

You start the DOS Editor by typing **EDIT** at the DOS prompt:

```
C> EDIT
```

After pressing Enter, you'll see the Editor's start-up screen, as shown in Figure 16-1. Press the Esc key, and you'll be ready to start typing.

- ✔ When you start the Editor with the EDIT command, a box appears on the screen asking if you want to use the Survival Guide (see Figure 16-1). My advice is to press the Esc (Escape) key to skip it. If you press Enter, the Survival Guide appears, offering tips and such for using the Editor. Major yawner.

- ✔ Refer to the section "Editing text" later in this chapter for tutorial typing tips.

- ✔ If you don't see the DOS Editor, or you get a bad command or file name error message, it's time to contact someone else for help. Double-check the instructions here first. Also, make sure to tell the person that you've already tried to do it yourself. Even the most surly of computer wizards appreciate effort.

Starting the Editor to edit a file

If you know the name of the text file you want to edit, you can follow EDIT with that filename. For example, if you felt a burning desire to edit the text file BLORF.TXT, you would type the following:

```
C> EDIT BLORF.TXT
```

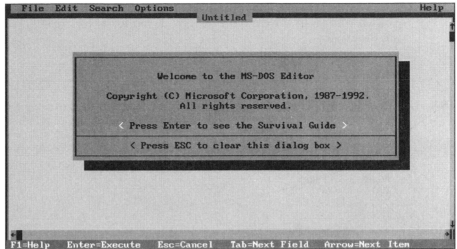

Figure 16-1:
The
DOS Editor's
start-up
screen.

First comes EDIT, a space, and then the name of the text file you want to edit, BLORF.TXT, as shown in the preceding line.

If the file already exists, the Editor will load it from disk, displaying it on the screen ready for editing. If the file doesn't exist, the Editor lets you create it from scratch. (Either way, no Survival Guide prompt — yeah!)

 ✔ Most text files end with the TXT extension. I use TXT when I create or save a text file because that lets me know a file is a text file. However, specifying a filename extension is optional when you load or save a file in the Editor. Refer to Chapter 18 for more information on filename extensions.

 ✔ If you do specify an extension on your text file, remember to specify it when you start the Editor.

 ✔ To quit the Editor, refer to the section "Quitting the Editor," later in this chapter.

 ✔ Another file to use with the Editor is README.TXT, the "read me" file included with most new software packages. You can easily view such files using the Editor. PgUp, PgDn at your leisure or print the whole ding-dang-doodle.

Editing the text

You use the Editor to either create a new file or edit a text file already on disk. This tutorial shows you how to create a new file on disk. Because you may be dry on ideas, I'm providing a sample file, though you should feel free to type in anything you like (a list of suggestions is nearby).

Start by firing up the Editor to work with a sample file. The one I've created is called WORDS.TXT. Here is the DOS command to use for creating WORDS.TXT in the Editor:

```
C> EDIT WORDS.TXT
```

Type in the EDIT command, followed by a space and then the name of the file you want to edit, such as WORDS.TXT above. Press Enter.

If the WORDS.TXT file already exists, you'll see it on your screen. Otherwise, you'll have to type in the file's contents. The following is what I typed in for my WORDS.TXT file:

```
Simon's words at age 7 months
Da = Daddy
Mamm = Mommy
Baba = Bottle
Up = Up
Duh = Duck
Bpbpbp = Is that Rush Limbaugh on the radio again?
```

Here are some general Editor typing and editing rules:

- ✔ Press Enter at the end of each line.
- ✔ No "word wrap" is available in the Editor.
- ✔ Use the Backspace key to back up and erase if you make a mistake.
- ✔ You can type long lines if you like, though they'll "scroll" to the right across the screen. Typing more than a screenful of text causes the Editor to scroll down.

- ✔ Lines of text in the Editor can be up to 255 characters long; the entire text file can be utterly huge — a size so boggling you'd have to be a pretty darn prolific writer to see the Editor full error message.

A list of Editor key commands, specifically those that move the cursor around, is shown in Table 16-1. Test these commands out. Press Ctrl-End to move to the end of your text, Ctrl-Home to move to the start, Ctrl→ to move right a word and Ctrl← to move left, and so on. Play, play, play!

Table 16-1	Editor Key Commands
Key Command	*Function*
↑ (Up arrow)	Move the cursor up one line
↓ (Down arrow)	Move the cursor down one line
← (Left arrow)	Move the cursor left (back) one character
→ (Right arrow)	Move the cursor right (forward) one character
PgUp	Move up to the previous page (screen)
PgDn	Move down to the next page (screen)
Ctrl-←	Move left one word
Ctrl-→	Move right one word
Ctrl-↑	Scroll the screen up one line
Ctrl-↓	Scroll the screen down one line
Delete	Delete current character
Backspace	Delete previous character
Insert	Switch between insert and overwrite editing modes
Ctrl-Home	Beginning of file
Ctrl-End	End of file

✔ In addition to using the arrow-key commands shown in Table 16-1, you can refer to Table 10-1 for a list of other, bizarre key commands used in the Editor.

✔ You can also use your mouse (if you have one) to position the cursor on the screen: Point the mouse where you want the cursor to be and click it once to move the cursor to that very spot.

✔ To save your all-important text file, refer to the section, "Saving your stuff to disk." Remember: Always save before you quit!

Playing with blocks

You can mark text in the Editor and treat that text as a single unit — a block, with which you can have lots of fun. For example, you can copy a block of text, cut and paste it, or just zap it all to kingdom come. There are two ways to mark a block:

1. Use your mouse to *drag* over the text you want marked as a block.

2. Hold down the Shift key and use the arrow keys to mark the block.

Suggestions for sample files to type

Drumming up ideas for sample text files to type in is the bane of the computer book author. I've seen some real losers in my time. To assist my fellow authors, as well as budding MS-DOS Editor enthusiasts, the following list contains some suggestions for li'l sample text files you can type in. Only titles are offered; it's up to you to devise content.

Four famous-but-not-dead people I'd like to invite over for dinner

What clouds smell like

What if Democrats ran the afterlife

Thoughts Freud might have on the things I doodle when I talk on the phone

If I were in charge of building a VCR, what I would put on the knobs

Why walking through a sandbox with wet socks on makes my skin crawl

Ten common, household objects a 2-year-old could stick in his ear

A promo for the new *Sports Illustrated* famous groin injuries football video

Ten things you'd find in an airplane lavatory

Several convincing reasons why aliens would prefer to land in your state instead of any place else

Either way, the marked block appears highlighted on the screen, typically shown with inverse text (such as blue text on a white background). After that block is highlighted, you can do the following things to it:

- ✔ Press Ctrl-Insert to copy the block, and then move the cursor to where you want to paste the copy and press Shift-Insert to paste it.

- ✔ Press Shift-Delete to cut the block, making it vanish from the screen. Move the cursor to where you want to paste the block, and then press Shift-Insert to paste it.

- ✔ Delete the block by pressing the Delete key.

- ✔ It's a lot easier to access these commands from the Edit menu, either by using the mouse or by pressing the Alt-E key combination. (See "Information about the Editor not worth reading.")

- ✔ Yeah, Ctrl-Insert to copy, Shift-Delete to cut, and Shift-Insert to paste are about as non-mnemonic as you can get. Fortunately, the people at Microsoft tell me that the guy who dreamt up all those dorky key combinations has long ago been fired. Relish that thought as you struggle to remember what's what.

Searching and Replacing

To search for a specific tidbit of text in your document, press Alt-S, F. This move drops down the Search menu and selects the Find command. A magical box then appears, where you can type in the text you're looking for. Type **Uganda** to find all references to that African nation. Press Enter to scope it out.

- ✔ The Find command locates text from the cursor's position to the end of the document. If the text isn't found, Find then starts looking at the start of the document. And if the text doesn't exist, you'll see a `Match not found` box displayed. Sigh deeply and press the Esc key.

- ✔ To find the next occurrence of your text tidbit, press the F3 key.

Information about the Editor not worth reading

The Editor uses drop-down menus to contain its commands. You activate the menu by pressing Alt and then the first letter of the menu you want to use. You can also press both the Alt key and the letter key at the same time; Alt-F drops down the File menu.

Each menu contains menu items, all of which pertain somehow to the title of the menu. For example, the File menu contains file commands. You select these commands by typing the highlighted letter in their name.

If you have a mouse, you can select menu items with it. This involves using a whole lot of mousy terms, which I don't really care to get into at this point in the book (but do get into in Chapter 10).

Printing with the Editor

To print your prose, use the Print command found in the File menu. Start by making sure you have a printer turned on and all ready to print. Then press Alt-F to get the File menu; then press P for the Print command. You'll see a li'l box displayed on the screen. Press Enter to print your whole ding-dang file. Zip, zip, zip. It's done.

- ✔ If the printer isn't turned on, or it's goofy or something, you'll see a *Device fault* error box. Fix the printer and try again.

- ✔ Chapter 11 has all the messy-messies on printing and using a printer.

Printing any Text File without Having to Bother with the Editor

You can print any text file by using the DOS Editor to edit it and then using the Print command as described above. You can also print any file at the handy DOS prompt by using the following command:

```
C> COPY WORDS.TXT PRN
```

Yes, this is the typical COPY command, which in this case is used to print the text file WORDS.TXT. First comes COPY, a space, and then the name of the file you want to print. Follow the file's name with another space, and then PRN. Make sure your printer is on and ready to print, and then press Enter.

✔ The COPY-PRN command can be used to print any text file on disk, not just those created by the Editor. These are the same files you can view with the TYPE command. Refer to Chapter 2 in the section "Looking at files."

✔ If you have a laser printer, you'll probably need to manually eject the page to see your work. Refer to Chapter 11, the section "Ejecting a page" for more information.

✔ If the printer isn't ready to print (such as when you forget to turn it on), you'll probably see a *Write fault error writing device PRN* error. Gadzooks! Turn the printer on and carefully type **R.** That should do the trick. If not, press **A** and you'll be safely back at the DOS prompt. (Refer to Chapter 11 for printer help.)

Saving your stuff to disk

Before you quit the Editor, you need to save your file back to disk. If you don't do this, all that work and your many precious words will not be saved for posterity.

To save your stuff, press and release the Alt key and then press **F**. This action *drops down* the File menu at the top of the screen.

Press **S** to save the file.

If you're editing a new file, a Save box-thing appears where you can type the name of the file you want to save. Type up to eight characters; be sure to use something memorable. Press Enter to save the file to disk.

✔ The file you save to disk is a text file, which means it contains readable text as opposed to unfathomable stuff or information only the computer can digest.

✔ The Editor does not automatically give your file a TXT extension. You'll need to type that into the Save box if you want your files to end in TXT.

✔ Refer to Chapter 18 for more information on naming files.

✔ If a box appears proclaiming that the file already exists, type **N** and select a different name. If you type **Y**, you'll overwrite the file already on disk. If that's what you want, OK. Otherwise, select another name because you may not be certain of what you're overwriting.

✔ Other application programs, text editors, and word processors can easily read the text files you create using the DOS Editor. Unfortunately, the Editor can only deal with basic, no-frills text files. You cannot edit a document from your word processor using the Editor unless you save it in the *plain text*, *DOS text*, or *ASCII* format first.

Quitting the Editor

You should quit the Editor only after saving your file to disk; refer to the previous section for the details on this operation. After the file is saved, you quit the Editor so that you can return to DOS and spend more time enjoying life at the DOS prompt.

To quit the Editor, press and release the Alt key, and then press **F**. This action drops down the File menu.

Press **X** to select the Exit item. This quits the Editor and returns you to the safe-but-not-warm-and-fuzzy DOS prompt.

✔ If you haven't saved your file before quitting, a message box or window appears asking if you want to save. Press **Y** in that instance; follow the steps listed in the previous section on saving a file.

✔ Never ever "quit" the Editor by pressing Ctrl-Alt-Delete or your PC's reset button.

It Tells Me to Edit My CONFIG.SYS or AUTOEXEC.BAT File!

One of the most puzzling DOS wild goose chases happens when a program says `Put the following into your config.sys file` or `Edit your autoexec.bat file and add the following`. To carry out these instructions, you're told to refer to your DOS manual. The DOS manual, on the other hand, says to refer to your application's manual. Herein we have the rumblings of any great bureaucracy: confusion and consistency in equal amounts.

Before diving into this, you should know two things: First, you should always know what it is you're adding to CONFIG.SYS or AUTOEXEC.BAT. The exact line of text you need to add should be specified somewhere. Never edit these files without a purpose.

Second, use this tutorial only as a last resort or when no other help is around. Especially in a business situation, someone should be in charge of the computers and they should be updating these two important files. If you're at home, or there isn't anyone else around to help, this is where you turn. But beware: This stuff is funky.

Hunting down the files

To get at CONFIG.SYS or AUTOEXEC.BAT, you must log to the root directory of your hard drive. Type the following two commands:

```
C> C:
```

Press Enter. You're logging to drive C. Now type

```
C> CD \
```

That's CD, followed by a space and the *backslash* character (\) — *not* the forward slash (/).

The two commands you use here ensure that you're logged to the root directory of drive C, your boot disk. You're now ready to edit either CONFIG.SYS or AUTOEXEC.BAT. The next step is to determine which *text editor* you have.

- ✔ If you want to make a duplicate, safety copy of the file you're editing, refer to "Duplicating a File" in Chapter 4.

- ✔ For more information on logging, refer to "Changing Drives" and "Changing Directories," both in Chapter 2.

- ✔ The CD command is covered in "Finding the Current Directory" and "Changing Directories," both in Chapter 17.

Editing the file

If the instructions told you to edit your CONFIG.SYS file, type the following:

```
C> EDIT CONFIG.SYS
```

That's EDIT followed by a space and then CONFIG.SYS, which is the name of the file you want to edit. This command starts the DOS Editor — the program that edits files on disk.

If you're told to edit your AUTOEXEC.BAT file, substitute AUTOEXEC.BAT for CONFIG.SYS as follows:

```
C> EDIT AUTOEXEC.BAT
```

After pressing Enter, you'll see the DOS Editor appear on your screen. It looks something like Figure 16-2.

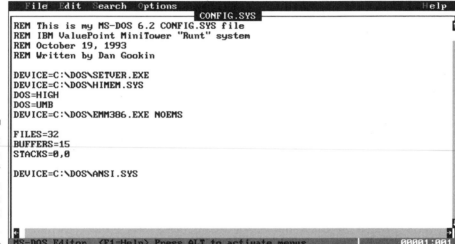

```
 File  Edit  Search  Options                                    Help
                            CONFIG.SYS
REM This is my MS-DOS 6.2 CONFIG.SYS file
REM IBM ValuePoint MiniTower "Runt" system
REM October 19, 1993
REM Written by Dan Gookin

DEVICE=C:\DOS\SETVER.EXE
DEVICE=C:\DOS\HIMEM.SYS
DOS=HIGH
DOS=UMB
DEVICE=C:\DOS\EMM386.EXE NOEMS

FILES=32
BUFFERS=15
STACKS=0,0

DEVICE=C:\DOS\ANSI.SYS




MS-DOS Editor  <F1=Help> Press ALT to activate menus          00001:001
```

Figure 16-2:
The
DOS Editor
with
someone's
CONFIG.SYS
file in it.

Adding the new line

Because I'm not going to make any assumptions here, put the new line at the end of the document, way down toward the bottom. If your instructions explicitly tell you where to put the new line, follow them as best you can — for example, if the instructions say to put the line at the very tippy top, do that.

To add the new line at the end of the file (which is where it goes if the instructions aren't specific), press Ctrl-End: press and hold down the Ctrl (Control) key and then press the End key. Release both keys. This moves you to the last line in the file. (It doesn't matter which Ctrl or End key you use.) Then press Enter.

To add the new line at the start of the file you . . . hey! You're already at the start of the file. Fancy that. (Press Ctrl-Home to move there if you aren't there already.)

Now type the line you need to add. For example, if you were adding the PROMPT command to AUTOEXEC.BAT, you would type in that command. If you were adding a command to CONFIG.SYS, type that command in as well.

After you enter the exact text of the command, double-check your work. Make sure you typed in exactly what you should have. After that's done, press Enter.

- ✔ The Ctrl and End key combination is often written Ctrl-End. Refer to "Alt-S Means What?" in Chapter 11 for more information about key combinations.

- ✔ If you make a mistake while you're typing, use the Backspace key to back up and erase.

- ✔ Sometimes commands in CONFIG.SYS require a full pathname in order for them to work properly. Refer to "What Is a Pathname?" in Chapter 17 for information on pathnames.

Saving and quitting

Before saving your CONFIG.SYS or AUTOEXEC.BAT file back to disk, first double-check your work. Make sure you typed in everything exactly and that no stray characters appear unexpectedly. (This takes a trained eye because, I'll admit, CONFIG.SYS and AUTOEXEC.BAT look like they have lots of sneeze marks in them.)

To save the file, press Alt-F to drop down the File menu. Press **S** to save the file. This saves the file on disk, making your changes permanent.

To quit the Editor and return to DOS, press Alt-F to drop down the File menu again. Press **X** to exit and return to DOS.

- ✔ Additional information on saving and quitting can be found earlier in this chapter.

Resetting

You're back at the DOS prompt, ready to continue working. Congratulations, your CONFIG.SYS or AUTOEXEC.BAT file is updated. Whew! But now comes the scary part.

You must reset your computer to see the results of any changes you've made to these files. This is only true for AUTOEXEC.BAT and CONFIG.SYS; any other file you edit or program you run doesn't require a reset. (I told you this would be funky.)

- You reset by pressing Ctrl-Alt-Delete or by punching that big red button on your PC. Refer to "Resetting" in Chapter 1 if you feel anxious about doing this.

- Oftentimes, it's a good idea to run the MemMaker memory management program after you update either CONFIG.SYS or AUTOEXEC.BAT. Refer to Chapter 8 for information on running the DOS MemMaker program.

- Anytime you add (or remove) a line from your CONFIG.SYS or AUTOEXEC.BAT file, you'll see (or miss) extra text displayed each time your PC starts.

- If you see any errors when the computer restarts, that means you may have typed something incorrectly. Go through these steps again and recheck your work. Make sure that what you typed is exactly what was required. Then call for help.

Mired in the Past with EDLIN

If you have an old, old version of DOS — before DOS 5 — then, boy, do I feel sorry for you. You don't have access to the fancy Editor program. Instead, you're stuck using DOS's old line editor, EDLIN. It's just the worst example of a text editor in the history of DOS. This program was originally written in 1981 — back when the only people using computers were puffy and pale Neanderthal nerds just rising from the mud swamps of the slide-rule age. It makes me shudder.

Editing your CONFIG.SYS or AUTOEXEC.BAT file with EDLIN

Follow EDLIN with the name of the file you want to edit. For example, when you're told to edit your CONFIG.SYS file, type in the following command:

```
C:\> EDLIN CONFIG.SYS
```

To edit your AUTOEXEC.BAT file, substitute AUTOEXEC.BAT for CONFIG.SYS. After pressing Enter, you'll see the following:

```
End of input file *
```

Yoikle! I shudder to think of the user hostility this program harbors. You see End of input file, which means God-knows-what, and then an asterisk on the next line. Is this like shaking hands with a snake or what?

To add a new line of text to a file, such as CONFIG.SYS or AUTOEXEC.BAT, you'll need to "move" to the end of the file. You do this by using the #I command. At the asterisk prompt, type a pound sign (#) and the letter **I** (no spaces!):

```
*#I
```

Press Enter. You'll see something like the following displayed:

```
13:*
```

There will be a number, a colon, and an asterisk. The number is a line number, the last line in the file. The asterisk is EDLIN's friendly prompt. And no, you don't see anything on the screen. (Ugly editor. Ugly.)

Type the line you need to add. For example, if you were adding the PROMPT command to AUTOEXEC.BAT, you would type in that command. If you were adding a command to CONFIG.SYS, you would type that in as well.

After you enter the exact text of the command, double-check your work.

After you've made sure that everything has been typed correctly, press Enter. You'll see something like the following:

```
14:*
```

The number will be one higher than the new line you entered. At this prompt, type a Ctrl-C: Press and hold the Ctrl (Control) key and, with that key held down, type a **C**. Release both keys. You'll see ^C displayed and then the main asterisk prompt two lines down.

You now need to save the edited file back to disk. In EDLIN you do this by quitting the program with the E command, which stands for *Exit back to DOS*. (Though I prefer that it stand for *Enough!*)

Press **E** and then press Enter. Soon you'll see the happy DOS prompt displayed.

✔ Note that EDLIN automatically makes a backup file: CONFIG.BAK for CONFIG.SYS or AUTOEXEC.BAK for AUTOEXEC.BAT. These files contain the original text that you edited.

✔ If you've totally screwed up, you can quit EDLIN using the Q command. EDLIN will ask if you want to Abort edit? Press **Y** to return to DOS and try again — if you dare!

The 5th Wave By Rich Tennant

"No thanks. But I <u>would</u> like one more chance to see if I can edit my AUTOEXEC. BAT file so my programs will appear when I start up my computer."

Chapter 17
The Hard Drive:
Where You Store Stuff

• •

In This Chapter

▶ Understanding how information is stored in separate work areas on the hard drive

▶ Understanding how the root directory fits into the big picture

▶ Learning about what the <DIR> thing in a directory listing means

▶ Creating and using a pathname

▶ Finding the current directory

▶ Changing from one directory to another

▶ Viewing your hard disk's tree structure

▶ Using the ScanDisk command

▶ Backing up your hard drive

▶ Understanding disk compression

• •

I've always been fascinated by hard disk management. Why isn't it *easy* disk management? Computers are supposed to make life easier, not harder. Yet computer nerds are fascinated by hard disk management. They've even come up with a whole row of verbal hurdles to leap over for anyone who attempts to understand hard disk management. Even given that it's a hard disk you're managing, the subject could easily be called hard hard-disk management. Ugh.

All kidding aside, hard disk management is simply using files on a hard drive. This involves some organization, and that's where the funky terms come into play. This chapter describes the ugly terms you'll encounter when you use a hard drive, what they mean, and why the heck you'd ever want to use them. This stuff is really important. If you learn only one thing — how to find your way around a hard disk — it will be worth the price of this book.

What Is a Subdirectory?

A *subdirectory* is workspace on a disk. It's almost like a disk within a disk. You can copy files and programs into a subdirectory or workspace, and you can use DOS commands. The advantage to subdirectories is that you can store information in a subdirectory and keep it separate from other files on the same disk. That keeps the disk from getting file-messy.

Any disk can have subdirectories, though they're used primarily on hard drives to keep files separate and your programs organized. So rather than let you suffer through a hard drive with bazillions of files all in one place, the subdirectories enable you to organize everything by placing information into separate areas.

- ✔ Subdirectories should just be called *directories*. The prefix *sub* means *under,* just as submarine means any large naval vessel that a marine is standing on. All the workspaces on a disk are really directories. However, when you refer to one directory in relation to another, the term *subdirectory* is used.

- ✔ If you want to create a directory to keep some of your files separate from other files, refer to "How to Name a Directory (the MKDIR Command)" in Chapter 18.

- ✔ All the directories on your disk create what's called a *tree structure*. For information refer to "The Tree Structure" later in this chapter.

The Root Directory

Every disk you use under DOS has one main directory, called the *root directory*. The root directory (often just called *the root*) exists on all DOS disks; it happens naturally, created when you first format the disk.

The symbol for the root directory is the single backslash (\). This is an abbreviation — shorthand — that DOS uses in reference to the root directory. It also plays an important role in the *pathname,* which is covered later in this chapter.

Additional directories on a disk are subdirectories under the root directory. They branch off of the root like branches of a tree. In fact, if you map out the directories on a disk linking each subdirectory, it looks like a family tree of sorts (see Figure 17-1).

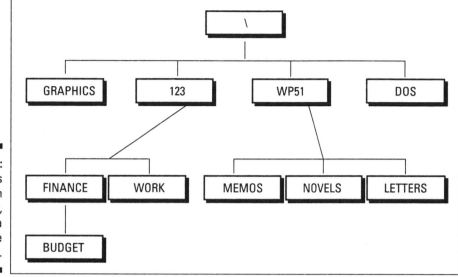

Figure 17-1:
Subdirectories
branch from
the root,
creating a
family tree
of sorts.

- The FORMAT command is used to prepare disks for use under DOS. It also creates the root directory. For more information, refer to "Formatting a Disk" in Chapter 13.

- Whenever you're using a disk, you're *logged to* or currently using a directory on that disk. To change to another subdirectory, refer to "Changing Directories" later in this chapter; to change to another disk, refer to "Changing Drives" in Chapter 2. To see which directory you're currently logged to, refer to "Finding the Current Directory" later in this chapter.

You are not required to know this stuff

Subdirectories are often called *child* directories. And from a subdirectory's point of view, it has a *parent* directory. For example, in Figure 17-1, DOS is a subdirectory of the root directory (\). DOS is the root directory's child directory. The root directory is the parent of the DOS directory.

If you were logged to or using the 123 directory in Figure 17-1, its parent directory would be the root. The 123 directory also has two child directories — or two subdirectories. They are named FINANCE and WORK.

The visual representation shown in Figure 17-1 is only for your head; you'll *see* nothing of the sort as you use your computer. However, it's a good visual representation of the relationships between various directories on a disk. The TREE command, covered later in this chapter, enables you to see the representation in a different format.

That Funny <DIR> Thing

To find a subdirectory on a disk, you use the DIR command. Directories are listed there, along with other files. The way you identify a directory name is by the <DIR> thing shown after its name (where other files would have their file size in bytes).

For example, consider the following output from the DIR command:

```
Volume in drive C is DOS HAPPY
Volume Serial Number is 16CE-9B67
Directory of C:\
123          <DIR>         03-18-92      9:33p
COMM         <DIR>         08-07-92      9:37p
DOS          <DIR>         09-20-93      10:52p
GAMES        <DIR>         09-22-93      5:18p
WP60         <DIR>         09-21-93      5:12p
AUTOEXEC  BAT      574     09-05-93      10:04a
COMMAND   COM   54,928 08-11-93         6:20a
CONFIG    SYS      464     07-25-93      10:20a
WINA20    386    9,349 08-11-93         6:20a
        9 file(s)     65,315 bytes
              36,468,736    bytes free
```

The *files* 123, COMM, DOS, GAMES, and WP60 are actually directories on disk. At the top of the output in the preceding example, Directory of C:\ tells you that you're looking at a directory of drive C (that's the C:), the root directory (shown by the backslash). The <DIR> entries in the listing are all subdirectories of the root directory.

- Subdirectories appear in the DIR command's listing because they're part of your disk, just like files. In fact, directories are named just like files and can even have an extension like a file. Refer to "How to Name a Directory (the MKDIR Command)" in Chapter 18 for more information (if you're curious).

- For more information on the DIR command, refer to "The DIR Command" in Chapter 2.

- ✔ For information on finding a lost directory on disk, refer to "Finding a Lost Subdirectory" in Chapter 18.

- ✔ The C:\ is actually a pathname.

- ✔ Commas in big numbers only appear if you have MS-DOS 6.2. Early versions of DOS don't use commas, which is just DOS's attempt to overwhelm you with large values.

What Is a Pathname?

A *pathname* is like a long filename. A filename is a name given only to a file; providing you're clever with eight characters, it also tells you something about the file's contents. A pathname, on the other hand, tells you where a file is located — it tells you on which disk the file has been saved and in which subdirectory.

A file's pathname is like a path to the file. It tells you how to get to a specific file or subdirectory — an exact location. For example, the following is a pathname, a full pathname to a specific file on disk:

```
C:\WORK\CHAP12.DOC
```

The filename CHAP12.DOC identifies a file on a disk. In the preceding example, the full pathname says it's a file on drive C, as seen by the C: at the start. Furthermore, the file CHAP12.DOC is located in the WORK subdirectory. The backslashes (\) in the pathname are provided as separating elements, keeping the drive letter, subdirectories, and filename from running into each other.

This breaks down as follows:

C:	Drive C
C:\	The root directory
C:\WORK	The WORK subdirectory
C:\WORK\CHAP12.DOC	The file CHAP12.DOC and its full pathname

Pathnames don't always have to end with a filename. They can also be used to identify a subdirectory located somewhere on a disk. In that case, the pathname tells you which drive it's on and all its parent directories on up to the root. For example, consider this pathname:

```
C:\WP60\DATA
```

To break this down, you have:

`C:`	The drive letter, C
`C:\`	The root directory of drive C
`C:\WP60`	The WP60 subdirectory on drive C, a subdirectory of the root
`C:\WP60\DATA`	The DATA subdirectory under the WP60 directory

- ✔ The backslash is used both as a symbol for the root directory and as a separator. A backslash always separates subdirectories from each other. There are no spaces in a pathname.

- ✔ A pathname that starts with a drive letter is called a *full pathname*. (Pathnames don't always need the drive letter.)

- ✔ The drive letter is optional in a pathname. However, I recommend using it because it's more specific.

- ✔ When you use the CD command by itself to locate the current directory, what it returns is a pathname; refer to the next section.

Finding the Current Directory

To find out which directory you're logged to or currently using, type the CD command:

```
C> CD
```

The directory you're using will be displayed on the following line. (Actually, what you will see is a pathname of the current directory.) You can change to any other subdirectory on the same drive by using the CD command followed by that directory's pathname. Refer to the next section for the specifics.

- ✔ CD has a longer form, CHDIR. Both do the same thing, but CD is quicker to type (and you can say *current directory* or *change directory* in your head instead of *chiddur*).

- ✔ For more information on changing drives, refer to "Changing Drives" in Chapter 2.

- ✔ For more information on pathnames, refer to "What Is a Pathname?" earlier in this chapter.

- ✔ The PROMPT command can be used to tell you the current directory at all times. Refer to "Prompt Styles of the Rich and Famous" in Chapter 3.

Technical background junk

Whenever you use a computer, you're using or attached to some specific disk drive. Though your system may have several drives, you're actually using only one of them at a time. That drive is said to be the *currently logged drive*. (*Logged* in computer lingo means *using*.) The same holds true with directories on a disk; you can use — or be logged to — only one directory at a time.

When you first use a disk, you're automatically logged to its root directory, the main directory on disk. After you've been using the computer for a while, you'll probably wind up elsewhere on the disk, say in some subdirectory somewhere. To find out the pathname of that subdirectory, use the CD command as just described.

Changing Directories

To change to another directory, type the CD (Change Directory) command followed by the pathname of the directory to which you want to change. In computer jargon, this *logs* you to that new directory.

For example, suppose you want to change to the root directory. Type this in:

```
C> CD \
```

That's the CD command, followed by a space and the root directory's name/ symbol, the backslash.

To change to the \WP60 subdirectory, type

```
C> CD \WP60
```

Try to type in a pathname that includes the root directory. This kind of pathname always starts with a backslash, which indicates the root. If you know the full pathname of the directory, type it in. Otherwise, you can refer to "Finding a Lost Subdirectory" in Chapter 18 for finding lost directories.

You can use the DIR command to find the name of a subdirectory to log to. If you find a name, a full pathname isn't needed. For example, if you use the DIR command and see the DATA directory (marked by <DIR> in the directory listing), you can log to (use) it by typing

```
C> CD DATA
```

Because DATA is a subdirectory, or child, of the current directory, there's no need to specify a full pathname.

You can take another shortcut to log to the parent directory:

```
C> CD ..
```

The dot-dot is an abbreviation for the parent directory — no matter where you are. This is much quicker than typing out the full pathname for the parent directory.

- ✓ You cannot use the CD command to change to a subdirectory on another drive. You must first log to that drive and then use the CD command. Refer to "Changing Drives" in Chapter 2 for how to log to another drive.

- ✓ If you see an Invalid directory error message, you didn't type in a full pathname or you mistyped something. It could also be that you're not logged to the proper drive. Refer to "Finding a Lost Subdirectory" in Chapter 18 for finding lost directories.

- ✓ You can also use the CHDIR command, the longer form of the CD command. CHDIR stands for Change Directory, supposedly.

- ✓ Refer to "What Is a Pathname?" earlier in this chapter for information on pathnames.

The Tree Structure

All the subdirectories on a disk make for a fairly complex arrangement. I know of no one, nerd or non-nerd, who actually knows exactly what's where on his or her system. So to find out, to get a view of the big picture, you use the TREE command.

Type the following command:

```
C> TREE C:\
```

That's the TREE command, a space, C, a colon, and a backslash character. The TREE command is followed by a pathname; C:\ means drive C's root directory. Press Enter and the TREE command displays a graphic representation of your tree structure, how your subdirectories are organized for drive C. Early versions of DOS don't have graphic trees; they use a confusing text display instead.

The display scrolls off the screen for a time. If you want to pause the display, press the Ctrl-S key combination; to continue, press Ctrl-S again. You can also use the following command:

```
C> TREE C:\ | MORE
```

That's the same command as before, followed by a space, the pipe character (|), another space, and the word MORE. This inserts an automatic *more prompt* at the bottom of each screen. Press the spacebar to look at the next screen.

If you want to print a copy of the output, turn on your printer and type this command:

```
C> TREE C:\ > PRN
```

That's the same TREE command described in the preceding example, a space, a greater-than symbol (>), another space, and the word PRN. Press Enter. If the printed output looks gross, try this variation of the command:

```
C> TREE C:\ /A > PRN
```

That's a slash-A in the middle of the command, surrounded by a space on each side. (Well, as you make more demands on DOS, it gets more cryptic. But at least your printed copy won't look so gross.) For more information on using a printer, refer to Chapter 11.

> ✔ For more information on Ctrl-S, refer to "Ctrl-S and the Pause Key" in Chapter 10.

Is My Disk Okay?

Computer disks are nothing like melons. You can't thump them to hear if they're ripe. You can't see any soft spots. And you can't slice into them to find a soupy-black mush of maggots to realize a disk is rotten. Instead, DOS gives you some disk-prodding tools that do the thumping, looking, and slicing for you — plus a bit of repair.

For almost everyone, the DOS disk fixer-upper tool is CHKDSK, the Check Disk command. CHKDSK is still around with MS-DOS 6.2, but a much better disk-checking tool, ScanDisk, is available instead. The following sections sort out the fruit.

Checking the disk (the CHKDSK command)

To check out a disk, hard or floppy, by using CHKDSK, type in **CHKDSK** at the DOS prompt, press Enter, and prepare to be overwhelmed:

```
C> CHKDSK
```

After pressing Enter you'll see something like this:

```
Volume DOS HAPPY created 09-21-1990 1:26p
Volume Serial Number is 16CE-9B67
42366976  bytes total disk space
   73728  bytes in 2 hidden files
  110592  bytes in 52 directories
25837568  bytes in 879 user files
16345088  bytes available on disk
    2048  bytes in each allocation unit
   20687  total allocation units on disk
    7981  available allocation units on disk
  655360  total bytes memory
  637984  bytes free
```

There are four chunks of information here. The first is trivia about your disk. The second, with five items, is more important. The first value tells you the size of your disk. It says there are 42,366,976 bytes of *total disk space.* That means the drive holds about 40MB of stuff. The last value tells you how much space you have left. That's 16,345,088 bytes *available on disk,* which means that drive has about 16MB of unused storage.

The third section is really useless, with *allocation unit* sounding like something the government would say about every 35 billion dollars it spends.

The final section tells you how much memory you have and how much is available for use by programs.

CHKDSK works on only one drive at a time. To use CHKDSK on another drive, first log to that drive and then run CHKDSK. Refer to "Changing Drives" in

Chapter 2 for information on logging to another drive. You can also use
CHKDSK on another drive by typing the following command:

```
C>CHKDSK A:
```

CHKDSK is often thought of as some form of cure-all for disk ailments. It's not.
CHKDSK merely reports information that the computer already knows about
itself, so if some computer weirdo says "run CHKDSK" to fix the problem, he or
she probably doesn't know what he or she is talking about. There is one
exception: refer to the next section.

If CHKDSK reports any errors, specifically `Missing files` or `unallocated
clusters` or `lost chains` or something along those lines, it will ask you a
question. Type **N** for no and then refer to the following section.

📖 For more information on available memory, refer to Chapter 8.

CHKDSK says I have lost files in clusters or something

The CHKDSK command is good at finding lost files on disk. These aren't
important files that you may have lost, but rather pieces of files that were
blown to bits by DOS. Usually, these files are shattered when you reset in the
middle of something or when the computer goes bonkers; there is typically
nothing CHKDSK finds that's important, so don't take its message as a bad
omen.

When CHKDSK does report something wrong, you should fix it. In order to fix
the problem, run CHKDSK a second time with its slash-F option. Type in the
following command:

```
C> CHKDSK /F
```

That's the CHKDSK command, a space, and then slash-F. Press Enter. CHKDSK
will discover the same errors. This time, however, press **Y** when it asks you the
Convert lost chains to files? question.

When you use slash-F and answer Yes to the question, CHKDSK gathers up all
the pieces of the lost files it finds and places them on your disk. There is really
nothing you can do with these files, so delete them. This command does the job:

```
C> DEL \FILE*.CHK
```

That's DEL, a space, a backslash, FILE, an asterisk, a period, and CHK. This is a
filename wildcard that matches all the files CHKDSK creates in your root
directory.

> ✔ For more information on deleting files, refer to "Deleting a Group of Files" in Chapter 4.
>
> ✔ For information on filename wildcards, refer to "Wildcards (or Poker Was Never This Much Fun)" in Chapter 18.

Scanning the disk with ScanDisk

To make sure your disk is in tip-top shape, you can use MS-DOS 6.2's ScanDisk command. This command takes a close look at your disk, and if it finds anything awry, it fixes it on the spot. This is something only available with MS-DOS 6.2.

To use ScanDisk, type the **SCANDISK** command at the DOS prompt, press Enter, and prepare to be overwhelmed:

```
C> SCANDISK
```

After pressing Enter, ScanDisk proceeds to smell, squeeze, and thump your disk, looking for any soft spots. You'll see an interesting screen with five tasks displayed and checked off as ScanDisk completes them (see Figure 17-2).

Before doing the fifth task, Surface scan, you'll see a box displayed asking whether or not you want a surface scan. My advice is to press **N** for No, then press **X** to exit (quit) ScanDisk. Only press Y if you've been having problems with the disk, such as *Read errors* or *Write errors* or if you've noticed a general increase in disk mayhem (beyond the normal).

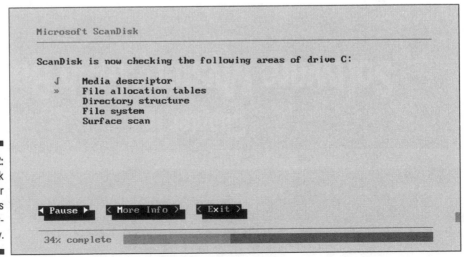

Figure 17-2: ScanDisk ensures your disk drives are hunky-dory.

If you press Y to perform a surface scan, ScanDisk will take a long, slow, careful look at your disk. This is a tedious process, but it's certain to find any errors and fix them. Because of the time involved, I recommend that you only answer Y to the surface scan question once a month or so.

ScanDisk works on only one drive at a time. To use it on another drive, first log to that drive and then run the SCANDISK command. Refer to "Changing Drives" in Chapter 2 for information on logging to another drive. You can also use ScanDisk on another drive by typing the following command:

```
C>SCANDISK A:
```

The preceding command scans a floppy disk in drive A. Substitute your favorite drive letter for A: to scan that drive.

If ScanDisk reports any errors, it's a good idea to select the Fix It option. This directs ScanDisk to repair the disk. Refer to the next section for details.

Having ScanDisk fix your disk

When ScanDisk finds something amiss with the disk it's scanning, you'll see a box appear on the screen. The box does its best to explain what's wrong and offers you several options at fixing the problem. Most of the time, when you're faced with such a box, pressing Enter patches things up nicely. You should also write the changes to an "undo" disk — and it's a good idea to keep an undo disk handy next to your computer. This is the course I recommend: When ScanDisk gives you the Fix It option, press Enter, read the screen carefully, shove in the undo disk as told, and the problem will be fixed.

A common disk boo-boo that ScanDisk locates is the old "lost files or directories" error. You'll see a box with text that starts off something like this:

```
ScanDisk found xxxx bytes of data on drive X that might be
one or more lost files or directories, but which is probably
just taking up space.
```

Normally, you should select the Delete option to remove the excess files ("probably just taking up space"). The exception here is when ScanDisk has been doing a lot of repair work for you, in which case the Save option is a better choice.

To select the `Delete` option, press **L** or click on the Delete "button" using your mouse. At this point you can stick your undo disk into drive A. Do so, and then ScanDisk continues to scan the disk. Before you quit, a summary screen is displayed telling you what ScanDisk did.

If you've been using ScanDisk a lot to repair a misguided disk, select the `Save` option when faced with the above error message box. ScanDisk then gathers up all the pieces of the lost files that it finds and places them on your disk. The files will be found in the root directory, named FILE0000.CHK, FILE0001.CHK, FILE0002.CHK — for as many files as ScanDisk rescued.

You can examine the files with the TYPE command if you like. This helps you to see what they were. For example:

```
C> TYPE FILE0000.CHK
```

Or you can use the following command when the file is inexcusably long:

```
C> MORE < FILE0000.CHK
```

That's MORE, a space, the less-than symbol, a space, then the name of the file you want to peer at.

As far as content goes, what's in the file could be anyone's guess. But if you recognize it, rename the file to its original name (using the REN command). Then copy the file to its proper location on disk. Kneel appropriately toward Microsoft Headquarters and chant "Bill is Good" several times in appreciation. (That's *Good* with two O's, mind you.)

✔ When you're reading the ScanDisk fix-it screens, remember to press the down arrow to see any additional information that may be lurking beneath the box.

✔ If you select the `Save` option to save the files and, lo, they're full of a lot of meaningless junk, then delete them. This is 100 percent okay; rogue files seem to litter people's disks like beer cans after a rodeo. Use the DEL command as covered in Chapter 4.

✔ If you use an undo disk, keep it handy next to your computer. Should the errors that ScanDisk detected turn out to not really be errors, sing "Whoomp, there it is" and then put the undo disk back into drive A. Type **SCANDISK /UNDO** at the DOS prompt and follow the instructions on the screen.

✔ For more information on renaming files, refer to "Renaming a file" in Chapter 4.

✔ For information on viewing files (the "MORE <" thing), refer to "Looking at files" in Chapter 2.

Backing Up

Backing up is making a safety copy of your data, typically the data on your hard drive. You make a copy of all the files on your hard drive on a large stack of floppy disks by using one of the most lonely commands in DOS: the BACKUP command (or MSBackup if you're using DOS 6). Yes, it's sad and lonely, but backing up is important and you'll definitely lead a life of woe and sorrow should you neglect it.

Backing up the hard drive using DOS BACKUP (before DOS 6)

If you don't have a convenient third-party backup program or haven't yet upgraded to DOS 6, you can still use DOS's BACKUP command to back up your hard disk. Why not just use COPY? Well, you could if you only need to back up a few files that change regularly, and if none of the files is bigger than a floppy disk. Backup programs can do what COPY can't: They can break up a file and put half on each of two separate disks.

> ✔ If you have DOS 6, refer to the section "Running MSBACKUP" later in this chapter.

Backing up the whole dang hard drive

To back up your entire hard drive using DOS BACKUP, the first thing you'll need is a stack of formatted disks. You should label each disk and sequentially number them, 1 through however many are in your stack. (I have no idea how many disks you'll need. Typically, a 40MB hard drive requires about 40 1.2MB disks; you can do the math for different-sized hard drives and larger or smaller disks.) The third-party backup programs usually give you an estimate, but not DOS — oh no, that would be too easy.

Given that you have a stack of formatted and numbered disks nearby, type the following command:

```
C> BACKUP C:\*.* A: /S
```

That's the BACKUP command, a space, and then C:*.*, which means all files in the root directory of drive C. That's followed by a space, A: for drive A, another space, and then a slash-S. In the preceding example, you're backing up drive C. If you're backing up another hard drive, substitute its letter for C:. If your backup is to another floppy drive, put B: in the same spot A: is in.

Press Enter and follow the directions on your screen.

If you're using DOS 3.3 or earlier and you don't have a stack of backup disks, use this version of the BACKUP command instead:

```
C> BACKUP C:\*.* A: /S /F
```

The extra slash-F tells BACKUP to format any blank disks you may insert into the drive.

- ✔ Refer to "Formatting a Disk" in Chapter 13 for more information on formatting.
- ✔ Refer to "Names and Versions" in Chapter 1 to see which version of DOS you have.

Backing up a single file

The BACKUP command can back up a whole hard drive, a subdirectory, or just a single file. Why would any sane person want to do this instead of just using the COPY command? Because BACKUP is the only method you have of copying a very large file to a floppy disk (or to more than one floppy disk, as is usually the case). Here is the format:

```
C> BACKUP C:\WORK\LARGE.FAT A:
```

Here you see the BACKUP command, a space, and then the full pathname of the large file that you want to back up. That's followed by a space and then the letter of the floppy drive you're backing up to, plus a colon. Press Enter and follow the instructions on the screen.

- ✔ Refer to "What Is a Pathname?" earlier in this chapter for more information on a file's full pathname.

Backing up today's work

You can back up the stuff you've worked on today, usually in one single subdirectory, using the following BACKUP command:

```
C> BACKUP C:\WORK\STUFF\*.* A:
```

Here you type the BACKUP command, a space, and then the name of the subdirectory (work area) that contains your files — plus a backslash and the star-dot-star wildcard. That's followed by a space and then the drive letter of the floppy drive to which you're backing up, plus the required colon.

- ✔ Refer to "Using *.* (star-dot-star)" in Chapter 18 for information on that wildcard.

Backing up modified files

A special type of backup command can be used to back up those files that have been changed or modified since the last *real* hard disk backup. This is what's known as an *incremental* backup. The following is the BACKUP command to perform an incremental backup of drive C.

```
C> BACKUP C:\*.* A: /S /M
```

The BACKUP command is followed by C:*.* for all the files on drive C. That's followed by a space and A:, meaning that you're backing up to drive A. Then comes a space, slash-S, another space, and finally a slash-M.

> ✔ If you're doing an incremental backup of another hard drive, substitute its letter for C: in the preceding example.

> ✔ If you're backing up to floppy drive B, substitute B: for A:.

Running MSBACKUP

MSBackup is a full-screened, pull-down menu, pop-up, graphical house of backup fun. If you were familiar with the old BACKUP command, stand back! Backups are faster, take fewer disks, and you don't even need to press "any key" after inserting the next backup disk with MSBackup.

Start the MSBackup program by typing the following command:

```
C> MSBACKUP
```

If the MSBackup program hasn't been configured, it will do so when you first run it. Follow the instructions on your screen (just press Enter during the appropriate lulls and you'll be okay). You'll need two or more disks to assist with the configuring: Stick them in the drive when the program tells you to — this will happen twice. Better still, let someone else do this because the configuration process is about as much fun as chewing on aluminum foil.

After MSBackup has been configured, you'll start it and see the main menu, as shown in Figure 17-3. To back up files, click on the Backup button with the mouse or press Alt-B on your keyboard.

> ✔ After you've configured MSBackup, you can reuse the one or two sample disks. The content of these disks is unimportant; reformat them with the FORMAT command if you like (refer to Chapter 13).

> ✔ To quit the MSBackup program, select Exit from the File menu: Press Alt-F and then the **X** key. Or if you're at the main screen (see Figure 17-3), press **Q** to quit.

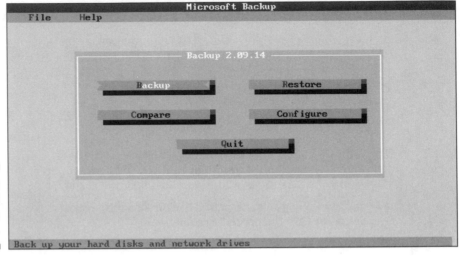

Figure 17-3:
MS-DOS
6.2's
MSBackup.

✔ For information on the Restore option in MSBackup, refer to "Restoring from a Backup" in Chapter 20.

✔ If you use Windows, back up using the DOS-based version of MSBackup over the Windows version. That way, if you ever need to restore your entire hard drive, the steps involved will be less than if you had to restore the hard drive *and* restore Windows.

✔ You can use a mouse with MSBackup if you're well-versed in mousy things. Refer to Chapter 10 for the jargon and such.

✔ Yes, MSBackup is a major pain in the ass.

Backing up the whole hard drive, all of it

Do this at least once a month.

Start out by procuring a stack of formatted disks. Label these disks 1 through however many you have. On the first one, write *Full Backup* and maybe the date.

How many disks do you need? Typically, a 40MB hard drive requires about 40 1.4MB disks; you can do the math for different sized hard drives and larger or smaller disks. But don't worry about that; MSBackup tells you approximately how many disks it takes once it gets under way.

Start MSBackup by typing **MSBACKUP** at the DOS prompt:

```
C> MSBACKUP
```

Steps: Backing up an entire hard drive

Step 1. At the main screen, press Alt-B to back up. The next screen is the backup configuration screen (see Figure 17-4). It's the second most complex screen in the program. (Don't worry, the first is coming your way.)

Step 2. Press Alt-K to highlight the Backup From area of the screen. Use the up- or down-arrow keys to highlight the hard drive that you want to back up. When the hard drive is highlighted, press the spacebar. Don't be distracted by any surprise pop-up windows. It will say All files by the drive letter after you press the spacebar.

After you select the hard drive, you'll see approximately how many disks the backup will take in the lower-right portion of the screen.

You can select more than one hard drive (if you have 'em) by using the up- or down-arrow keys and pressing the spacebar when that hard drive letter is highlighted. I recommend this approach if you have more than one hard drive.

Step 3. Press Alt-Y. Make sure the Full item is dotted. Use the up- or down-arrow key and press the spacebar to move the dot. Press Enter when Full has the dot by it.

Step 4. Press Alt-S to start the backup. (Then you get to see the most complex screen in the program — which isn't malevolent, just boggling.)

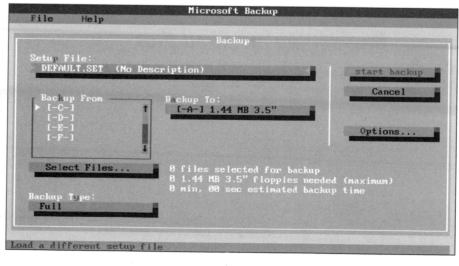

Figure 17-4:
The backup configuration screen bothers you before you actually back anything up.

Step 5. Follow the directions on the screen: Insert your first backup disk. When you hear the beep, remove the disk from the drive and replace it with the next disk in the stack. Keep doing this until all the disks are done or your arm gets sore.

Step 6. When you're done you'll see a summary screen. Oogle over the statistics. Then rubber-band your backup diskettes and keep them in a safe place. Those disks will come in handy should anything abominable happen to the hard drive.

Not required reading on setup files

Setup files are special files on disk that record your settings in the MSBackup program. They save you a wee amount of time since they record certain options that you select in the backup configuration screen (Figure 17-4 and steps 2 and 3 above). If you want to save your own custom setup files, before step 4, press Alt-F, A and then give your setup file a name. Then, the next time you use MSBackup, press Alt-F, O and select your setup file from disk. Or, you can start MSBackup with the name of a setup file. For example:

```
C>MSBACKUP FULLHD
```

Above, FULLHD is the name of a setup file, possibly one that backs up your whole hard drive. This would mean that you wouldn't need to go through steps 2 and 3 each time you backed up the whole hard drive; the setup file would make those selections for you "automagically."

Backing up modified files

This is something you should do every day or at least once a week.

You can use a special variation of the MSBackup command to back up only those files that have been changed since the last backup. This is called an *incremental backup,* and it takes less time than the full hard disk backup and fewer disks.

To perform an incremental backup, follow the same steps as outlined in the previous section. The only difference is that after step 3, you use the up- or down-arrow keys to highlight the word Incremental instead of Full. Press the spacebar to put a dot into the circle. You're cool now; press Enter. After that, everything works the same.

Backing up today's work

This is something you would do to backup a work subdirectory. For example, at the end of every day I back up the ELMO directory, which is where the files for this book are stored. (Write me if you want to know why it's called ELMO.)

To back up only a specific subdirectory, follow the same steps as outlined in the section on backing up the whole hard disk. Replace that step 2 with the following:

Press Alt-K to highlight the Backup From area of the screen. Use the up- or down-arrow keys to highlight the drive containing the subdirectory that you want to back up.

Press Alt-L. This displays another overwhelming screen — but only pay attention to the lefthand side. There you'll see a directory "tree." Use the up- or down-arrow keys to highlight the subdirectories that you want to back up. To select a directory, press the spacebar. You can select more than one directory if you like. Press Enter when you're done.

Continue on with Step 3 in the section on backing up the whole hard drive.

✔ I recommend backing up your work directory every day. I do.

✔ You may want to save a custom setup file with your subdirectory selections. Refer to the section "Not required reading on setup files."

Understanding Disk Compression

A keen way to squeeze out an extra few megabytes on a full (or near bursting) hard disk is to use disk-compression software, such as the ever popular Stacker or the DoubleSpace program that comes with DOS 6. Programs of this type can be a godsend when you need a few extra megabytes but can't afford (or don't have room) to add another hard drive. And it's truly magical how it all works.

The drawn-out details of using MS-DOS's DoubleSpace are covered in Chapter 28. Stacker isn't covered here because either I don't have the space or I'm lazy. Still, the following sections are designed to help you understand the concept of disk compression and how it fits into the big, hard drive picture — whether you're using Stacker, DoubleSpace, or some other disk-squishing program.

Dealing with compressed disks

The most important thing to keep in your head when dealing with a compressed disk is that there's really nothing you should keep in your head about it. Instead, ruminate upon the following:

- ✔ Your compressed drive works exactly the same as any other hard drive. There's no difference really, other than the compressed drive has more space available.

- ✔ Files and programs on a compressed drive are just the same as files on any other drive. You can copy, rename, delete, and mutilate them just like regular files — indeed, they *are* regular files. Nothing different 'tal.

- ✔ You can copy a file from a compressed drive to an uncompressed drive (or a floppy disk) and vice versa. Files on a compressed drive are normal in all respects.

How dey do dat?

DOS works in conjunction with disk-compression software to make more space available on your hard drive. It does this by using complex mathematical compression algorithms and lots of pleading with God. In the end, you get more room on your hard drive without your having to worry about it.

If you need a mental picture, imagine the disk-compression software as a girdle. Your hard drive is a nice but pleasantly plump person who has eaten too many files. The girdle is bursting. What disk compression does is to give you a larger girdle, allowing more files to be digested. So don't think of your files as being compressed or made special in any way; just think of your hard drive — like the girdle — as getting larger.

Disk-compression lingo

When you deal with DoubleSpace compressed drives or Stacker *stacked* drives, you'll occasionally encounter the term *CVF*. That stands for *Compressed Volume File*. Ugly.

The CVF is really a secret file that the disk-compression program uses for disk compression. For example, if you've compressed your drive C, then you'll have what the nerds would call a CVF for drive C. You'll see the term used with MS-DOS's DBLSPACE program (see Chapter 28), as well as when discussing DoubleSpace with loftier humans who are adept at such talk.

Stacker doesn't call their secret files CVFs. This is probably because people from Carlsbad, California, aren't as nerdy as folks from Redmond, Washington.

Never delete the CVF! You may see it if you monkey around with some advanced hard-disk tools. It will be named something like DBLSPACE.000 or STACVOL.DSK on most computers. Don't delete that file or any file starting with DBLSPACE or STACVOL.

Backing up a compressed disk

Backing up a compressed drive works just like backing up any other disk in your system. If you want to back up your compressed drive C, just follow the steps outlined earlier in this chapter for backing up drive C. It all works the same.

- ✔ Don't bother backing up to compressed floppies (if you create them). This just doesn't work for reasons I won't bother explaining here.

- ✔ There is no need to backup the CVF (Compressed Volume File) on your hard drive.

- ✔ Information on restoring an obliterated DoubleSpace drive is offered in Chapter 28.

Freeing up space on a hard disk

Disk-compression software is your main weapon in the battle of shrinking disk space. This battle is currently raging because programs keep getting bigger and bigger while everyone's hard drives stay the same size. It's not your fault that you bought an 80-megabyte hard drive when you really needed 150 megs; and now there's something you can do about it.

In addition to using disk-compression software, like Stacker or DOS's DoubleSpace, you can also help ease the hard drive space crunch by occasionally deleting files. No, not randomly; every hard drive has a few extra gross of files just lying around that aren't needed for anything, and that can quickly vanish with deft use of the DEL command. The problem is knowing which files you can safely delete without fouling up the whole system.

Generally speaking, you can delete any of the following types of files:

- ✔ Backup files (ending with the BAK extension)

- ✔ Temporary or junk files

- ✔ Any files that start with a tilde (~) and end with the TMP extension (but only after you run Windows)

After deleting those types of files, you can free up disk space by doing what the nerds call *archiving*. That's taking old data files that you don't need anymore but don't want to delete and copying them to floppy disks. For example, if you store all of last year's budget files and proposals in a specific place, copy them all to floppies, properly label the floppies, and then delete the old files from your hard drive. That way you'll still have the files on floppy disks, but lots more room will be made available on your hard drive. This technique usually frees up the most space, and you can use the MSBackup program as discussed in this chapter to make the job easier.

You can also archive old programs and especially games from your system. I found a copy of an old disk utility on my hard drive that was eating up 8 megabytes — and I hadn't used the program in over a year!

Dot to dot

How many times have you seen something like the following in the DIR command's listing?

```
.      <DIR>   8-24-93        4:44p

..     <DIR>   8-24-93        4:44p
```

Doesn't that just bug you? A single period, or dot, isn't the name of a file, and dot-dot isn't the name of a file either. (Filenames, legal and illegal, are covered in "Use These Filenames, Go Directly to Jail!" in Chapter 18.) By now you know that these are both directories on disk. Where are they? What are they?!

The dot and dot-dot entries are abbreviations. Dot, the first entry here, is an abbreviation for the current directory. Dot-dot refers to the parent directory.

You can use these abbreviations to refer to the current or parent directory in various DOS commands. This, however, is an advanced and secretive subject, best left up to the loftier books on using computers. But if dot and dot-dot ever bugged the heck out of you, now you know what they represent.

Chapter 18
Files — Lost and Found

Did you know that the word *file* can be anagrammed into the word *life*? Aside from that, there's really nothing interesting about files. Well, actually only two things: what you can and cannot name a file (which is much akin to getting a 14-letter last name on a vanity license plate) and that files, like certain socks, occasionally get sucked into some parallel universe since the last time you saw them. It's like the car-keys gremlin who goes around snatching up your keys for a few seconds. There's also a file gremlin who steals files — even though you just saved them to disk.

This chapter contains instructions for defeating the file gremlin. Actually, this chapter contains tidbits of information about using files, naming files, and all that file stuff. It doesn't contain information on copying, renaming, or deleting files, which is conveniently stored in Chapter 4.

Name That File!

When you create a file, you give it a name. The name should reflect what's in the file or somehow be able to describe the file's contents. After all, it's that name that gives you the clue as to what the file is when you are looking at a directory listing. But rather than grant you poetic license to create highly accurate and descriptive filenames, DOS puts on the blinders and gives you only so many letters to use. It's frustrating.

All filenames fit into a specific pattern, called the *eight-dot-three pattern:*

```
FILENAME.EXT
```

The first part of the filename can have up to eight characters. This can be followed by an optional dot (period) plus up to three additional characters. This is where they get the eight-dot-three (which really sounds like Mr. Spock calling out photon torpedo spreads).

The first eight characters of a filename are the descriptive part. These characters can be any number or letter. For example, the following are all OK filenames:

```
TEST
A
80PROOF
HELLO
1040
LETTER
KINGFISH
```

If you want to add an extension (a definition follows) to a filename, you must specify the dot (or period) and then up to three more characters. Here is the same group of rowdy files with extensions added:

```
TEST.OUT
A.1
80PROOF.GIN
HELLO.MOM
1040.X
LETTER.DOC
KINGFISH.ME
```

The extension is normally used to identify file types, for example, whether a file is a word processing document or a spreadsheet. Here are some common file extensions:

BAK	A copy of a data file as a backup
BAT	A special type of program; a batch file
COM	A command program or command file (program file)
DBF	A database file
DOC	A document or word processing file
EXE	An executable file or another type of program
FON	A font file
GRA	A graphics file
PIC	A picture file
SYS	A system file
TXT	A text file
WKS	A worksheet file
YUK	A collection of jokes

Of course, the list goes on and on. None of this is etched in stone anywhere, so feel free to give a file whatever extension you want — save for the dreaded COM, EXE, or BAT extensions (which are covered in "Significant Filenames" later in this chapter).

✔ Some programs supply their own extensions automatically; you simply type in the first part of the filename, and the program adds the rest as it creates or loads the file.

✔ You can enter a filename in upper- or lowercase; DOS doesn't care. The DIR command displays filenames in uppercase.

Use These Filenames, Go Directly to Jail!

If you goof when you name a file, you'll usually get some pleasing error message or an idle threat. Generally speaking, as long as you stick to naming a file using letters and numbers, you'll be OK.

You cannot, however, under any circumstances — even if the building were on fire and St. Peter appeared to you, winked, and said it was OK just this once — use the following characters in a filename:

. " / \ [ ] : * | < > + = ; , ?

- ✔ The biggest boo-boo most users make is putting a space in a filename. A space! Heavens! Filenames cannot contain spaces.
- ✔ The period cannot be used, unless it's the separator between the filename and the extension.
- ✔ The special characters asterisk (*) and question mark (?) are actually filename wildcards, covered later in this chapter.
- ✔ The colon (:) is only used after a letter of the alphabet to identify a disk drive, so it cannot appear in a filename.
- ✔ The special characters less-than (<), greater-than (>), and the pipe character (|) are all used by DOS for other, confusing purposes.
- ✔ And the rest of the characters have special meanings to DOS as well, so using them offends your operating system. (Not a nice thing to do to something that holds life-and-death control over your data!)

Significant Filenames

Filenames that end with a COM, EXE, or BAT extension are special. Those are actually programs that do things on your computer. As such, please don't name any of your files with those extensions. You can use any other extension or three-letter combination you can dream up. But COM, EXE, and BAT are for programs only.

How to Name a Directory (the MKDIR Command)

Directories are given names just like files. They can contain numbers and letters, and they can have up to eight characters, plus an optional period and a three-letter extension. As a rule, however, directories usually lack extensions.

Directories are named as they're created. You do this by using the MD command. Here's an example:

```
C> MD JUNK
```

This command is MD, for *Make Directory*, followed by a space and the name of the directory to create. In this case, DOS creates a subdirectory named JUNK. (For more on subdirectories, refer to Chapter 17.)

- ✔ There is no visual feedback for creating a directory.

- ✔ Creating directories is a job best left to someone else. However, you can create your own directories to store your favorite files, thus keeping them together. More information on subdirectories is offered in Chapter 17.

Renaming a directory

OK, everyone makes mistakes. Just as you can rename a file, you can rename a directory after it's been created. The insanity here is that, unlike renaming a file, you don't use the REN command. Instead, to rename a directory, you use the MOVE command. To wit:

```
C> MOVE JUNK TRASH
```

The MOVE command is followed by a space and the name of the directory you want to rename. Then comes another space and the directory's new name (following proper file naming procedures, of course). In this example, the directory named JUNK is renamed to the more apropos TRASH. Something like the following would be displayed on your screen:

```
C:\JUNK => C:\TRASH [ok]
```

That "OK" means that the directory was successfully renamed.

- ✔ Because this trick uses the MOVE command, and because that command is only available with DOS 6, well, you get the idea.

- ✔ No, nothing is moved here; the directory is just renamed.

- ✔ It's typically not a healthy idea to go around renaming directories. The reason is that many programs are set up to find certain directory names, and changing them makes the computer goofy.

- ✔ For information on using the MOVE command to move files, refer to Chapter 4, "Moving a file." Information on using the REN command to rename files is found in the same chapter under the section, "Renaming a file."

Using the DIR Command

The DIR command is used to see a list of files on disk. You just type **DIR** and press Enter:

```
C> DIR
```

The files are listed in a special format, shown with their size and date and time of creation or last update. But note that the special format separates the filename from the extension, padding the distance between them with spaces. Although this lines up the directory listing nice and pretty, it doesn't show you how to accurately type in the filename.

To see a list of files on another drive, use the DIR command with the drive letter and a colon:

```
C> DIR A:
```

In this example, you'll see a listing of all files on the disk in drive A. If you want to look at drive B, substitute B: for A:.

To see a list of files in another directory on the same disk, specify that directory's pathname after the DIR command:

```
C> DIR \WP60\DATA
```

Here the DIR command lists all the files in the \WP60\data subdirectory.

To see a single file's information, just type that file's name after the DIR command:

```
C> DIR BLOOP.NOF
```

Here the DIR command is followed by the file named BLOOP.NOF. Only that single file (and its associated and miscellaneous information) will be displayed.

To see only a specific group of files, follow the DIR command with the proper, matching wildcard:

```
C> DIR *.COM
```

In this example, DIR is followed by a space, an asterisk, a period, and then COM. This command displays only those files with the COM extension.

> ✔ For more information on subdirectories and pathnames, refer to Chapter 17.
>
> ✔ For more information on using wildcards, refer to "Wildcards (or Poker Was Never This Much Fun)" later in this chapter.

The wide DIR command

When you long for the wide open spaces of the Big Sky country, you can use the following DIR command:

```
C> DIR /W
```

That's the DIR command, a space, and slash-W. Pressing Enter displays the directory listing in the wide format, with only the filenames marching across the screen five abreast.

If you want to display a wide directory of another drive or a subdirectory, sandwich the drive letter or subdirectory pathname between the DIR and the /W. For example:

```
C> DIR A: /W
```

or:

```
C> DIR \WP60\DATA /W
```

Refer to the previous section for more details.

Making DIR display one screen at a time

When the DIR command scrolls and scrolls, rolling up and up the screen and you cannot find the file — not to mention that you've completely forgotten about the Ctrl-S key combination mentioned in Chapter 10 — you can use the following DIR command at the next DOS prompt:

```
C> DIR /P
```

That's the DIR command, followed by a space and a slash-P. The P means *page* or *pause*, and DOS will insert a friendly press any key message after each screen of filenames. Press the spacebar to continue.

✔ To cancel the listing, press Ctrl-C. Refer to "Canceling a DOS Command" in Chapter 3.

✔ If you're just hunting down a specific file, follow the DIR command with that filename. Refer to "Using the DIR Command" earlier in this chapter.

✔ If you're looking for a group of files that can be matched with a wildcard, refer to "Wildcards (or Poker Was Never This Much Fun)" later in this chapter.

✔ You can use this DIR command to see a directory listing of another drive or subdirectory. Just sandwich that drive letter or subdirectory pathname between DIR and the /P. Here's an example:

```
C> DIR A: /P
```

or:

```
C> DIR \WP60\DATA /P
```

Refer to the section "Using the DIR Command" earlier in this chapter if you care to fondle the DIR command further.

Displaying a sorted directory

Have you ever gotten the impression that DOS could just care less? It's true. When DOS displays a list of files, it shows them to you in any old order. To sort the files in the listing alphabetically, use the following DIR command:

```
C> DIR /O
```

That's the DIR command, a space, and then slash-O. The O must stand for *Oh, sort these,* or maybe the word *sort* in a foreign language. (It may mean *order* — naaa.)

Finding a Lost File

In some cases, losing a file is worse than losing a pet or a small child in the mall. Pets and children have legs and wander off. Files? Where do they go? (And would one expect to find them in the video arcade?)

The first step in locating a lost file is knowing its name. If you want to copy said file and are greeted with the happy `File not found` error message, you may have mistyped the name. (It happens.) Check your typing. Furthermore, you may want to check the directory listing to see if the file is there. Type this command:

```
C> DIR /P
```

The slash-P pauses the listing, enabling you to scan each entry. Even the author of this book has transposed filenames as he's saved them. (Here's a hint: The new files are usually listed at the end of the directory, though that's not a hard-and-fast rule.)

If the file still doesn't show up, use this command:

```
C> DIR \WHERE.AMI /S
```

That's the DIR command, followed by a space, and then a backslash and the filename. In this example, the filename, WHERE.AMI, is used. After the filename comes a space and then slash-S.

By pressing Enter, you tell DOS to search the entire hard drive for the file you've specified. If it's found, you'll see it on the screen as follows:

```
Directory of C:\LOST\FOUND
WHERE AMI   574 08-01-94 10:04a
  1 file(s)  574 bytes
```

Here DOS has found the lost file in the subdirectory \LOST\FOUND. You then need to use the CD command to move to that subdirectory and from there you can get at the file. (The CD command is covered in "Changing Directories" in Chapter 17.)

- ✔ If any additional matching files are found, they're listed as well, along with their directory.

- ✔ When you find the lost file, consider copying it to the proper location, or use the REN command to rename the file to the name you originally thought you used. Refer to "Copying a Single File" in Chapter 4 for information on the COPY command; refer to "Renaming a File," also in Chapter 4, for information on REN.

- ✔ If the list scrolls off the screen, you can tack on the slash-P option. Here's an example:

```
C> DIR \WHERE.AMI /S /P
```

Everything else in the command remains the same.

  ✔ If the file still isn't found, it may be on another disk drive. Log to another drive and then type the same DIR command again.

  ✔ If you still cannot find the file on any drive, you probably saved it under a different name. Because I don't know what that name is, it's up to you to scour your drive looking for it. Use the CD and DIR commands to move around and find the file.

Finding a Lost Subdirectory

A lost subdirectory is a bit harder to find than a lost file, especially when you know that it's somewhere on the drive — but where? As with finding a lost file, the first step is to use the DIR command. Look for the telltale <DIR> in the listing. That shows you all the subdirectories.

If you don't find your subdirectory, you can use the DIR command to search for it. Type in the following (this is bizarre, so watch your fingers):

```
C> DIR \*.* /A:D /S | FIND "MARSPROB"
```

That's the DIR command, a space, and then a backslash and star-dot-star. That's followed by another space, a slash-A, a colon and D, and then a space and a slash-S. A space follows slash-S, and then the pipe or vertical bar character, another space, the find command, a space, and then the name of the subdirectory you're looking for (MARSPROB in the example). The subdirectory name *must* be in uppercase (all caps) and have a double quote character (") on either side.

Press Enter and DOS scours the drive, looking for your subdirectory. If it's found, it is displayed as follows:

```
MARSPROB   <DIR>  09-23-92 7:23p
Directory of C:\LOST\MARSPROB
```

The subdirectory's name comes first — as it would in a directory listing. That's followed by the pathname. To change to that subdirectory, you would type in the pathname following the CD command. In the example, that would be

```
C> CD \LOST\MARSPROB
```

✔ If more than one subdirectory appears, you may have to log or change to each one in turn to find the one you're looking for.

✔ There is a chance that this command may not find your subdirectory. In that case, you can use the TREE command to view your hard disk's tree structure. Refer to "The Tree Structure" in Chapter 17.

✔ Refer to Chapter 17 for more information on the CD command and pathnames.

Wildcards (or Poker Was Never This Much Fun)

Wildcards enable you to manipulate a group of files using a single DOS command. The object here, just like using wildcards in poker, is to specify wildcards in a filename in such as way as to match other files on disk. That way you can wrangle a group of files — the whole lot of them — with only one command. This is the convenience aspect of computers they promised in the brochure.

For example, if you've named all the chapters in your Great American Novel with the DOC extension, you can treat all of them as a group using a wildcard. If all your special project files start with PROJ, you can do things to those files en masse — even if the rest of the files are named something completely different.

There are two wildcards DOS uses, the question mark (?) and the asterisk (*). They are covered in the following two sections.

✔ Wildcards are generally used with DOS commands. They can seldom be used inside programs.

✔ Not all DOS commands will swallow wildcards. The TYPE command, for one, must be followed by a single filename. Refer to "Looking at Files" in Chapter 2.

Using the ? wildcard

The ? wildcard is used to match any single letter in a filename. It can be used by itself or in multiples of however many characters you want to match. For example:

The wildcard filename TH?? matches all four-letter filenames starting with TH, including THIS and THAT.

The wildcard filename CHAP?? matches all files starting with CHAP and having one or two more letters in their name. This includes CHAP00 through CHAP99 and any other combination of characters in those two positions.

You can also use the ? wildcard in the second part of a filename:

The wildcard filename BOOK.D?? matches all filenames starting with BOOK and having D as the first letter of their extension.

You can even mix and match the ? wildcard:

The wildcard filename JULY????.WK? matches all files starting with JULY that have WK as the first two letters of their extension.

All of these wildcard combinations can be used with DOS's file exploitation commands: DIR, DEL, COPY, REN, and so on. Refer to Chapter 4 for more information on manipulating groups of files.

Using the * wildcard

The * wildcard is more powerful than the single-character ? wildcard. The asterisk is used to match groups of one or more characters in a filename. Here's an example:

The wildcard filename *.DOC matches all files that have DOC as their second part. The first part of the filename can have any number of characters in it; *.DOC matches them all.

The wildcard filename PROJECT.* matches all files with PROJECT as their first part, with any second part — even if they don't have any second part.

But beware! The * wildcard is rather lame when it comes to being used in the middle of a filename. For example:

The wildcard filename B*ING matches all filenames that start with the letter B. DOS ignores the ING part of the name because it comes *after* the wildcard. I know. It's dumb. But that's the way DOS is.

Quirky yet easily skippable stuff

If you want to match all filenames that start with B, use this wildcard:

```
B*
```

This matches all files, whether or not they have a second part. True, you could use B*.*, but DOS matches the same files, so why bother with the extra dot-star?

The wildcard *. (star-dot) matches only filenames *without* an extension. This is the only time under DOS that a command could end in a period. Here's an example:

```
C> DIR *.
```

In this example, the DIR command shows only files without any extension (typically only the subdirectories).

*Using *.* (star-dot-star)*

The most popular wildcard is the "Everyone out of the pool!" wildcard, *.*, which is pronounced *star-dot-star*. It means everything, all files, no matter what their name (but usually not directories).

Since star-dot-star matches everything, you should be careful when using it. This is that one rare occasion in your life when you can get everyone's attention. It's like: You can't fool all of the files some of the time, but you can fool all of them all of the time with star-dot-star.

- The COPY *.* command copies all files in the directory. Refer to "Copying a Group of Files" in Chapter 4.

- The DEL *.* command is deadly; it ruthlessly destroys all files in the directory; refer to "Deleting a Group of Files" in Chapter 4.

- The REN command with *.* is tricky. You must specify a wildcard as the second part of the REN command; you cannot give every file in the directory the same name. Here's an example:

```
C> REN *.DOC *.WP
```

In this example, all files with the DOC extension are renamed to have a WP extension. That's about the most you can do with the REN command and wildcards.

Part IV
Yikes!
(or, Help Me Out of This One!)

The 5th Wave   By Rich Tennant

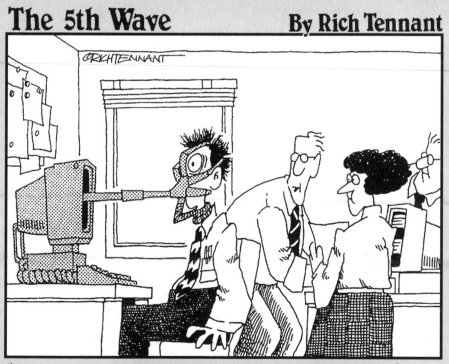

"ALRIGHT, STEADY EVERYONE. MARGO, GO OVER TO TOM'S PC AND PRESS 'ESCAPE',...VERY CAREFULLY."

In this part...

There is a certain level of fear required when using a computer. Don't worry, even the DOS gurus have it. It must come from watching all those Irwin Allen TV shows of the 1960s. They were kind of science fictiony and they all had computers — computers that loved to explode and pop sparks whenever they didn't like something. Today's computers are much more powerful and produce much better explosions.

Seriously, computers don't explode. But they will do some unfriendly things that will make your heart drop a few flights. Some of this stuff isn't serious at all, which is what this part of the book tries to explain. But there are times when it pays to call in an expert. This part is where you'll learn how to tell the difference between the two situations.

Chapter 19

When It's Time to Toss in the Towel (and Call a DOS Guru)

· ·

In This Chapter

▶ Spotting computer problems and narrowing down the causes

▶ Detecting and dealing with software problems

▶ Fixing a broken battery (when the computer forgets the time)

▶ Locating a lost hard drive

▶ Determining when it's time to reset the system

▶ Learning what you should do after you've reset your computer (in a panic)

▶ Preparing to get help

▶ Dealing with some form of beverage spilt into the keyboard

· ·

Computers, like anything made by the human hand, aren't perfect. For the most part, they work flawlessly. But suddenly you feel that something is wrong — like when you're driving your car and it feels a little sluggish. Then you hear the noise. Computers won't usually make noises when they go south, but they will start behaving oddly. This chapter tells you what you can do in those situations, and it gives you an idea of when it's time to yell out for a professional to deal with the situation.

My Computer's Down and I Can't Get It Up!

You have a problem. Your computer isn't working the way it should. Something is definitely amiss.

The first step is to analyze the problem. Break everything down and find out what is working. Even if you can't fix the problem, you're better prepared to tell an expert about it and have him or her deal with it.

Check the following items first:

- ✔ Is the computer plugged in? Seriously, check to see if it is. If the computer is plugged into a power strip, make sure that the power strip is plugged in and switched on. Furthermore, you may want to check other items plugged into the same socket. Bad sockets happen. And check the circuit breaker.

- ✔ Is everything else plugged in? Monitors, modems, and printers all need to be plugged in. Are there power cords attached? Are they turned on?

- ✔ Note that most power cords on your computer have two connections: one end plugs into the wall (or a power strip) and the other plugs into the computer, printer, modem, and so on. Believe it or not, *both* ends need to be plugged in for the computer to work. One end is *not* built into the computer the way it is in an iron or TV set.

Check the following connections:

- ✔ Computers have a ganglia of cables attached. There are power supply cables, and then there are data cables. A printer has two cables: a power cable and a printer cable. The power cable connects to the wall socket; the printer cable connects to the computer.

- ✔ Modems can have three or four cables attached: a power supply; a data line between the modem and the computer's serial port; one phone line from the modem to your telephone; and, often, a second phone line from your modem to the phone company's wall socket.

- ✔ Make sure that all the cables are connected to their proper ports on the PC's rump. You may have to trace each cable with your finger, seeing as how the back of a PC resembles the tail end of a squid. Also, serial and parallel ports look similar on some PCs. If your modem or printer isn't working, try swapping the plug around a few times (of course, this is assuming that it did work before).

- ✔ Keyboard cables can become loose, especially given the unique design of most PCs where the keyboard is connected to the back (which never made sense). But be careful here: only plug or unplug the keyboard connector when the computer is turned off.

Here are some other things to check:

- ✔ Is the computer locked? There's a key on the front of most PCs. It must be turned to the unlocked or open position for you to use the computer.

- ✔ Is the monitor off or dimmed? Monitors have their own on/off switch; make sure that the monitor switch is on. Also, monitors can be dimmed, so check the brightness knob. Furthermore, some computers have *screen dimming* programs. Try pressing the spacebar to see if the monitor comes back on.

✔ Is there a blackout? If so, you won't be able to use the computer. Sorry.

✔ Is there a brownout? A brownout happens when the electric company isn't sending enough juice through the power lines. A computer won't turn on if the required number of volts isn't present. If the system is already on, a brownout will force the system to shut itself off. This is unusual because, during a brownout, the lights in the room and all your clocks may continue to work.

The following items are all general things to look for and quick items to check if you're not a professional computer doctor. They're also all hardware items. If your problem is in software, refer to the discussion under "It's Just Acting Weird" later in this chapter.

✔ If possible, you can further narrow the problem down to a specific part of the computer: the computer box, disk drives, keyboard, monitor, printer, or some other peripheral. If everything works OK except for one part of the computer, you've narrowed down the problem far enough to tell the repair person about it over the phone.

✔ Fixing this stuff isn't hard. Most repair places or computer consultants will simply replace a defective part with a brand new one. In fact, I would go out on a limb here and say: Never trust anyone who claims to be able to fix what you have without needing to replace anything. I speak from personal experience here. Some bozo claimed he could fix my $4,000 laser printer. After $600 of his attempts, it ended up costing me only (relatively speaking) $1,000 to fully replace the defective part. An expensive lesson, but one worth passing on.

✔ For more information on ports, refer to "What Are Ports?" in Chapter 7. A general discussion of all types of computer hardware is offered throughout Part II of this book.

It's Just Acting Weird

Computers act weird all the time. Sometimes, however, they act more weird than usual. If you've gone through the previous section and have determined that your hardware works fine, then what you may have is a software problem.

The best thing to check for with a software problem is any recent changes made to the system, specifically the CONFIG.SYS and AUTOEXEC.BAT files. Adding new items or deleting old ones can drastically affect how the system works: you can lose disk drives, some programs won't find enough memory, and some applications will refuse to work. To remedy the problem, undo the changes to either file (CONFIG.SYS or AUTOEXEC.BAT), or call someone else for help. For more details on editing CONFIG.SYS and AUTOEXEC.BAT files, see Chapter 16.

Frequently, weirdness can occur after a period of time. The longest I've been able to continuously run my word processing software (without shutting the computer off) is about three weeks. (OK, I slept a little every night.) After three weeks, mold must grow on the circuits because the computer suddenly stops working. The same thing happens to other programs as well, but with different time periods involved. Resetting the computer seems to solve the problem.

Be wary of *memory-resident programs* (also called *TSRs*). If you notice your computer locking up tight, a memory-resident program may be to blame. Also, *popping up* a memory-resident program while your computer is in graphics mode may cause the screen to tweak — if not right away, then definitely when you return to graphics mode.

The mouse has been known to cause many problems, sometimes even with programs that don't use a mouse. If you notice any random characters on your screen, they're probably due to a misbehaving mouse. The only real cure for this is to turn the *mouse driver* off, which should be done by your local computer guru.

> ✔ Don't be surprised if you suspect a hardware problem and it turns out to be software. For example, losing your hard drive is really a software problem; the physical hard disk hasn't left your computer to go outside and frolic through the garden. Instead, DOS has mislaid its map of what equipment it's got on board.

> ✔ Any program you're just learning (including DOS) will act weird until it's used to you. You'll experience at least three confounding, unreproducible errors that your guru never heard of in the first month you use a program intensively — then they'll never occur again. Try not to get too mad at the machine or the software.

> ✔ Refer to "Resetting" in Chapter 1 for more information on resetting the computer.

The Computer Has Lost Track of the Time

About 99 percent of the computers sold today have battery-backed-up clocks inside. They keep the time no matter what, even if you unplug the PC. So when you notice that the time isn't correct — or the computer thinks it's January 1, 1980 (and Jimmy Carter is still in office!), you need to check your battery.

Replacing a computer's battery is as easy as replacing the battery in a clock or camera. Of course, if you don't particularly think that's easy, make someone else do it for you.

✔ If you have an AT or later computer, you'll also need to run your PC's setup program to reset the clock. You may further need to reset other information in the SETUP program, which means that this operation should be performed by your dealer or a computer "expert."

✔ Every once in a while you should type the word **DATE** at the DOS prompt, just to make sure your PC hasn't drifted. It's annoying to look for files by date only to find your computer has been date-stamping everything for 1951. Type **TIME** too and see if it thinks it's 1:15 in the morning.

Gulp! The Hard Drive Is Gone!

Hard drives do have a tendency to wander. Normally, no one would care, but hard drives do contain all sorts of important information. So concern over their whereabouts is justified.

There are two reasons a hard drive suddenly disappears. The first is related to the computer's battery. In addition to maintaining the current time, the battery keeps a special area of memory active. In that area of memory, the computer remembers a few things about itself, including whether or not it has a hard drive. When the battery goes, the computer forgets about the hard drive. Oops!

To fix the battery problem, replace the battery. This requires opening up the computer, so it's OK to pay someone else to do this if the thought of opening up the computer makes you wince.

After the battery is replaced, you need to run your computer's hardware setup program. You'll need to tell the computer all about itself again; give it the current time, tell it about its floppy drives, memory configuration, and what *type* of hard drive is installed. Most hard drives are type 17, though they tell me this just isn't true any more. If you're in doubt, make someone else do this.

The second reason a hard drive suddenly disappears is age. The average PC hard drive can run flawlessly for about four years. After that, you're going to start experiencing problems, typically `Access`, `Seek`, `Read`, or `Write` errors in DOS. This is a sign that the hard drive is on its last legs. If you see these ominous words, back up all your work and start hunting for a new drive.

Read this if you care about your data

Buy a new drive when the old one starts to go. Sure, you can run special software utilities to fix these intermittent problems. But that's not going to do much for a hard drive that's truly on its way south for retirement at a reef off Florida. Look at it this way: An old, failing hard drive is like a bald tire. You need a new tire to replace it — not a toupee.

Keeping the old, worn-out hard drive around is a bad idea as well. Even if it's only marginal, there's no sense in keeping it for games or as a "temporary" files disk. That's like keeping your old bald tire as a spare.

A Record of Your Hardware Setup Program

Because your hardware setup program's information is so important, run that program right now and jot down this important information. If running the hardware setup isn't obvious to you, refer to Chapter 21 on running diagnostic programs and get the information from there.

Program name to run SETUP: _____

Keys to press to run SETUP: _____

First floppy drive: _____

Second floppy drive: _____

First hard drive (type): _____

Second hard drive (type): _____

Main (motherboard memory): _____

Extra memory: _____

Total memory: _____

Monitor/display: _____

Keyboard: _____

Serial port 1: _____

Serial port 2: _____

Printer port 1: _____

Printer port 2: _____

Math coprocessor: _____

Other stuff: _____

Other stuff: _____

Other stuff: _____

Note that not every computer has all of these items. If there are any extra items mentioned, write them down on the blank lines provided.

Steps to Take for a Locked Computer

The Reset button is not a panic button, but it's the next best thing. When your computer is all locked up and the programs appear to have flown to Orlando, try the following steps:

Steps: Dealing with a computer that is locked up

Step 1. Press the Esc (Escape) key. Or if the program uses a different cancel key and you know what it is, press it. For example, the old WordPerfect program uses F1.

Step 2. Press the Ctrl-C (Control-C) or Ctrl-Break (Control-Break) key combination. This usually (and safely) cancels any DOS command.

Step 3. In Windows, you can press the Alt-Esc key combination to leave a window and move to the next window. To get rid of a program run amok, press Ctrl-Esc to bring up the Task List and then click on the End Task button to close the highlighted task (program). As a last resort, press Ctrl-Alt-Delete. On the screen that appears, select whichever option carefully blows the errant program out of the water.

Step 4. In DESQview, you can press and release the Alt key to pop up the DESQ menu. Select the Close Window item to close a window. Or you can press Ctrl-Alt-Delete to close any DESQview session. (Under DESQview, Ctrl-Alt-Delete doesn't reset the computer.)

Step 5. If none of these tricks work, try Ctrl-Alt-Delete to reset your computer. If that doesn't work, or if your keyboard is beeping at you, punch your Reset button.

Note that you only resort to resetting after trying all the alternatives. Resetting is such a drastic measure that you should really run through your options before trying it. Never act in haste.

- ✔ If your system lacks a reset button and Ctrl-Alt-Delete doesn't reset, you'll have to turn off the PC. Refer to "Turning the Computer Off" in Chapter 1.

- ✔ Information on using the Ctrl-C cancel key is covered in "Canceling a DOS Command" in Chapter 3.

- ✔ What does the Reset button do? It interrupts power to the main chip, which causes it to restart.

I Had to Reset My Computer

OK. So you had to reset. I'm going to assume that you've reset in the middle of something. Resetting at the DOS prompt is OK and generally doesn't do anything bad. But resetting in the middle of a program isn't nice. It's not a sin, but it's not nice (see the following for why).

After your system comes up again, get to the DOS prompt. This means you should quit any automatic startup program, such as WordPerfect or (especially) Windows. Then type the following at the DOS prompt:

```
C> CHKDSK C: /F
```

That's the CHKDSK command, followed by a space and drive C: (C and a colon), and then another space and a slash-F. Press Enter. If you're asked the question `Convert lost chains into files?` or something similar to that, press **Y**.

After CHKDSK is done running, you need to delete some *garbage* files it created. Type the following command:

```
C> DEL C:\FILE*.CHK
```

That's the DEL command to delete a file, followed by a space, C, a colon, a backslash, and the filename wildcard FILE*.CHK. You only need to type this command if you told Check Disk to convert the lost chains into files. Otherwise, you can skip this step.

- ✔ You may want to repeat this CHKDSK (Check Disk) procedure for each hard drive in your system. If so, substitute the proper drive letter for C: in the first command listed here. Remember, you only need to use the second DEL command if CHKDSK says it found lost clusters or files.

- ✔ Refer to "CHKDSK says I have lost files in clusters or something" in Chapter 17 for additional information about CHKDSK.

Now go back to your program, open the file you were working on, and see how much work you lost. (And they say computers are time-saving devices!)

A specific, MS-DOS 6.2 solution

If you have MS-DOS 6.2 — and only if you have that version of DOS — you can run the ScanDisk program instead of Check Disk to ensure that everything is hunky-dory after a reset. Type the following:

```
C> SCANDISK /ALL
```

That's the ScanDisk command, a space, then slash-ALL. This command will check all your hard drives. Do a surface scan on each one. And obey the instructions in Chapter 17 if any missing files or clusters or whatever are found by ScanDisk.

Freely skip this stuff on why you need to reset

When you reset in the middle of something, you often catch some programs with their pants down, so to speak. These programs may have created temporary files or may have some files that are "half open" on disk. Resetting leaves the files on disk, but not officially saved in any directory. The result is the lost chains or lost clusters that the CHKDSK command is designed to look for.

Running CHKDSK with its slash-F option (or SCANDISK /ALL) scours the drive and puts missing clusters and file fragments into real files on disk. They're named FILE0000.CHK, FILE0001.CHK, and on up through however many files were found. There's nothing most of us can do with these files, so they're OK to delete.

If you don't delete the files, nothing drastic happens. However, two negative things will take place after a time: First, the files do occupy space on disk, even though they never appear in any directory. Over time, your disk will be full and you won't be able to figure out why. The second long-term bad thing to happen is that your hard drive will become very sluggish. Only by deleting these files will things speed up.

When to Scream for Help

There comes a time when you must scream for help. When that happens, and when you've exhausted all other options mentioned in this book, be a good computer user and obey the following:

- ✔ First, get mad. Get it out of your system.

- ✔ Know the problem. Be able to offer a full report on what you were doing, what you just did, and what happened. If you've narrowed down the problem, don't be afraid to say what you suspect it is.

- ✔ Be at the computer when you call for help. They'll always ask you questions you can only really answer while at the computer.

- ✔ Tell the person you're begging for help from about anything new or changed on your PC. Always let him or her know if you attempted to modify something or changed something yourself.

✔ In order of preference, contact the following people: your office computer specialist or MIS manager, a friend who knows something about computers (and is still willing to help you), your computer dealer, the manufacturer, the Almighty.

✔ If the problem cannot be fixed over the phone, take the computer to the shop. If possible, try to back up your data before you do this (refer to "Backing Up" in Chapter 17). Remember to bring along cables and any necessary peripherals. Ask the computer fix-it person what he or she would like you to bring in, just to be sure.

✔ Always opt for the diagnostic first. Typical repair places will do a look-see for about $30 to $60. Then they should call you with an estimate. If they fix anything else "voluntarily" (for example, items not mentioned in the estimate or items they have not phoned you about), then it's free. Check with the laws in your state or county, but, generally speaking, repairing a computer is covered by the same laws that protect people at car repair places.

✔ It's easier to replace something than to fix it. If possible, try to order a bigger, faster, and better version of the thing you're replacing.

I Just Spilled Java into the Keyboard

I've added this as a special section because, believe it or not, many people spill things into their keyboards. Maybe not coffee (my personal favorite is lemonade), but something liquid that makes your eyes bulge out for a few comic moments.

OK. Suppose you've just spilled something into your keyboard. (You'll be reading this fast, so I'll type it in as quickly as I can.)

Just turn the computer off!

Never, under any circumstances, should you unplug the keyboard with the computer light still on!

Depending on the size of the spill, you may be able to save your information and quit the application; it's always better to turn off the PC at the DOS prompt. If not, it's OK to just flip the power switch. Try to pour any excess liquid out. Use a paper towel to sop up any remaining excess liquid.

Let the keyboard dry out. For coffee, this should take about 24 hours. After that time, turn on your PC and refer to the section "I Had to Reset My Computer" earlier in this chapter. Everything else should work as before.

If you've spilled something sugary into your keyboard, the dry-out time is still 24 hours. However, sugary stuff tends to create a sticky film. It won't interfere too heavily with the electronics, but it will make your keys stick. I've heard of people giving their keyboards a "bath" in a special solution. However, I recommend taking the keyboard to a pro for cleaning. In fact, this is a good thing to do on a regular basis, given all the cookie crumbs, chip fragments, and hair (ugh!) that ends up in your keyboard.

- ✔ If you have to unplug your keyboard, do it with the computer turned off.

- ✔ If you're accident-prone and you expect to spill other liquids into your keyboard from time to time, you can buy a clear plastic cover molded to fit the keyboard's contour. You can still type and use the keyboard, but it's sealed.

Chapter 20
After You Panic, Do This

● ●

In This Chapter

▶ Determining where you are when you suddenly find yourself there

▶ Returning to where you were before

▶ Finding a lost file

▶ Finding a lost program

▶ Recovering from DEL *.*

▶ Undeleting an entire subdirectory

▶ Unformatting a disk

▶ Restoring from a backup disk

● ●

*I*f you're still in a panicky mode, refer to the preceding chapter. That's more of a panic-stricken chapter. This chapter is about what to do *after* you panic. The situation can always be resolved, no matter what. Even if the system is making popping noises and you see smoke, there's nothing to worry about (unless the drapery catches fire).

Where Am I?

Has this ever happened to you: You're driving your car and suddenly you realize that you've been under highway hypnosis? What happened during the last few miles? Where are you? Well, that's never happened to me. But sometimes I do wake up in the middle of the night screaming (if that makes you feel any better).

Getting lost is part of using a computer. If you ever find yourself lost, try one of the following remedies:

✔ If you are using a familiar program and suddenly find yourself in the unfamiliar — but still in the program — try pressing Esc to *back out* (or press whatever the cancel key is, such as F1 in the old WordPerfect).

✔ If pressing Esc doesn't work, check the keyboard. Type a few keys. If the keyboard starts beeping, the system is locked. You'll need to reset. Refer to "Resetting" in Chapter 1.

✔ If you're suddenly out at the DOS prompt, refer to the next section.

✔ If you find yourself lost at the DOS prompt, use the CD command to find out where you are. Typing **CD** tells you the current drive and directory, and it may explain why the program you were trying to run doesn't work. Refer to Chapter 17 for more information.

✔ If you notice that your DOS commands aren't working, or the display doesn't quite look right, you may want to check the DOS version. Type in the VER command and DOS dutifully tells you its make and model number. Refer to "Names and Versions" in Chapter 3 for more information.

✔ Finally, if nothing works at all, try resetting. Computers do, occasionally, pick up and go to Hawaii to watch the surf. Pressing the Reset button or Ctrl-Alt-Delete brings them back to reality.

How Do I Get Back?

Sometimes you may find yourself in a different place. Say you are working in Lotus 1-2-3 and trying to save a worksheet when suddenly you find yourself at the DOS prompt. What happened? Or maybe you were at the DOS prompt just a moment ago, and now there's a strange program on the screen.

In the latter case, you probably just brought up a *pop-up* program by accident. These programs are triggered by certain key presses and you may have stumbled across one of them. Press Esc to exit. This should work and return you to the DOS prompt. (I've never seen a pop-up program that didn't pop back down after you press Esc.)

If you were just in a program and are now at a DOS prompt, and you know you didn't purposefully quit the program, look at the screen. Do you see the MS-DOS copyright notice? If so, type the following:

```
C> EXIT
```

This command returns you to your program. (If you're wrong, typing **EXIT** won't hurt anything.)

If you don't see the copyright notice, you've probably been dumped out of the program. To reenter the program, press F3 and then Enter. If you press F3 and don't see anything, try typing **MENU** or whatever command you normally type to use your computer (or the application you were so rudely ejected from).

Some programs require you to type in two things when the program starts. For example, if you were running an accounting package in Basic, you may have to type:

```
C> BASIC GL
```

or:

```
C> QBASIC /RUN GL
```

dBASE also requires you to type in two things to run a dBASE program. If you know the name of the program to run, put it after DBASE at the DOS prompt:

```
C> DBASE PAYROLL
```

- ✔ Refer to "The Handy F3 key" in Chapter 3 for information on using the F3 key.
- ✔ The section "Running a Program" in Chapter 2 has a list of popular program names and the commands required to run them.
- ✔ Refer to Chapter 15 for more information on restarting dBASE, menu systems, and other black boxes.

Where Is My File?

If you just saved a file or are looking for one you absolutely know exists somewhere, it may just be out of sight for now. Refer to the section "Finding a Lost File" in Chapter 18 for details on getting the file back.

Where Is My Program?

Programs are harder to lose than files, but it happens. The approach to finding a lost program depends on how you run the program.

If you run a program manually, you may just be lost on the disk. The manual way usually involves typing in a CD command and then typing in the name of the program at the next DOS prompt. If you type in the CD command and get an

`Invalid directory` error message, you're probably in the wrong place. Type this command:

```
C> CD \
```

This command logs you to the root directory. Try running your program again. If it still doesn't work, try logging to the proper drive. For example, to log to drive C, type in the following:

```
D> C:
```

That's C and a colon. To log to any other drive, type its letter and a colon, and then type the preceding CD command. That should get you on the proper footing.

If you normally run your program by typing its name at the prompt, and you get a `Bad command or file name` error message, DOS may not remember where it put your program. This usually happens because, somehow, the *search path* has been changed. I won't explain how that can be undone here; simply reset your computer to get the proper search path back. Press the Reset button or Ctrl-Alt-Delete.

- ✔ If you notice that DOS loses your files a lot, yet resetting seems to bring them back, tell someone about it. Let that person know that some program on your system is "resetting the search path" and that you aren't particularly fond of it. He or she should be able to fix the problem for you.

- ✔ Refer to "I Had to Reset My Computer" in Chapter 19 if you do reset.

- ✔ Information on the CD command and your disk's directory structure can be found all over Chapter 17.

The Perils of DEL *.*

Yeah, deleting all your files can be a drastic thing. The DEL *.* command will raze every file in a directory with abandon. However, there is a warning before this happens. DOS will tell you that all files in the directory are about to be churned to dust. It asks you if this is OK. You must type a **Y** to go on. Simple enough; you've been warned. Yet too many DOS beginners and experts alike are quick to press the Y key.

Before typing **DEL *.*** make sure you're in the proper directory. Use the CD command if the prompt doesn't display the current directory. (Refer to "Finding the Current Directory" in Chapter 17 and to "Prompt Styles of the Rich and Famous" in Chapter 3.) All too often you mean to delete all the files in one directory, but you happen to be in another directory when that happens.

If the files were accidentally deleted, they can be recovered using the UNDELETE command. As soon as you've recognized your mistake, type in the following command:

```
C> UNDELETE *.* /ALL
```

This command should bring back as many of your files as possible. Note that each may have a funky name, with the # character replacing the first letter. Use the REN command to rename the files one by one back to their original states.

> ✔ Refer to "Undeleting a File" in Chapter 4 for more information on the UNDELETE command; refer to "Renaming a File" in the same chapter for information on REN.

> ✔ If a file cannot be recovered, then it cannot be recovered. DOS knows about these things and won't push the subject any further.

I Just Deleted an Entire Subdirectory!

Neat. This result really requires effort on your behalf. Not only must you delete all files in a subdirectory, but you also have to use the RD (or RMDIR) command to peel off a directory (or the wicked DELTREE command). That command isn't even covered in this book! Congratulations.

Now the bad news: You cannot use the UNDELETE command to recover a lost subdirectory. It should be able to, but it doesn't.

The only way to recover a subdirectory is to *restore* it from a recent backup. Depending on how recent your backup is and how new the files were in the subdirectory, you may or may not get a full recovery.

Restoring a directory using MSBackup

There are eight steps involved with restoring a subdirectory. Most importantly, you must restore from a recent backup. Older backups will work, but like those two guys trapped in the Time Tunnel, you'll be missing a lot of stuff that's happened since you last backed up. Still, it's better than having to retype all the stuff in the subdirectories or reinstall software.

To restore a subdirectory "branch" using the MSBackup command, follow these tedious steps:

Steps: Restoring a subdirectory you accidentally blew away

Step 1. Type the **MSBACKUP** command at the DOS prompt.

Step 2. Select Restore from the main menu; press **R**.

Step 3. Select a recent backup catalog. This is displayed in the area on the screen titled `Backup Set Catalog`. Odds are good that what's displayed there now is the most recent backup. (The date of the backup is "hidden" inside the catalog filename in the last five characters. For example, 1214A means that the backup was made on December 14th.) If that's not the catalog you want, press Alt-K and select another catalog from the list.

Step 4. Select the Select Files button, or press Alt-L.

Step 5. Look for the files you want to restore. In this case, you'll be looking for the subdirectory you decimated. Use the up- or down-arrow keys to highlight that directory. Press the spacebar when that directory is highlighted, to select the directory and all its files.

Step 6. Press Enter to lock in your selection.

Step 7. Press **S** to select the Start Restore button.

Step 8. Follow the instructions on the screen and insert your backup diskettes as they're called for. (This step is where you're glad you numbered the diskettes before you started the backup.)

Yes, this isn't a pleasant, happy task. But consider that without MSBackup you'd never get a subdirectory back in any shape. And while you're stewing over swapping diskettes, remind yourself to be more careful when deleting subdirectories next time.

Restoring using the pre-DOS 6 RESTORE command

Ah, the cruddy old DOS RESTORE command. Those were the days: cryptic command lines, options and switches, one command did the job. None of that mouse stuff. Be thankful that you don't have to contend with the new MSBACKUP program. It's new! It's different! It makes opera seem enjoyable!

Suppose that, in a massive Freudian slip, you just deleted the C:\FAMILY\FATHER directory. To restore this directory from a recent backup disk set, place the first backup disk into drive A and type the following command:

```
C> RESTORE A: C:\FAMILY\FATHER\*.* /S
```

That's the RESTORE command, a space, the drive you're restoring from (A) and a colon. That's followed by a space and the name of the subdirectory you deleted — plus a backslash and star-dot-star. Then comes another space and finally a slash-S.

DOS will scan your backup disks, asking you to remove each one and insert the next one in sequence. It will do this until all the files are restored.

I Just Reformatted My Disk!

This is why disks are labeled: so you know what's on them. Before you reformat a disk, check to see that it's empty. Refer to "Reformatting Disks" in Chapter 13. But if you do reformat a disk, type the following:

```
C> UNFORMAT A:
```

If you're unformatting a disk in drive B, substitute B: for A: here. Press Enter and follow the instructions on the screen. Be patient: it takes a few minutes to unformat a disk.

Your disk may not be in the best of shape after it's unformatted. For example, most of the files in the root directory may be gone. If they're found, they will probably be given generic names, as will any of your subdirectories. On the bright side, the data in your subdirectories, and all the subsubdirectories, will be totally intact.

Unformatting a disk only works if you use the UNFORMAT command on the disk before putting any new files on it.

  ✔ Information on restoring a hard drive that was compressed using DoubleSpace is offered in Chapter 28.

Restoring from a Backup

Backing up is something you should do often. Your computer manager probably has you set up on some kind of backup schedule or, if you're on your own, you should back up your important stuff every day and do a full backup on a weekly or monthly basis, depending on how much you use your computer.

Rarely is the restore part of backup done. It happens only in those few circumstances where something goes wrong with the hard drive, you lose files or a subdirectory, or you need to recall an older version of a program.

How to restore using the DOS 6 MSBackup utility

Steps: Restoring a subdirectory you accidentally blew away

Step 1. Your hard disk is gone. Weep bitterly.

Step 2. Locate your MS-DOS 6 diskettes.

Step 3. Re-install MS-DOS 6 on your hard drive, all over again.

Step 4. Type the **MSBACKUP** command at the DOS prompt.

Step 5. Select Restore from the main menu; press **R**.

Step 6. Select a recent backup catalog. Only look at those catalogs whose filenames end in FUL. These are files that record your full hard disk backups, the best source for restoring the whole ding-dong hard drive.

The catalog files are displayed in the area titled *Backup Set Catalog*. It's usually a safe bet that what you see there now is what you want. If not, press Alt-K and select another catalog from the list displayed.

Step 7. Press Alt-I to highlight the Restore Files area. Use the up- or down-arrow keys to highlight the hard drive you want to restore — the one you blew away. Press the spacebar when that drive letter is highlighted to restore *All files*.

Step 8. Press **S** to start restoring files to the hard drive.

Step 9. Keep an eye on the screen and swap out and in your backup diskettes as they're called for.

✔ This technique works best when you back up often.

✔ Information on restoring a hard drive that was compressed using DoubleSpace is offered in Chapter 28.

How to restore using the pre-DOS 6 RESTORE command

If you need to restore a single file, and you're fortunate not to have DOS 6's MSBACKUP utility, use the following command:

```
C> RESTORE A: C:\WORK\PROJECT\FILE1.DAT
```

Here A: is the drive containing your backup disk(s). You can use B: if the backup disks are to be placed in drive B. The full pathname of the file follows the drive letter, a colon, and a space. In this example, the file FILE1.DAT is to be restored. You must specify a full pathname and the file can be restored to that directory only. Wildcards can also be used to restore a group of files.

If you need to restore a subdirectory, specify that directory's name plus a backslash (\) and star-dot-star:

```
C> RESTORE A: C:\MISC\*.* /S
```

Here A: indicates the drive containing the backup disk(s). Substitute B: if the backup disks will be placed in that drive. The drive letter is followed by a colon, a space, and then the full pathname of the subdirectory to restore. Do you see how star-dot-star is used here? It restores all files in the subdirectory. Furthermore, a space and a slash-S are added to the command.

I recommend that you use a third-party backup program. If you've been using the DOS Backup command anyway, here is how to restore your entire hard drive. Use this command:

```
C> RESTORE A: C:\*.* /S
```

That's RESTORE, and then A: to indicate the drive containing the backup disks (use B: if you're putting the disks into that drive). That's followed by a space, C, a colon, and star-dot-star, which indicates all files on drive C. If you're restoring to another hard drive, substitute its drive letter for C:. Finally, a space and a slash-S ends the command.

In all circumstances, you should start restoring by putting the first backup disk into the proper floppy drive. The RESTORE command will tell you when to swap disks — that is, when to remove the current disk and replace it with the next disk in sequence. This happens until all the files are restored.

✔ Backing up is covered in Chapter 17, starting with the section titled "Backing Up."

✔ Refer to Chapter 17 for more information on directories and pathnames.

✔ Refer to "Using *.* (star-dot-star)" in Chapter 18 for information on using that wildcard.

Chapter 21
Diagnosing, Disinfecting, and Getting Help

● ●

In This Chapter

▶ Using a diagnostic program

▶ Scanning for viruses

▶ Using DOS's feeble on-line help

▶ Getting technical support

● ●

*T*his chapter covers a broad canvas but does it with color, style, and a boldness even Bob Ross can't match.[1] First comes the majestic background—diagnostic programs that tell you what's what inside your PC. These programs are followed by some bold foliage, the anti-virus programs. The anti-virus programs can help you fight the viral plague we're supposed to be having all the time (at least according to the media). Finally, I've added a waterfall and lots of "little friends"—the various ways DOS gives you help. There. I painted that whole thing without once using the words *Titanium White* or *Burnt Umber*.

MS-DOS 6.0 and 6.2 are the only DOS versions that offer you the tools mentioned in this chapter. Otherwise, consider the information here for enlightenment purposes only.

What's Up Doc?

No matter how long you stare at the computer, you just can't tell what's inside it. This is why the medical profession invented X-rays. Doctors just couldn't tell what was wrong inside you unless they cut you up and poked around. Then, after they found out, they'd have to stitch you back together again and hope you'd live so you could pay the bill. Then along came X-rays and the ever-popular MRI scan, and they could see inside you, well-assured that you'd live to pay the bill. Computers are different.

---

[1]Bob Ross is the frizzy-headed guy who has a half-hour painting program on PBS. He's much more fun to watch than the "Oil Painting on Old Saw Blades" Lady.

First off, computers can't be X-rayed unless you take them to the airport. I'm not going to drone on here about how airport security people go all verclempt when they see a computer. Rule out X-rays. Secondly, computers can't talk. People can talk. "Doctor, my appendix is on my front side." Computers can barely muster "Hello, I'm now going to be rude to you" — so that's out as well.

On the up side, though, computers are pretty self-aware. Given the right type of program, they can fill you in on all sorts of internal tidbits without your every having to wield a screwdriver (or an MRI scanner). This is done by using a program called a *diagnostic utility*.

Many diagnostic utilities exist in the DOS universe. Chances are you already have one and don't even know it; both PC Tools and the Norton Utilities come with diagnostics. More likely than not, however, you probably have the MSD, Microsoft Diagnostic, program that comes with both MS-DOS and Windows. Since that's the case, I'll ramble on about it here at length.

> ✔ Diagnostic programs don't fix things so much as they tell you what's inside your PC.

Running MSD

You start MSD by typing **MSD** at the command prompt:

```
C> MSD
```

After you press Enter, the computer will rummage around inside of itself for a few tense moments (no need to step behind the lead wall here). Then it will pronounce its prognosis in a screen that looks dreadfully like Figure 21-1.

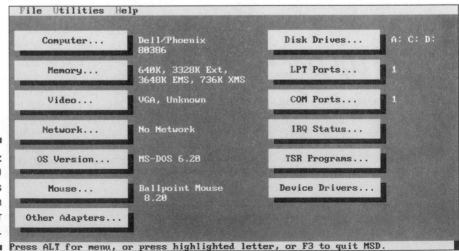

Figure 21-1: MSD displays information about your PC's guts.

The first screen shows you only the basics: `Computer` tells you which micropro-cessor lives in your PC; `Memory` gives a cryptic memory summary; `Video` tells you about your display; and so on.

If you select a specific area, such as pressing **P** for `Computer` (or clicking on that button with your mouse), you'll see more detailed information. Most of the stuff displayed is pretty nerdy, so proceed at your own risk.

To quit MSD, press the F3 key. You may have to first press the Esc key a few times to close any open windows or panels.

OK, you really want to know which microprocessor you have?

A key thing to know about your PC is which microprocessor, or CPU, dwells within its off-white case. To find out that, start MSD (see preceding) then press **P** to activate the Computer screen-panel thing. There you'll see a lot of detailed information on your computer's basic bones. For example, some tech support people may want to know your "BIOS version." There it is on the screen. The microprocessor info is found in the middle of the list — `Processor`. Press Esc to clean the screen away when you're bored with it.

More Than Bugs: Viruses

Protect your system against the evil virus. Wicked they are! Chances you'll get one? Not as great as you fear. Viruses are real, but unless you're swapping a lot of disks that contain illegal or *pirated* software — especially games — you'll probably never see a virus.

We have the media to thank for the proliferation of virus phobia among com-puter users. The hype may be a bit heavy, yet sadly viruses aren't a myth. On the up side, there is something you can do about them. Many companies now sell anti-virus software. These programs (utilities) will go out and hunt for viruses infecting your files and painlessly remove them. Again, MS-DOS 6 — the "utility" DOS — comes with a program called the Microsoft Anti-Virus, MSAV. MSAV devours viruses quite nicely, and I'll ramble on about it here at length.

> ✔ What is commonly called a *computer virus* could really be one of a hoard of nasty programs that all do sad things to your computer, specifically the files you store on your hard drive. There's no need to go into the detail or all the cutesy names given these programs. Suffice it to say that you don't want one.

> ✔ In addition to Anti-Virus, MS-DOS 6 provides another program to aid in anti-virus protection. The VSafe program is a TSR, sitting in memory and keeping a sharp eye on important parts of your disk. If any tampering occurs, VSafe lets you know instantly. The reason VSafe isn't covered here is that it's a bit of an alarmist, screaming "Wolf" once too often. The use of VSafe is covered in the DOS 6 manual (cough, hack!); also refer to the HELP command for more information on VSafe should you dare to use it.

Some common questions about computer viruses

What can I do to prevent viruses from invading my computer? Safe computing practices are listed in the nearby sidebar "Steps to avoid nasty programs." Most important among them is to never boot (start your computer) using a strange floppy disk.

How can I tell if my PC is infected with a virus? Don't be too quick to blame quirkiness on a "virus." Unfortunately, most viruses are specifically nasty and display appropriate messages telling you of your peril — *after* the damage is done. Before doing any damage, most viruses lurk inside your PC. The only way to be sure is to run a virus-scanning program.

I hear my PC caught a virus in the Orient. Should I wear a mask while I compute? No, the bugs the PC catches are electronic. People don't "catch" computer viruses. Spray some Lysol around your computer room if it makes you feel good.

Will copying files from my friend's disk infect my PC? Probably not, however, it's a good idea to scan the disk with your anti-virus software before you copy the files. Most viruses infect your computer when you run an infected program, so merely copying files doesn't have a risk. Running an infected program or — this is the most deadly way — booting from an infected floppy disk is what leads to infection.

How can I be sure that files I download with my modem don't have viruses? Run Anti-Virus on the files. If the files are contained in a ZIP file or other archive, "explode" them first and then run your anti-virus software on the lot. You'll know in a matter of seconds whether the files are free from infection.

How do I get rid of a virus? There are many techniques for virus removal, from "peeling" the virus from your disk to utterly destroying the infected file. Most anti-virus software handles the removal process for you should any infected files be found. After that, you'll be safe from impending doom (unless your PC becomes infected again).

Steps to avoid nasty programs

1. Never start your computer using a strange or unmarked floppy disk. Even if a well-meaning friend gave you the disk (to examine some game or leer at some graphics files), never start your computer with it. This is the number one way viruses are spread among PCs. (Also, such unmarked floppy disks are usually pirated copies of software and their use is illegal.)

2. Avoid software that comes on unlabeled diskettes. Software that you buy in the store should come in a shrink-wrapped box and be properly labeled. Some shareware software or freebie stuff may come crudely labeled — but be careful; run MSAV on that disk as described in this chapter. Again, software on an unlabeled diskette is probably pirated and you shouldn't use it anyway.

3. Okay, enough beating around the bush: Pirated software, stuff that people copy and distribute illegally, is often rife with viral infections. Don't pirate; don't get a virus.

4. If possible, ensure you're the only person who uses your computer. If the PC is out in the open, someone may happen by and ungraciously infect it for you. (Indeed, around my old office computer pranks were popular to the point of memorandum and condemnation by The Powers That Be.) When someone asks to borrow your PC, just say no!

5. Run virus-scanning and removal software often. The Microsoft Anti-Virus program is a great tool for this purpose.

If I have a virus, should I restore from a backup to delete it? Generally speaking, no. The reason is that the virus may have been backed up, and restoring the file would restore the infection. You should first remove the virus, then do an immediate, full, hard disk backup.

It's said that a virus affects your computer's behavior, making it run slowly and often impeding your ability to get work done. If so, then isn't Microsoft Windows a virus? No comment.

Running Anti-Virus

MS-DOS 6 comes with MSAV, the Microsoft Anti-Virus. To run it and scan your computer for viruses, type the following at your DOS prompt:

```
C> MSAV
```

Type **MSAV** and press Enter. The program starts and displays all sorts of wondrous information (see Figure 21-2). Pressing the F5 key makes it look for and remove any virus-infected files on the hard drive.

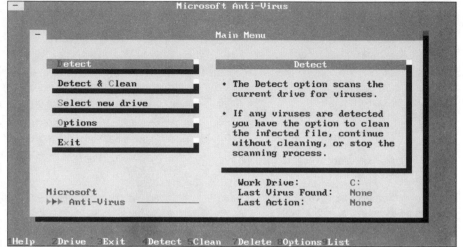

Figure 21-2:
Anti-Virus
(like Auntie
Em but not
as obsessed
with
counting
chicks).

- ✔ If MSAV finds a virus, follow the instructions on the screen for virus removal. Then phone up a friend and brag that you had a virus but MSAV saved your butt.

- ✔ I don't have any infected files, otherwise I'd show you what the "I found one and would you like it removed" screen looks like.

- ✔ Press F3 followed by Enter when you're ready to quit MSAV.

- ✔ Run MSAV as often as you like. But chances are, as long as you don't use illegal software or run programs somebody gave you "for free," you'll be safe from the virus.

- ✔ Information on the Windows-based version of MSAV is offered in Chapter 6.

Keeping your anti-virus software up-to-date

To scan for viruses, most anti-virus software looks for what are called *virus signatures*. These are tell-tale pieces of computer code that identify viral infections. Most anti-virus software can recognize hundreds of computer virus signatures. Unfortunately, the deviants are out there busily dreaming up new viruses whose signatures your software may not recognize.

Don't panic about this! As fast as they're churning out new viruses, the boys and girls who write anti-virus software are working on solutions that recognize those new virus signatures. To obtain this new information, you need to either fill out and return the update coupon that came with your anti-virus software or you can use a modem to access the software developers (or often their *forum* on CompuServe) and grab the new signature files. Using a modem to get the files can be easy, though I recommend that you have your guru do it.

Yes, You Can Believe It, DOS Has Lots of Help for You

No more can DOS be called uncivilized. Rude, perhaps, but definitely not as rigid and cold as in versions past. With DOS versions 5 and later you get help. MS-DOS 6? Hey, you get perhaps the most helpful hand DOS has ever extended to a beginner. Not only does DOS offer on-line help with its many commands and utilities, you also get command-line help plus a nifty full-screen help thing with examples and suggestions and, O, lots of fun.

Help with DOS 5

DOS 5 was the first version of DOS to even think about offering help. Not only do you get the nifty /? command line help (covered next), but there's a program called HELP that lists all the DOS commands and can display more information on each of them. It works like this:

```
C> HELP
```

Type in **HELP**. Avoid the temptation to type an exclamation point after that. Then press Enter. You'll see a list of all of DOS's commands plus a brief description of what each does.

You can also type HELP followed by a space and the name of a DOS command to see what that command does. Wow. Whodathot.

The /? command-line switch

For DOS's command-line commands, there is the universal /? option or *help switch*. You use this dealie after any DOS command to see a list of requirements and options for that command. This is what the techno-types call the *command format*. To see it, follow any DOS command with /? and no other options. Here's an example:

```
C> COPY /?
```

Here the COPY command is followed by a space and then slash-question mark. Instead of copying anything (or displaying the "huh?" error message), DOS instead spits out a list of command options and formats for the COPY command.

The good thing about /? help is that it's there! It works with all DOS commands! The bad thing is that the help is no more useful than the DOS manual. Hey! It *is* the DOS manual! Right on the screen. How con*veee*nient.

- ✔ The information /? displays is rather terse — not friendly at all. If you want something more friendly, refer to the next section on the HELP command.

- ✔ What? The /? switch doesn't work? Then it's one of two things. First, you have DOS 4 or earlier. If that's not the case, then what you probably have isn't a DOS command. Some third-party utilities work on the command line just like DOS commands. If /? doesn't work, most likely you've found one of those. Refer to its manual for the help you need.

- ✔ Refer to Chapter 14, the section "About the darn command formats," for more information on deciphering the darn command formats.

The F1 help key

DOS 6 has two types of commands. First are the traditional commands, such as COPY, MOVE, and REN. Then come commands that should really be called *utilities*. These include MSBackup, Anti-Virus, DoubleSpace, and a few others. For those commands — MS-DOS 6's utilities — you can get helpful information by pressing the F1 key. This is a standard help convention for most applications: Press F1 and you get help. Easy 'nuff.

The full-on, high-power, calmly desperate HELP command

Like DOS 5, DOS version 6 has a HELP command. But unlike DOS 5's pitiful help command, with DOS 6 you get what is essentially the manual — nerd meat and potatoes — right on your hard drive. Yet this command is actually better than having a real manual because it's very specific, provides lots of good examples, and doesn't smell as bad as the real manual.

Two ways to use the HELP command are available. First, you can just type **HELP** at the DOS prompt:

```
C> HELP
```

Do not follow HELP with an exclamation point. Just type **HELP** and press Enter.

When you type HELP by itself you'll see a list of DOS commands plus some "topics" on which you can get extra help (see Figure 21-3). Use the arrow keys or the Tab key to highlight the various help subjects and press Enter to see the helpful information. You can also double-click on the topics if you have a mouse.

Figure 21-3:
HELP as
MS-DOS 6.2
dishes it up.

When you need help with a specific DOS command, type **HELP** and then that DOS command. Here's an example:

```
C> HELP ANSI.SYS
```

Type HELP, a space, then the DOS command or topic of interest. Above, HELP is followed by ANSI.SYS. After pressing Enter, you'll see oodles of information about ANSI.SYS and all that.

- ✔ To quit HELP, press Alt-F, X. This action selects the Exit item from the File menu and returns you back to the cozy DOS prompt.

- ✔ As you read the helpful information, there will be two items at the top of the HELP screen, just below the menu bar. The items will be two of the following: Syntax, Notes, or Examples. The Syntax item displays a screen that describes the command's format and options; Notes displays information about using the command, plus tips; and Examples shows you how the command can be used and what it can do. Always look to the Examples screen. In most cases, what you're looking for will be illustrated right there.

- ✔ You move around in the HELP program using the Tab key. Press Tab to highlight an item on the screen; press Enter to see more information. Other key combinations are displayed on the bottom of the screen.

- ✔ Lamenting the loss of DOS 5's timid HELP command? It's still around. Type **FASTHELP** at the prompt.

- ✔ HELP's Find command can be used to find itsy bitsy information on specific subjects. For example, if you see the STACKS=0,0 thing in your CONFIG.SYS file, you can start the HELP command and press Alt-S, F to bring up the Find box. Type STACKS into the Find What box and press Enter. DOS will scour the HELP command's archives for matching information and display it right there on the screen.

Your Last Resort: Calling for Technical Support

There is no rule that says a company must offer you phone support for your computer or its software. However, some companies are nice and offer it to you — sometimes for free — when you need it. For this you should be thankful.

Never use tech support as a first resort.

Support lines are often flooded with people asking lame questions, which bogs down support for those people who are really in a bind. This book contains the answers to most of your questions and will help you piece together quite a lot of PC puzzles. Still, when the time comes, and you feel the urge to call technical support, do them a favor and run through this list first:

1. **Look up your question in this book or your software manual.**

   Use the index. Refer to the table of contents. Don't be lazy and just read the first few sentences or just pieces of paragraphs. In this book, related information is always listed in the check marks that conclude each section.

2. **Ask your guru for help.**

   If it's your office, then that's what they pay the gurus for. At home, call your crazy neighbor Earl and see if he's still willing to help you.

3. **Check the on-line help.**

   Most modern software gives you help by pressing the F1 key. In DOS, you can use the HELP command, as discussed earlier in this chapter. Don't neglect scoping out the "Examples" in the HELP for DOS 6.

4. **Refer to the README file.**

   Nearly every software program sold today comes with a lengthy README.TXT file, which you're usually exposed to right after installation. Refer to it again if you need to — especially for hardware (computer or printer) problems. There's a lot of specific information in there.

5. **Try the situation again and take notes.**

   Providing you've been diligent to this point, try the operation again. For some dumb reason, it almost always works the second time. If not, take some notes. Write down any error messages or numbers. Also, recall the last thing you did to your PC. I have a friend whom I won't name (okay, it's Tom) and he always messes with his PC and then seems surprised when things foul up afterwards. If you mess, expect weirdness. The two *are* related.

6. Run a diagnostic program.

This isn't to solve any problem. Instead, the diagnostic comes in handy when telling tech support people what's where inside your PC. (Don't forget the MSD program that comes with most versions of DOS and Windows.)

7. Dial tech support.

- Most software manuals bury the tech support numbers. If so, write them down on the blank pages provided in the back of this book.

- Note that often several ways exist to get tech support. The best is to call up and talk to a real live human. However, some automated tech-support systems ("voice menus") exist that are quite good. Consider calling those first because the lines aren't as busy as the real human type of tech support.

- Tech support calls come in three types: Free 800 number lines; toll calls (where you pay for the phone call); and expensive calls, where you pay for the call *and* for the person's time on the other end of the line.

- Printer problem? Call your printer's tech support. DOS problem? Call whoever sold you DOS. Word processor problem? Call the word processor developer.

- Pay attention when you call! Be at your computer with it on and ready to go. The tech support people can help you best when you're helpful to them as well.

- Be careful when dialing any 1-900 tech support numbers. If you misdial you might get the 1-900 Tech Guy Party Line or the Psychic Nerds Network.

- Tech support hours are usually from Monday though Friday (but not on holidays) during business hours. Check to see whether the times are Eastern, Central, Mountain, or Pacific.

- Modem support is available from the majority of computer companies. You can download files or pose questions on-line. Many developers also have forums on CompuServe. There are also FAX lines for tech support questions, as well as FAX-back lines, where the other computer calls your FAX machines and sends you the information you requested.

- Software companies often sell more than one product. Make sure you're calling the right number for that product. Also, Microsoft sells both DOS and Windows. Only call those support lines with your specific DOS and Windows questions. If you're having a problem with a Lotus or Borland product, call them instead.

- For heaven's sake, don't call up and play "Stump the Support Guy."

- Don't forget to have your serial number handy! Many places ask for a product's serial number before you get support.

Chapter 22
DOS Error Messages
(What They Mean, What to Do)

● ●

In This Chapter

▶ Abort, Retry, Fail?

▶ Access denied

▶ Bad command or file name

▶ Bad or missing command interpreter

▶ Divide overflow

▶ Drive not ready error

▶ Duplicate file name or file not found

▶ File cannot be copied onto itself

▶ File creation error

▶ File not found

▶ General failure

▶ Insufficient disk space

▶ Internal stack overflow

▶ Invalid directory

▶ Invalid drive specification

▶ Invalid file name or file not found

▶ Invalid media, track 0 bad or unusable

▶ Invalid number of parameters

▶ Invalid parameter

▶ Invalid switch

▶ Non-system disk or disk error

▶ Not ready, reading drive X

▶ Write protect

● ●

*T*he list of possible error messages you may see DOS display is massive — truly huge. This isn't because DOS is riddled with mistakes; it's because DOS is so vast. When you consider the bonus programs included with DOS 6, such as DoubleSpace, MSBackup, and Anti-Virus, the potential for error messages is staggering. But rather than have you stagger about, this chapter contains 20-something common error messages you might see while you're running your PC. Each error message is explained according to its meaning and probable cause, with a suggested solution for each. Nothing here is really fatal, though a few of the error messages will scare the bejesus out of you. Never fear, a solution is always at hand.

Note that DOS error messages tend to be kind of vague. This is because neither DOS nor the PC hardware is built to perform the kind of defaulted diagnostics that would result in messages like, "There's no disk in drive A; please put one in," or "Press A to cancel that last command." Oh well.

You'll find extended discussions of some issues or solutions in other chapters. I've cross-referenced them here.

Abort, Retry, Fail?

Meaning: The latest missile launched by the Air Force is careening out of control toward Moscow. Actually, this is a generic response to a variety of what DOS calls *fatal errors*. DOS has taken its best stab at doing something and just can't figure out what's wrong.

Probable cause: Typically, this message is preceded by a line of text explaining what DOS tried to do: read from a disk, write to a disk, touch its toes, and so on. Nine times out of ten you'll see this message when you attempt to access a floppy disk in drive A or B and the drive door is open or there is no disk in the drive.

Solution: If you can remedy the situation, such as closing the drive door or putting a disk into the drive, do so. Then press **R** to Retry. If nothing can be done, press **A** for Abort (which means Cancel, but most programmers don't know if Cancel has one or two *l*'s in it).

Pressing **F**, the Fail option, can be used in a few rare circumstances. For example, suppose you type **A:** to switch to drive A and there's no disk in there. When that happens, the `Abort, Retry, Fail` error appears and you'll never see a DOS prompt again — unless you type **F** to fail. Then you'll see `Current drive is no longer valid`. OK. Type **C:** to log back to drive C.

Tales from real life you don't have to read

Most often I get the `Abort, Retry, Fail` error message when I type **A:**
instead of **B:** and there is no disk in drive A. My solution is to have a formatted
disk (any disk will do) handy. I slip that disk into drive A and then press **R** to
retry. After the DOS command is done (or whatever), I retype the command
again specifying **B:** or whichever letter I originally meant to type.

Skip this only if you don't take the hard drive seriously

When you get the `Abort, Retry, Fail` message and the error DOS displays
seems more drastic, it's time to worry a bit. Situations such as a `read error`,
`write error`, or `seek error` could be the rumblings of a major disk disaster
(especially if the disk you're trying to access is the hard disk). If the errors are
consistent, refer to the nearest PC-knowledgeable person and scream "Help"
quietly into his or her ear.

Access Denied

Meaning: You've tried to change a file that DOS is not allowed to change.

Probable cause: The file you've specified, or one of several files in a group, has
its read-only file protection set. You cannot rename the command with REN;
you cannot delete it with DEL; and you cannot use any applications to change
the file's contents. This error may also occur if you've specified a subdirectory
name in a command that normally manipulates files.

Solution: Just ignore the file. Chances are the file's not meant to be touched,
anyway. (You can refer to "The File! I Cannot Kill It!" in Chapter 4 if you're
desperate.)

Bad Command or File Name

Meaning: DOS doesn't understand the command you just typed.

Probable cause: You mistyped a command name, misspelled the name of a
program on disk, or DOS cannot find the named program. This is also DOS's
typical response when you type in a dirty word or hurl it an insult via the
command line.

Solution: Check your typing. You can also refer to "Where Is My Program?" in Chapter 20 if you're certain the program worked before.

Bad or Missing Command Interpreter

Meaning: DOS cannot locate the file named COMMAND.COM, which contains its basic operations, and so it cannot proceed. Sounds worse than it is.

Probable Cause A: One of two categories are usually the culprit. If you were exiting a program to return to the DOS prompt and you got this message, or a similar one referring to an inability to locate COMMAND.COM, this just means DOS has gotten confused, probably because your program decided to drop DOS off at a different drive than DOS was expecting (like the A, B, or D drive, when the C drive is the one that has the COMMAND.COM program on it).

Solution A: Just reboot, reset, or push the Reset button. Everything should be fine at this point because the program was exiting normally anyway.

Probable Cause B: This happens when you're starting your computer. It might mean that you left a disk in drive A; you don't have a disk in drive A and the hard disk hasn't been set up to start DOS; or COMMAND.COM isn't in the root directory of your hard drive where it's supposed to be because it's been moved or deleted (a major no-no).

Solution B: If there's a disk in drive A, take it out and push the Reset button. If this isn't the problem, or it doesn't work, get help from a knowledgeable user. This user will probably dig out your original DOS floppy disk and copy COMMAND.COM back onto the hard drive's main directory where it belongs. This assumes you have a *bootable* copy of the DOS disks around. Just stick your DOS Setup Disk 1 into your A drive and press the Reset button. When the Setup program runs, press F3 twice to quit, and then copy COMMAND.COM back to drive C's root directory. An easier solution is to make a bootable disk just for such emergencies. Make a bootable disk by putting a fresh floppy in drive A and typing

```
C> FORMAT A:/S/U
```

S stands for *system,* which is what COMMAND.COM is part of — the DOS system file group. If FORMAT burps and won't do its job, or you only have a low-density floppy in a high-density drive, refer to "Formatting a Disk" in Chapter 13.

Divide Overflow

Meaning: A program — not necessarily DOS — has tried to divide some number by zero. On a calculator, that produces the infamous E error. On your PC, it's called *divide overflow*.

Probable cause: The program screwed up. Yeah! This isn't your fault. In fact, it's usually a sign that the program wasn't very well written or tested. Another cause could be computer fatigue; these things happen more often if the PC has been on for a long, long period of time.

Solution: Because this error message usually is followed by a DOS prompt, it means that you can try to run your program again. If you care, see if you can duplicate the error, and then proudly call up the software developer to report a *bug*. (This is real advanced user stuff — your guru will be jealous.) Sometimes a reset will solve the problem, especially if it's due to computer fatigue.

Drive Not Ready Error

Refer to "Not Ready, Reading Drive *X*" later in this chapter.

Duplicate File Name or File Not Found

Meaning: You've used the REN command to rename a file and something went wrong.

Probable cause: You've specified a new filename with improper characters in it; you've specified the new name and that file already exists; or the file you want to rename doesn't exist.

Solution: Try the command again. Check to see that a file with the new name doesn't already exist. (Refer to "Renaming a File" in Chapter 4 for more information.)

File Cannot Be Copied onto Itself

Meaning: You've forgotten something with the COPY command. This isn't a major boo-boo. In fact, nothing bad has happened (which is ironic, given the insincere nature of the COPY command).

Probable cause: You've used the COPY command to duplicate a file and given the duplicate the same name as the original. While COPY will overwrite a file that already exists, you cannot use COPY to overwrite the source file. For example, you probably typed something along the lines of

```
C> COPY MYSELF MYSELF
```

when what you meant to type was

```
C> COPY MYSELF B:
```

and you left off the B:.

Solution: Don't specify the same name twice. Refer to "Duplicating a File" in Chapter 4 for the proper ways and means.

File Creation Error

Meaning: For some unspecified reason, DOS will not make a new file.

Probable cause: Using the COPY command to copy or duplicate a file and the filename is already used by a directory; or if a file already exists by that name, but it's a read-only file; or if the disk or directory is full and can't contain any additional files. This error can also be produced by any program as it saves a file, though File creation error is an error message specific to DOS.

Solution: If the filename is already taken by a directory or some other file, try creating the file using a new name. If the file is read-only, refer to the section "The File! I Cannot Kill It!" in Chapter 4. If the disk is full, delete some superfluous files or try using another disk or making a subdirectory.

File Not Found

Meaning: DOS is unable to locate the file you've named.

Probable cause: You mistyped the name, or the file isn't on that drive, in the current directory, or on the path you've specified.

Solution: Check your typing. Refer to "Finding a Lost File" in Chapter 18.

General Failure

Meaning: DOS has lots of specific error messages. When it tosses General failure at you, it means something bad has happened but DOS has nothing specific to say about it. This is like DOS saying "all hell's breaking loose," but it's not that serious.

Probable cause: Typical things that cause DOS to report General failure include an incompatible floppy disk; the floppy drive door being left open; an attempt to read from an unformatted disk; or the absence of a disk from a floppy drive.

Solution: Check to see if there is a disk in the drive or if the drive's door latch is open. Try again by pressing **R** for Retry. If there is a disk present, it's not properly formatted; press **A** for Abort. Use the FORMAT command to format the disk — but make sure the disk is formatted to its proper size and capacity. Refer to Chapter 13 and the sections "What Kind of Disk Is This?," "Formatting a Disk," and "Formatting a Low-Capacity Disk in a High-Capacity Drive."

Insufficient Disk Space

Meaning: The disk is full. There is no more room left to create or copy any files.

Probable cause: You've used the COPY command to copy too many files to the disk. Various other DOS commands and programs may produce this error.

Solution: Use a different disk, or delete some unneeded files, or start copying to another disk. If you notice that the disk still seems to have ample space available, you've simply filled up the root directory. Delete a few files (or copy them to another disk), and then create subdirectories for the extra files. Refer to "How to Name a Directory (the MKDIR Command)" in Chapter 18. Run ScanDisk (see Chapter 17) to see if your disk is filled with loose fragments that take up space but don't do any good. Also refer to "Freeing up hard disk space" in Chapter 17.

Internal Stack Overflow

Meaning: Hey! What's that stuff leaking out of the computer? No, this means one of DOS's internal storage areas — the *stack* — is full and needs more room. Everything grinds to a halt.

Probable cause: You have the command STACKS=0,0 in your CONFIG.SYS file. Either that, or the two values just aren't large enough.

Solution: You'll need to bribe your guru for this one. If you want to, refer to Chapter 15 and edit your CONFIG.SYS file. Look for the line that says STACKS=0,0 and delete it. If that's beyond you — or it doesn't solve the problem — get on your knees and plead for help.

Invalid Directory

Meaning: You've specified a directory that doesn't exist. (DOS is big on using the term *invalid,* which it takes to mean illegal.)

Probable cause: You used the CD command to change to a directory that you don't have. If not that, then you may have specified a full pathname to a file or directory and something in the pathname isn't right.

Solution: Check your typing. Refer to "Finding a Lost Subdirectory" in Chapter 18 for hunting down lost directories.

Invalid Drive Specification

Meaning: What the hell kind of drive is that?

Probable cause: You've typed in a drive letter that isn't assigned to any disk drive on your system. For example, if you have drives A, B, and C, and you type **D:**, you'll get this message.

Solution: Check your typing. The colon (:) is a sacred character under DOS. It only follows a drive letter, which can be any letter of the alphabet. If that drive doesn't exist, DOS will spit back a variation of the Invalid drive specification error message. P.S.: If it gives this message when you try to log (switch) to drive C, that means DOS has lost track of your hard drive. Oops. See Chapter 19, "When It's Time to Toss in the Towel (and Call a DOS Guru)."

Invalid File Name or File Not Found

Meaning: You've specified a filename with an illegal character, one that DOS cannot find.

Probable cause: You've used the REN command to give a file a new name that has an illegal character in it. This error also appears when you try to use the TYPE command with a wildcard filename; you can only view one file at a time using the TYPE command. (Refer to "Looking at Files" in Chapter 2.)

Solution: Check your typing. Refer to "Use These Filenames — Go Directly to Jail!" in Chapter 18. Also see the error message "Duplicate File Name or File Not Found" in this chapter.

Invalid Media, Track 0 Bad or Unusable

Meaning: The FORMAT command cannot format the disk. At least, it cannot format it to the specific capacity.

Probable cause: You're trying to format a disk at the wrong capacity, for example, a 360K disk to 1.2MB or a 1.2MB disk at 360K. Or you may have successfully formatted a high-capacity disk at low capacity and now are attempting to reformat it to high capacity. Or you have a bad disk.

Solution: You can try the FORMAT command again, but add the slash-U (/U) option. If that doesn't work, try taking a bulk eraser, one that you may use to erase a video tape, and erase the disk. That may allow the disk to be formatted — but always format disks to their proper capacity. Refer to Chapter 13.

Invalid Number of Parameters, Invalid Parameter, Invalid Switch

Meaning: You typed something improperly at the DOS prompt, left something required out of a command, or mistyped an option.

Probable cause: Usually a typo. If one of these errors pops up, you're on the right track, but you may need to check the format of the command again.

Solution: Check your typing. You may have forgotten a space. If you've forgotten an option with some DOS command, enter the command again but with its help switch, slash-?, supplied instead. Here's an example:

```
C> FORMAT /?
```

Or type

```
C> HELP FORMAT
```

Either way displays all the options and requirements of the command. Check for the one you want and then specify it properly. Refer to "About the Darn Command Formats" in Chapter 14 and "The ever-gracious HELP command" in Chapter 21 for more information.

Non-System Disk or Disk Error

Meaning: You're trying to start the computer from a nonboot disk. It may be formatted, but there is no copy of DOS on the disk.

Probable cause: You've left a floppy disk in drive A while starting your computer.

Solution: Make sure that drive A is empty, or open the drive door latch. Press the spacebar to allow DOS to boot from the hard drive.

Other versions of DOS, some third-party utilities that have their own disk formatting programs, and diskettes that come preformatted will put subtly different error messages on their diskettes. The general gist here is `Non-System Disk`. What you see on the screen may be different than what's shown above.

Not Ready, Reading Drive X

Meaning: You've tried to access or log to either of your floppy drives, and DOS found only air where it expected a disk.

Probable cause: There's no disk in the drive, or the drive door latch is open.

Solution: Stick a disk into the drive or close the drive door, and then type **R** to retry.

Write Protect

Meaning: You've attempted to write to or alter a disk that's been tagged as write-protected.

Probable cause: The disk has a write-protect tab on it, or the 3½-inch disk has its little tile off the hole. This prevents any information from being written to the disk or information on the disk from being changed.

Solution: Answer A for Abort. If you really want to change the information, remove the disk's write-protection and try again (press **R** for Retry instead of **A** for Abort). Refer to "Write-Protecting Disks" in Chapter 13 for additional information.

Part V
The Part
of Tens

"OH YEAH, AND TRY NOT TO ENTER THE WRONG PASSWORD."

In this part...

If you love to read trivia, world records, or books containing lists, then this is the part of the book you've been waiting for. These aren't meaningless lists of tens, such as Ten People Who Have Plunged to Their Deaths Over Niagara Falls, Ten Otherwise Ugly People I've Seen on "Geraldo," or Ten Things Liberals Would Like to Do with William F. Buckley's Severed Head. Instead, these are interesting lists of dos and don'ts, suggestions, tips, and other helpful information for people who have computers sitting on their desks.

Note that there won't always be ten items in each category, and in some cases there may be more. After all, if one more misguided soul died while going over the falls, why leave him off the list?

Chapter 23
Ten Things You Should Do All the Time

In This Chapter

▶ Back up

▶ Always quit a program properly and return to DOS

▶ Keep your disks away from magnets

▶ Keep your PC in a well-ventilated place

▶ When you get a box of disks, format them

▶ Change your printer's ribbon or toner when it gets low

▶ Label your disks

▶ Wait at least 30 to 40 seconds before turning the computer on again

▶ Buy supplies

▶ Buy more books

*T*he rest of the lists of tens in this book are all fairly negative things, so why not start on an upbeat note? You may not have to do these things every second of the day, but keep each of these things in mind as you use your PC. Some of these items are elaborated on elsewhere in this book — that is duly noted here.

Care for Your Files

There are three things you should do to ensure that you, your PC, and the files you create always live in harmony: Back up, check your disk, and check for viruses. Refer to Chapter 17 for information on backing up. Information on checking the disk (using CHKDSK or ScanDisk) is in Chapter 17 as well. Checking for viruses is covered in Chapter 21.

Always Quit a Program Properly and Return to DOS

There is no reason to quit a program by punching the Reset button — or worse, by turning the computer off and then on again. Just as in social circles, there's always a proper method of exiting any situation. Know what it is and use it to quit your programs. Believe it or not, it's faster to quit back to the DOS prompt than to reset anyway.

Keep Your Disks Away from Magnets

A magnet erases a disk faster than looking at Medusa turns you to stone. Magnets are everywhere, so be careful. For example, the mouthpiece on most phones and phone handsets has a big magnet in it; rest the phone down on your desktop and THWOOP! the data on the disk is gone.

Other popular desk items that contain magnets are listed below. Please try to keep your disks away from the following:

- Modems
- Paperclip holders
- Compasses
- Those things that pick up cars at the junk yard
- The planet Jupiter

Keep Your PC in a Well-Ventilated Place

PCs need to breathe. The internal fan needs to suck air in through the front of the computer box, and it needs to wheeze that air back out again through the rear of the box. Make sure nothing covers the front of the computer (where it breathes in) or the back of the computer (where it coughs it back out).

The purpose of the fan is to keep the computer cool. Just like men in the Kinsey Report, electrical components perform better under cold conditions than hot. So it may be a good idea to keep your computer out of direct sunlight — and keep your meltable disks out of the sun as well. Even for security reasons, try not to place computers directly beneath a window. (I've seen too many computers disappear from various offices thanks to the old smash-n-grab.)

When You Get a Box of Disks, Format Them

You are never more desperate than when you need a disk on which to store a file but you don't have any formatted. There is no way around that problem. In fact, I've even driven to another location just to format a disk so I could take it back to the office and use it. The only way to avoid this problem is to format the whole box of disks after you buy it. Yeah, that takes time. But so does driving seven miles to format a disk.

Label Your Disks

I'm in the habit of sticking a label on a disk after it's been formatted. I may just label it with the date or the word *Formatted*. Later, as the information on the disk changes, the name can be changed to reflect its contents. You can label some disks to reflect their purpose, such as *Work to Home* or *Today's Stuff*. The purpose is to help you keep track of your disks and the information on them. (Refer to Chapter 13 for more information on formatting disks.)

Wait at Least 30 to 40 Seconds Before Turning the Computer On Again

Nothing screws up a computer faster than rapidly flipping the On/Off switch a few times. Computers should be allowed time to *power down* (which is a term the Sunday Paper Grammarians love to harp on). You should allow the fan to stop spinning and those torrentially turning hard drives to gracefully wind down to silence. Only then is it 100 percent OK to turn the system back on again.

Change Your Printer's Ribbon or Toner When It Gets Low

In the Hall of I'm Too Cheap, near the Display of Irony, there's a plaque devoted to those who pay $2,000 for a laser printer but are too cheap to go out and buy a new $90 toner cartridge when one gets low. Don't do this. If your printing starts to fade, buy a new printer toner cartridge or ribbon. In most cases, using an old one has a negative effect on both the printer and your hard copy. This is something you shouldn't neglect.

Buy Supplies

In the same vein as changing a printer ribbon, you should always keep handy plenty of supplies for your computer: this includes disks, labels, printer ribbons or toner cartridges, paper for the printer, and other goodies you can find hanging from the racks at any software store.

Buy More Books

Speaking from experience, and as an author of computer books, I can't recommend anything better. Seriously, keep a sharp eye out for computer books. Definitely give the computer and software manuals a try before you buy a computer book on the subject. Some books are long-winded rewrites of the manual. Avoid them. Instead, try to find books with personal insight, plenty of tips, and those written in a language you understand. The computer press reviews books but rarely keeps those items in mind. So be your own critic.

Chapter 24
Ten Common Beginner Mistakes

. . . .

In This Chapter

▶ Assuming it's your own fault

▶ Mistyping commands

▶ Buying the wrong thing

▶ Buying too much software

▶ Assuming it will be easy (just because the program says so)

▶ Incorrectly inserting disks

▶ Logged to the wrong drive or directory

▶ Pressing Y too quickly

▶ Reformatting an important disk

▶ No organization or housekeeping

. . . .

*G*olly, if there really were only ten common beginner mistakes, life would be so much easier with computers. Sad to say, the following only highlights a few common beginner faults, but there's nothing that can't be cured. Review this list and reduce your problems.

Assuming It's Your Own Fault

The first thing most beginners assume is that when something doesn't go right, it's their own fault. Usually it isn't. Computers don't always work as advertised. If you type in a command exactly as it's listed in the book or manual and it doesn't work, the manual is wrong, not you. How do you find out what is right? You can check the program's README file, or you can call the developer for technical support. Or experiment, especially if it's your own computer (so you delete your own files and not your coworker's).

Mistyping Commands

Making typing mistakes is a common problem for all computer users. Beginners typically forget spaces on the command line, sandwiching separate parts of a DOS command together, which doesn't make sense to DOS. The result: You get an error message. Also, never end any DOS command with a period. Even though the manual may have a period after the command (in obeisance to English grammar), few, if any, DOS commands ever end with a period. And be aware of the differences between the forward slash (/) and the backslash (\), as well as the colon (:) and the semicolon (;).

Buying the Wrong Thing

Hardware and software must be compatible with your computer. In particular, this means that software must run *under DOS,* and your computer must have the proper innards to support the software. The problem primarily exists with PC graphics and memory. If you don't have enough or the proper type of either, some software may not work. Don't try too hard to save money by buying bargain hardware from remainder catalogs if you don't know enough about computers to tell the difference.

Buying Too Much Software

It's fun to go crazy in a software store, wielding your VISA card like a samurai sword. Bringing home all those applications and getting started with them takes time, however. Don't give yourself too much to do, or you may neglect some of the programs you've bought. Start by buying software with the basics, maybe one or two packages. Learn those, and then expand with other programs as needed. Your brain and your monthly VISA bill will be easier to live with.

Assuming It Will Be Easy (Just Because the Program Says So)

This goes right along with buying too much software. You need time to learn a program, get comfortable with it, and become productive with it. With today's overwhelming applications, you may never master everything (no one does). Still, give yourself time to learn. You can get your work done far more quickly if you take those extra few days to experiment and play with the software, work the tutorials, and practice. (Be sure to tell the boss about that.) Most of all, don't buy software on deadline. I mean, don't think you can buy the program on

The 5th Wave By Rich Tennant

Monday, install it on Tuesday, and produce the divisional report that's due on Wednesday. Programs save time only after you've learned them — until then, they eat time.

A corollary to this is: Don't expect to learn the program if you refuse to look at the manual (or a book about the program). There's no such thing as an intuitive program, no matter what they say. At least take the introductory tutorial.

Incorrectly Inserting Disks

The handy 3 ½-inch disks can only fit into a floppy drive one way. Even though there are potentially eight ways to insert a disk, only one of them meets with success. The 5 ¼-inch disks are different. You can fit them into a drive on any of four sides both right-side-up and upside-down. The correct method of inserting both types of disks is with the label up and toward you. The notch on the 5 ¼-inch disk is to the left and the oblong hole on the disk goes in first. Nothing heinous happens if you insert a 5 ¼-inch disk the wrong way — it just doesn't work.

Logging to the Wrong Drive or Directory

As you work with a computer, you'll always be using, or *logged to,* one directory on one disk drive. Never assume that you know where you are. If you do, you may delete files you don't want to delete or be unable to find files you expect to be there. Refer to "Finding the Current Directory" in Chapter 17.

Another common variant of this mistake is logging to a floppy drive that doesn't have a disk in it. If you do that, you'll see a `General failure` error message; put the proper disk into the drive and then press **R** to Retry.

Pressing Y Too Quickly

DOS asks a Y/N (yes or no) question for a reason; what's about to take place has serious consequences. Are you *sure* you want to go ahead? Only press **Y** if you really do. If you're uncertain, press **N** or Ctrl-C and reexamine your situation. This question happens more often than not with the DEL*.* command; make sure you're logged to the proper directory before typing DEL*.* to delete all the files.

Reformatting an Important Disk

Eventually, like all computer users, you will accumulate some 10,000 or so floppy disks, which you'll keep in a drawer, on a tabletop, tossed onto a shelf, or in cityscape-like piles on the floor. Grabbing one of these disks and reformatting it is cheaper than buying a new disk. But make sure that old disk doesn't contain anything valuable first. How do you do that? Label the disks properly and run the DIR command to see what's there before you format.

No Organization or Housekeeping

Organization and housekeeping are two duties that the intermediate-to-advanced DOS users learn to take upon themselves. It's routine stuff, actually part of the larger picture of hard disk management. Not performing housekeeping or being unorganized are things beginners are good at. But over the long run, picking up after yourself now can save you massive problems in the near future.

Unless you want to pick up a good book on hard disk management (which implies taking that first step toward computer nerdhood), my suggestion is to let your favorite computer expert have a crack at your computer. Tell him or her to check out the system, organize things, and clean up your hard drive. (But tell him or her not to get too fancy — you don't want to plow through six layers of subdirectories to find something.) The end result will be a faster system — and maybe even some more disk space. That's a plus, but getting more disk space isn't something beginners need to concern themselves with.

Chapter 25
Ten Things
You Should Never Do

● ●

In This Chapter

▶ Don't switch disks

▶ Don't work from a floppy disk

▶ Don't take a disk out of the drive when the light is on

▶ Don't turn off the computer when the hard drive light is on

▶ Don't reset to leave an application

▶ Don't plug anything into the computer while it's on

▶ Don't force a disk into the drive

▶ Never format a high-capacity disk to low capacity

▶ Never format a low-capacity disk to high capacity

▶ Never load software from an alien disk

▶ Never use these DOS commands: CTTY, DEBUG, FDISK, FORMAT C:, RECOVER

● ●

*U*h-oh. Here is a list of ten big no-nos (OK, there are 11, but who's counting?). Actually, there are a lot of bad things you can do to a nice computer. For some of them I'm hoping you don't need a written warning. For example, it's a bad idea to attempt to fix your own monitor. You can, conceivably, upgrade your computer, but being able to do something and wanting to do it are two different things.

Here then are ten unhealthy things you don't even want to consider doing.

Don't Switch Disks

This isn't that obvious a warning. Basically, it means don't switch disks while you're still using the one in the drive. For example, suppose you're working on a file in drive A and you haven't yet saved the file back to disk. Then, for some reason, you switch disks and try to save the file on the second disk. The result is that you've ruined the second disk and not truly saved your file.

Always save a file on the same disk from which you've loaded it. If you want a second copy of the file on another disk, use the COPY command after you've returned to DOS. Refer to "Copying a Single File" in Chapter 4.

Don't Work from a Floppy Disk

I am often amazed that people whose computers have nice, big, fast hard drives do their work on floppy disks. It's almost impossible to find a program any more that can be run from a floppy. And, for heaven's sake, don't start your PC from a floppy disk when you can do it using the hard disk. This leads to nothing but trouble.

Floppy disks are still useful. You can read and write files on a floppy, send work back and forth between two distant computers, and so on. Using floppies is slow, and floppies are less reliable than hard disks, but they work. Back up your data files to your floppies and use the floppies to move files to another machine — but do your day-to-day work on your hard drive.

Don't Take a Disk Out of the Drive When the Light Is On

The drive light is on only when the computer is writing to or reading from the disk. As with humans, the computer becomes annoyed when you remove its reading material before it's finished reading it. The result could be a damaged disk or lost information.

If you remove a disk before the light goes out, the computer displays a What's going on? error message. Replace the disk and press R to Retry the operation.

Don't Turn Off the Computer When the Hard Drive Light Is On

The only safe time to turn off the computer is when you're at the DOS prompt. However, if the hard drive light is still on, that means the computer is accessing the hard disk. It's only safe to turn off the system when the hard drive light is off, meaning that the computer is done writing to disk. (You should also refer to "Turning the Computer Off" in Chapter 1, as well as "Black Box Program Rules" in Chapter 15.)

Don't Reset to Leave an Application

This goes along with not turning off the PC in the middle of something. Always properly quit a program and return to the DOS prompt. From the DOS prompt you can quickly run your next program. Of course, you can reset if the program has run amok and pressing Ctrl-C or Esc can't stop it.

Don't Plug Anything into the Computer While It's On

Connect any external goodies to your computer only when your computer is off. This especially goes for the keyboard, monitor, and printer. Plugging in any of those items while the computer's power is on can "fry" something you've paid a lot of money for. It's best to turn off the computer, plug in your goodies, and then turn the computer back on again.

Don't Force a Disk into the Drive

If it doesn't go in, the disk is probably pointed in the wrong direction. Or worse, what you're sticking the disk into is probably not a disk drive, or there's a disk already *in* the drive. Refer to "Changing Disks" in Chapter 1 for the details.

Never Format a High-Capacity Disk to Low Capacity

First, it's a waste of money. Second, many low-capacity drives can't read high-capacity disks formatted to low capacity. Third, it's hard to force the machine into reformatting the disk back to high capacity later.

Never Format a Low-Capacity Disk to High Capacity

Oh, you can try. The results are usually a disk that's riddled with errors, or a disk that fails miserably over time and loses lots of data. Don't be fooled by some huckster into thinking that a $19.95 hole-punching device can do the trick for you; don't be cheap with your disks or your prized data.

Never Load Software from an Alien Disk

Only buy software *shrink-wrapped* from a reputable computer dealer. Any other program you get, especially those on cheaply labeled disks, is suspect. Don't trust it! This is how computer viruses are spread, so it's best not to load anything from an alien disk. And, for God's sake, never boot from such a disk.

Never Use These Dangerous DOS Commands

The following commands serve special purposes way beyond the reach of most beginning computer users. It's OK to let someone who knows what they're doing use these commands, but you should never try them yourself. The consequences are just too horrible to think of.

CTTY   This command unhooks DOS from the keyboard and screen. Don't
              try it.

DEBUG   This is a programmer's tool used to create programs, modify
              memory, and, if you're careless, mess up a disk drive. Don't run
              this program. (If you do, type **Q** to quit.)

FDISK   This command could destroy all information on your hard drive if
              used improperly.

FORMAT C: The FORMAT command should only be used with drives A and B
              to format floppy disks. Never format drive C, or any drive letter
              higher than C.

RECOVER   This command sounds healthy, but RECOVER is dumb and
              deadly. If you type this command it will destroy all files on your
              disk and remove all your subdirectories, replacing them with
              garbage — all without a Y/N warning. Don't try it.

Chapter 26
Ten Programs
That Make Life Easier

● ●

In This Chapter

I review some neat programs (and give them an IQ rating where 100 takes DOS talent — so the lower the better):

▶ COPYCON — a quick text file editor/creator (IQ: 60)

▶ Direct Access — a menu system (IQ: 50)

▶ DOS Shell — a free menu system (IQ: 100)

▶ LIST — a quick file viewer (IQ: 70)

▶ Magellan — a point-and-shoot disk manager (IQ: 90)

▶ PC Shell — everything but the kitchen sink (IQ: 100)

▶ Windows — makes the entire computer easier to use (IQ: 90)

▶ XTree Easy — an easy file maintenance program (IQ: 80)

▶ Other cutesy shells, as stated

● ●

*O*K. Some people are just going to hate everything. You may hate your car, but you use it. Even so, one of those rolly-bead back things you put on your seat can make driving more comfortable. And a good stereo system can make you forget that everyone else is passing you on the freeway. Enjoy life, be comfortable, and consider some of the following programs that can make life easier for any DOS user (though they're not as cool as fuzzy dice).

COPYCON (IQ: 60)

The COPYCON (pronounced copy-con) program is used to edit text files (those files you can view with the TYPE command). It gets its name from a handy DOS trick used to create quick-and-dirty text files: You can use the COPY command to copy information from the keyboard (the CON) to a file. For example:

```
C> COPY CON FUNSTUFF
```

After pressing Enter you're in a *dumb typewriter* sort of mode. Everything you type goes into a file on disk (FUNSTUFF in this example) or whatever file you specify. You can only backspace to edit, you must press Enter at the end of each line (there is no word processor-like word wrap), and when you're done you press the F6 function key. Nothing big.

The major drawback is that you cannot edit a file with the above COPY command. Remember, COPY always erases the target file, so the file FUNSTUFF would be overwritten if you used COPYCON. (Refer to Chapter 4 for more information on the COPY command.)

The COPYCON program takes the simple elegance of DOS's COPY CON and makes it into a real bone-headed editor. I give it a 60 on the DOS IQ chart (where anything over 100 requires real brains to get the work done). With COPYCON on your disk, you can quickly edit files — including CONFIG.SYS and AUTOEXEC.BAT — and never have to learn the DOS Editor, EDLIN, or any other gross text editor. You also don't have to wait 60 seconds while your big, hulking word processor loads.

For example, to edit the file FUNSTUFF, you would type the following:

```
C> COPYCON FUNSTUFF
```

Note that there's no space between COPY and CON. It's all one word. You're running the COPYCON program. If all goes well, you'll see your file in a handy editing screen, similar to that shown in Figure 26-1.

✔ If you get a `Bad command or file name` error message, you probably don't have COPYCON on your computer. You can order it directly from the author for $10 at JB Technology Inc., 28701 N. Main St., Ridgefield, WA 98642. Or you can check with your local computer user group or a national software distributor, such as PC-SIG (800-245-6717, or 800-222-2996 in California, and ask for disk #2029).

✔ Know the differences: the COPYCON program has no space and doesn't erase files; DOS's COPY CON has a space and will erase files. If you don't see COPYCON's screen (Figure 26-1), press Ctrl-C at once!

✔ Press F6 to end editing and save your file.

✔ Press F1 for a quickie help screen.

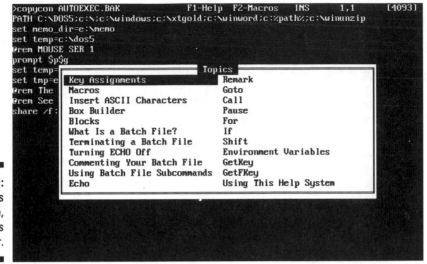

Figure 26-1:
COPYCON is
a simple,
no-brains
editor.

Direct Access (IQ: 50)

Direct Access is a menu program and is probably the simplest and most elegant way to use a PC: no graphics, no beeps and zooming windows, no "486 required," just a list of programs to choose from. Ahhh. Figure 26-2 shows a sample screen from Direct Access.

Figure 26-2:
Direct
Access
begs you to
get some
work done.

The beauty of Direct Access is that it enables you to use your computer and all your software without having to mess with DOS. Once you set it up (or pull out someone else's hair until he or she sets it up for you), your system is as easy to use as pressing a button. On the DOS IQ scale, Direct Access gets a 50 — less if someone else does the setup.

✔ Make sure Direct Access is part of your AUTOEXEC.BAT file, so that it runs each time you start up your PC. (Tell your computer expert to set it up that way, or refer to Chapter 15.)

✔ Direct Access is available at nearly all software stores, or you can order it directly from Fifth Generation Systems. Call them at 800-766-7283.

The DOS Shell (IQ: 100)

Shells and menu programs are popular ways of avoiding DOS. The most common shell that needs mentioning is the DOS Shell, the program that's included with DOS versions 4 through 6.0 (unfortunately, it's not included in DOS 6.2 — you have to order it from Microsoft. Unlike Direct Access, however, the DOS Shell is a bit more technical. It gets a 100 on the DOS IQ scale (see Figure 26-3).

You can use the DOS Shell to circumvent DOS's ugly command line. In the shell, you can copy, move, delete, and rename files. This is all done using the shell's menu system and fancy graphics — plus a mouse if you have one installed. Of course, this may be overwhelming to you. If so, you can have someone configure the shell to show only a list of programs to run. Then you can select which programs you want and entirely avoid DOS.

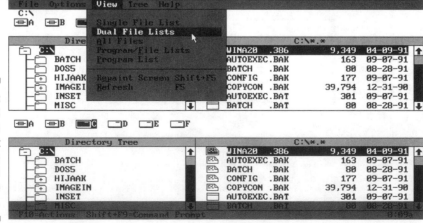

Figure 26-3:
The DOS
Shell is fun
to look at
but may be
a tad
complex to
use.

✔ The shell is a pain to set up, so make someone else do it for you. Tell your friend which programs you want installed. Then have him or her configure the shell so that it shows only the program list window on the screen. Furthermore, have them edit AUTOEXEC.BAT so that the DOS Shell always comes up when you start your PC.

✔ Chapter 5 waxes romantic about the virtues of the DOS Shell.

✔ Gotta have a mouse. No mouse, no fun.

LIST (IQ: 70)

The LIST program is basically a better version of DOS's TYPE command. Unlike TYPE, LIST shows you a file using the entire screen, enabling you to scroll through the file using the arrow keys. This is perhaps the best thought-out program ever; just use LIST instead of TYPE. Figure 26-4 shows how LIST displays a file.

LIST gets a 70 on the DOS IQ scale. I would rank it lower (and lower is better), but LIST does more than just look at files, which will make it beneficial to you in the future (if you care to expand your DOS knowledge). With LIST you can copy, delete, move, and rename files, which gives this program lots of power beyond being a simple file viewer.

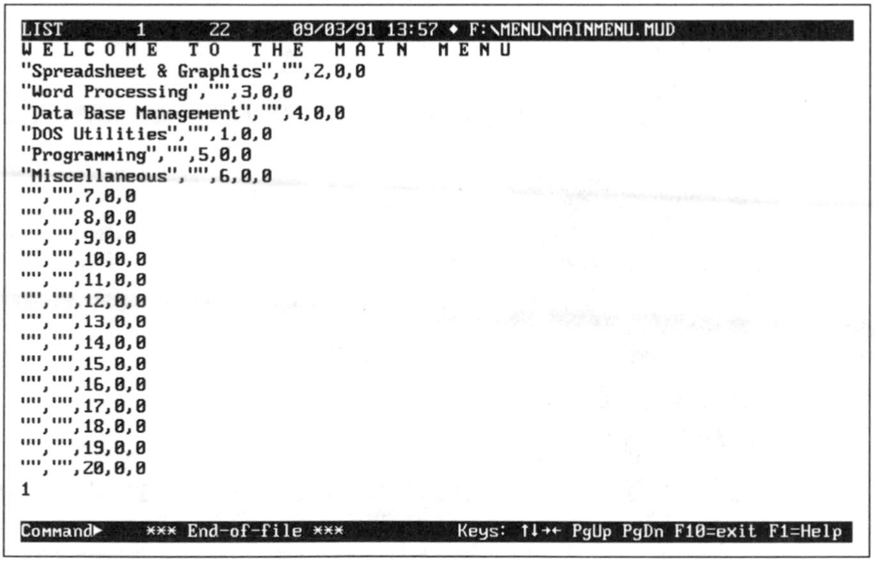

Figure 26-4: The LIST program beats the pants off of the TYPE command.

```
LIST        1      22      09/03/91 13:57 ♦ F:\MENU\MAINMENU.MUD
W E L C O M E   T O   T H E   M A I N   M E N U
"Spreadsheet & Graphics","",2,0,0
"Word Processing","",3,0,0
"Data Base Management","",4,0,0
"DOS Utilities","",1,0,0
"Programming","",5,0,0
"Miscellaneous","",6,0,0
"","",7,0,0
"","",8,0,0
"","",9,0,0
"","",10,0,0
"","",11,0,0
"","",12,0,0
"","",13,0,0
"","",14,0,0
"","",15,0,0
"","",16,0,0
"","",17,0,0
"","",18,0,0
"","",19,0,0
"","",20,0,0
1
Command▶   *** End-of-file ***         Keys: ↑↓→← PgUp PgDn F10=exit F1=Help
```

TIP

> ✔ If you don't have LIST, you can pick it up from a user group or a shareware library. You can also order it directly from the author (who wants $20 for it): Vernon D. Buerg, 139 White Oak Circle, Petaluma, CA 94952. A "professional" version is available, which means it comes in a shrink-wrapped box and costs a lot more; ask your local software-o-rama dealer for more information.

Magellan (IQ: 90)

Magellan is an interesting tool, but it's hard to describe. It's like the DOS Shell in that you can copy, move, delete, and rename files. Yet it's also like the LIST program in that you can see a file's contents — even in the same format in which the file was created (which is a real help). Furthermore, Magellan is smart enough to know which program created any file on disk and, at the touch of a key, it will run that program and load your file. How's that for magic?

Figure 26-5 shows Magellan at what it does best. A list of files is on one side of the screen. The highlighted file is a worksheet, which is shown on the other side of the screen as if it were in the program that created it (Quattro Pro). That's remarkable because spreadsheet programs store their files in Greek, so a TYPE or LIST just shows garbage. If you were to press a special launch key at this point, Magellan would run Quattro Pro and load the highlighted worksheet.

Figure 26-5: Magellan is shown here displaying a spreadsheet in context.

```
Magellan MENU          Use ↑↓←→ to navigate                    TREE
◄ Tree: F:\QPRO
   DUTB.SFO       A1: [W13]
   DUTI.SFO              A        B        C        D        E
   EGASPL.PCX    1
   EMSTEST.COM   2
   ENVELOPE.CLP  3                      EXPENSE REPORT FOR ALLISON SPRINGS
   EURO.CHR      4                      WEEK ENDING JUNE 24, 1989
   EUROPE.CLP    5
   EXPENSES.WQ1  6  DAY OF WEEK   DATE    LOCATION   TRANSPORT   HOTEL
   FANFARE.SND   7  MONDAY       06-18  SAN DIEGO      $89.00    $0.00
   FILELIST.DOC  8  TUESDAY      06-19  SAN DIEGO       $9.00   $67.00
   FONTS.BGI     9  WEDNESDAY    06-20  SAN DIEGO      $27.55   $67.00
   FRANCE.CLP   10  THURSDAY     06-21  SAN DIEGO      $12.50   $67.00
   FRWK!.TRN    11  FRIDAY       06-22  SAN DIEGO       $0.00   $67.00
   FRWK$.TRN    12  SATURDAY     06-23  SAN DIEGO       $0.00   $67.00
   FRWKZ.TRN    13  SUNDAY       06-24  SAN JOSE      $133.00   $67.00
   FRWQ!.TRN    14  TOTAL                             $271.05  $402.00
   FSWK!.TRN    15
   FSWK$.TRN    16
   FSWKZ.TRN    17
   FSWQ!.TRN                                                     READY
   File 36 of 117   ↔   F:\QPRO\EXPENSES.WQ1     Quattro Pro   3,776 Bytes
ALT  F1      F2      F3      F4      F5      F6     F7      F8       F9    F10
   Compose  Move   Mark  Rename  Index   Tree  Macro  Options   Path   Dos
```

Magellan gets a 90 on the DOS IQ scale, primarily because it can be overwhelming. Even so, Magellan is the best utility for keeping track of all the stuff on your hard drive. It can find lost files not only by their names, but also by what's in them (and that's severely nifty in my opinion). But for some beginners, particularly those who may just want a menu system like Direct Access, Magellan would be a bit much.

> ✓ You may still be able to find a copy of Magellan at just about any software store. Lotus has stopped manufacturing it, so if you see a copy, buy it.

PC Shell (IQ: 100)

Central Point's PC Tools started out as a meek Albania-size program. Currently, it's bigger than the whole of Eurasia thanks to dozens of useful little programs, most of which are way beyond the abilities of beginning DOS users. PC Tools is massive. Yet, the shell program, PC Shell, can be a much better way of using a computer than staring at a DOS prompt (see Figure 26-6).

PC Shell gets an IQ rating of 100, which some will consider a bit low. However, with the program in the basic mode, and forgetting the 10,000 other DOS utilities that come in the PC Tools package, PC Shell does rate a 100. It's quite similar to DOS's DOS Shell, but it has many more features and capabilities.

Figure 26-6:
PC Tools' PC Shell helps you organize and examine files.

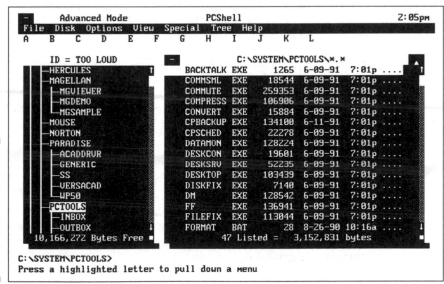

About the biggest advantage to PC Shell is the sheer immensity of PC Tools. There are lots of useful programs bundled together, including a backup program, computer-to-computer file transfer and modem programs, disaster recovery and prevention, and stuff that will boggle the mind. Impressive, but maybe a bit high on the IQ scale for some of us.

✔ You can get PC Tools at any software store; it's often heavily discounted (and well worth the price). Or you can order it directory from Central Point Software.

Windows (IQ: 90)

We're all supposed to be using graphical computers in the future. Toss out that old command line and DOS prompt! The computer industry will have everyone using a PC with a mouse soon, and Windows is the way that's done on a PC. This is kind of like a Greek tragedy where ugly DOS spawns and nurtures the beautiful Windows only to have Windows grow insane with its own beauty and, in a fit of rage, kill its mother DOS. Windows then wanders the land in search of meaning and love, but it gets no attention because news travels fast in ancient Greece.

Windows can totally replace DOS. With the WIN command stuck at the end of your AUTOEXEC.BAT file (see Chapter 15), you'll never see a DOS prompt while you use your computer (see Figure 26-7). Want to run an application? Just point the mouse at it and click. (Mouse stuff is provided in Chapter 10; more information on Windows is raked over in Chapter 6).

Windows gets a 90 on the IQ scale. It should get a 100, or even higher, because Windows can at times be quite a load to bear. But by itself, Windows is intuitive, obvious, and I'll admit, a little fun to use. And it may require someone else to set it up just the way you like, which is why Windows scores a bit high on the IQ thermometer.

✔ Windows can be purchased all over; refer to your local software dealer or a national mail-order house. Note that sometimes Windows is bundled with other products, such as Windows-specific programs, a computer mouse, or other goodies.

✔ Windows works best when it runs Windows-specific programs, such as Word for Windows, Microsoft Excel, Ami, WordPerfect for Windows, and so on. It can run other DOS programs as well, though you won't get all those fancy graphics.

✔ Gotta use a mouse.

✔ Gotta read the manual. Bill Gates (president of Microsoft, billionaire, and boy genius) thinks it's intuitive. Enough said.

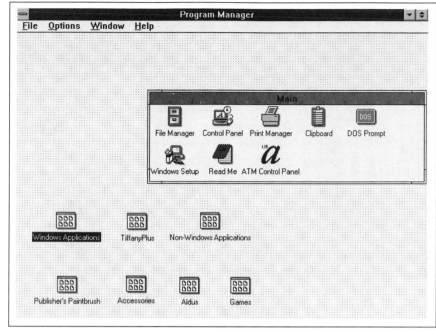

Figure 26-7:
Here is
Windows'
happy,
friendly,
graphical
face.

XTree Easy (IQ: 80)

XTree Easy is the easiest to use of several XTree-brand programs, all designed to make file management a snap. Using XTree Easy you can copy, delete, rename, and move files all around your hard drive; you can compare two different subdirectories and work with files between them; or you can "prune and graft" various subdirectories to help keep yourself organized.

But forget all that: When you start XTree Easy, it presents you with a list of all the programs on your computer. To run one you just point and shoot. Nothing could be easier. It even sets all that up for you.

The nice thing about XTree Easy is that it always gives you a visual representation of your files and hard disk's tree structure (see Figure 26-8). This makes it easy to zip around and see where things are as well as run those programs you have stashed all over the place.

This isn't straightforward like Direct Access, but it's still easy to use. Therefore, XTree Easy gets a big 80 on the DOS IQ scale. Especially if you've been using your computer for years and have no idea what's where, or you prefer a more visual way of working with files. Consider it.

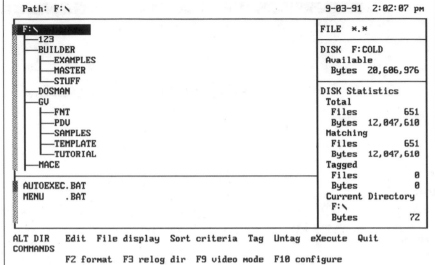

> ✔ XTree Easy is available all over — software stores, computer dealers, and national mail-order places. But beware: XTree Pro, its big brother, is a wee bit more complex than XTree Easy. If that's what you want, great. But for a DOS beginner, I'd recommend XTree Easy.

Other Cutesy Shells

There are many, many programs available that make DOS easier to use. Windows is the front-runner, followed by Direct Access. Everything else that claims to be a menu system or DOS shell falls in between (though Magellan is really an information management program). Out there in the real world, you'll find even more programs. I could list about 50 or so here. Instead, the following are some items you may want to mull over before you decide to buy a program that professes to make DOS easier to use.

Purpose

Discover what the program does. How does it make DOS easier to use? Is it a menu program, such as Direct Access? Or is it more along the lines of PC Shell or the DOS Shell — or even Windows? A menu system lists your programs; a DOS shell makes it easier to perform basic DOS functions. Both usually do some of each. If what the program does matches your needs, you're halfway home.

The 5th Wave By Rich Tennant

"OH SURE, $1.8 MILLION DOLLARS SEEMS LIKE ALOT RIGHT NOW, BUT WHAT ABOUT RANDY? WHAT ABOUT HIS FUTURE? THINK WHAT A COMPUTER LIKE THIS WILL DO FOR HIS SAT. SCORE SOMEDAY."

Ease of installation

How easy is the program to set up? For example, some menu programs will scan your hard drive for programs and automatically set up your own menu system. That saves you a big step. Also remember to check the program's requirements. For example, Windows makes a computer easy to use, but it's taxing on memory, graphics, and computer horsepower (you really need a 386). Does your system meet the requirements?

Ease of use

You would think this a redundant category. After all, some of these programs have the word *easy* on the package several times too many. But what the developer thinks is easy and what you find easy could be two different things. Up front, anything is easier than using DOS. So see what else it is the program does and how it makes that one thing so much more "easy."

If you're buying from a software store, try to see a demonstration of the program. That's the true gauge of whether or not something is easy. And here you can chalk up a big point for Direct Access: It's the program that your typical software store uses to run the other demo programs.

Support

Support comes from three places: the dealer or computer store, the software developer, and from people who are willing to help you. Sometimes the store can't be counted on; they sell hundreds of software programs and no one can really be an expert in all of them. Instead, take a hard look at developer support. Do they have a phone-in support line? Is it toll free? For how long can you call? Then ask your friends: The best program to buy is the one all your friends have because they know it and can answer questions. Presto, free tech support.

Price

Finally comes the issue of price. The "other cutesy shells" can range in price from a couple of hundred dollars to free. What you're getting for that price is more important than comparing individual prices. After all, programs like PC Tools offer you more than Direct Access, so there's going to be a difference in price.

Just about anything that makes a computer easier to use can be a blessing. Even DOS experts will use shells and menu systems simply because they make things quicker and less painful than using DOS. Finding the right one can be complicated. But it's a big field, full of competition, so there's bound to be a way to make DOS easier to use for everyone. Keep looking.

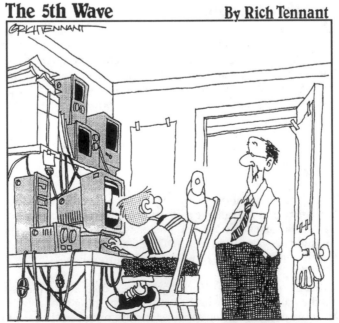

"I SUPPOSE THIS ALL HAS SOMETHING TO DO WITH THE NEW MATH."

Chapter 27
Ten Otherwise Worthless Acronyms to Impress Your Friends

●●●

●●●

*T*ired of talking about IRAs, RBIs, and STDs at your local YMCA or YWCA? Get in the loop; learn a little computerspeak. Amaze and delight your friends at your next social by talking about the real issues of today — FUDs, IDEs, and SVGAs, for example. Use some of the following acronyms to impress your friends. (After all, what are friends for if not to bolster your image by making them appear ignorant?)

ASCII

What it stands for: American Standard Code for Information Interchange.

Pronunciation: ASK-ee.

Meaning: Usually used to identify a type of file that contains only readable text, one that can be displayed with the TYPE command and read by a human.

As used in a sentence: Here is the ASCII version of that file because I know you're too lame to buy a real word processor.

Please don't read this

ASCII is a coding scheme used to identify characters in a computer. Each character, letter, number, or symbol is assigned a code number from zero through 127. All personal computers use the same coding scheme to represent these characters, which means that basic (text-only) files can be transferred between two computers without the need for translation.

DOS

What it stands for: Disk Operating System.

Pronunciation: It rhymes with boss. (Don't pronounce it *dose.*)

Meaning: The main program that controls all PCs; your computer environment on the computer.

As used in a sentence: The Microsoft Legal Department would be oh so pleased if we all called it MS-DOS instead of just DOS.

EMS

What it stands for: Expanded Memory Specification.

Pronunciation: Letters only, E-M-S.

Meaning: Extra memory in a PC, particularly memory that can be used by graphics programs, spreadsheets, and most applications that are severe memory hogs.

As used in a sentence: I have four megabytes of EMS memory, so I can run bigger spreadsheets. Ha ha.

FUD

What it stands for: Fear, Uncertainty, Doubt.

Pronunciation: Fud, rhymes with dud.

Meaning: The reasons why people don't buy computers, or hesitate to upgrade. It's the FUD factor.

As used in a sentence: Naa, there's no point in the company laying down hard cash to buy a laser printer. I'm just too full of FUD.

GUI

What it stands for: Graphical User Interface.

Pronunciation: People think it's cute to say *gooey* as in that soft, slimy pink thing you never eat at a Chinese restaurant. I personally say G-U-I (letters only) because I believe *gooey* is just too cute for a computer term.

Meaning: A program that uses graphics to display information, such as Windows. (Refer to Chapter 6.)

As used in a sentence: Me? Go GUI? Never! I'm a real man! Give me the DOS prompt any day!

IDE

What it stands for: Integrated Drive Environment (or Electronics).

Pronunciation: Letters only, I-D-E.

Meaning: A type of fast hard drive typically found on most laptop computers though popular on desktop systems, too.

As used in a sentence: Golly, those IDE drives are cheap and fast.

SCSI

What it stands for: Small Computer System Interface.

Pronunciation: Scuzzy (believe it or not).

Meaning: It's like a fast and versatile serial port onto which you can *chain* a variety of devices: hard drives, scanners, tape-backup systems, CD-ROM drives, and so on. The standard for hard drives on Macintoshes; common on PCs with large hard drives.

As used in a sentence: I never thought I'd pay that kind of money for a SCSI WORM drive.

TSR

What it stands for: Terminate and Stay Resident.

Pronunciation: Letters only, T-S-R.

Meaning: A special type of program that stays in memory after it quits. The *real* term is *memory-resident program,* though the marketing droids use the programmer's acronym instead (because they're in marketing and don't know much about real life). A TSR is a program that does something special: helps you use a mouse, gives you more control over your keyboard, or in some way augments what DOS does.

As used in a sentence: I loaded all my TSRs into UMBs, which saved me some 45K of conventional memory. Don't ask me how I did it, though. My brain hurts and I need more Ritz crackers with the brown-flavored stuff on top.

SVGA

What it stands for: Super VGA (Video Graphics Array).

Pronunciation: Sooper Vee Gee Ay, or letters only: S-V-G-A

Meaning: The current, top-o'-the-line in PC graphics. (Refer to "Graph-a-Bits Soup" in Chapter 9.)

As used in a sentence: Now that I have SVGA graphics, I can stop buying those forbidden magazines!

WYSIWYG

What it stands for: What You See Is What You Get.

Pronunciation: WIZZY-wig (yup, it's true).

Meaning: The stuff you see on the screen looks identical to the way it will appear when printed. Sort of.

As used in a sentence: The more you pay, the more WYSIWYG lives up to its name.

The 5th Wave

By Rich Tennant

"YES, I THINK IT'S AN ERROR MESSAGE."

Part VI
DOS Reference for Real People

The 5th Wave

In this part...

*I*s there really a need for a DOS reference for beginners? Yes. Don't think this is your standard DOS reference, such as those endless pages with cryptic notations muddying up your DOS manual. This reference contains three chapters: Chapter 28 contains a scenic tour of the key elements — the utilities — of DOS 6 and 6.2, the meat of this DOS sandwich. Chapter 29 has ten common DOS commands you may be using every day, with information on how they work. Chapter 30 contains commands beyond the everyday use of DOS beginners. This information is simply an explanation of what the command does; formatting and command examples have been cheerfully omitted.

Chapter 28
The MS-DOS 6
Scenic Tour

- -

In This Chapter

▶ Understanding DoubleSpace

▶ Using SmartDrive

▶ Feeling good about Defrag

▶ Talking PC-to-PC with InterLink

▶ Going on-the-road with Power

- -

*I*n DOSs of years past, the new version was often introduced with a few, feeble new DOS commands, some mild improvements on older commands, plus the ability to access some exciting new disk formats: DOS 3.0 heralded the age of the 1.2MB 5¼-inch floppy diskette; DOS 3.2, the 720K 3½-inch disk; DOS 3.3, the 1.4MB disk; DOS 5.0 the 2.8MB diskette. DOS 6.0? Hey! They ran out of disk formats!

Not to worry, MS-DOS version 6 comes with 'bout half a dozen cool programs that you wouldn't expect from dreary ol' DOS. These are heavy hitting programs — real doozies such as MSBackup, DoubleSpace, and Defrag. Before MS-DOS 6.0, you had to pay serious money to other people for that stuff. Now it comes "free" with DOS.

This chapter mentions several of the new utility programs that come with MS-DOS 6. A few of them have been discussed in detail elsewhere in this book. For example, you can find out about MSBackup in Chapters 17 and 20; Anti-Virus is discussed in Chapter 21. Other key utilities are right here, presented as a scenic bus tour of the DOS 6 countryside. Your bus driver is Virgil — ready with a joke and always friendly. Just don't talk to him while he's driving, thanks.

Day 1 — The DoubleSpace Expanse

Nothing is more beautiful than the wide open spaces. Lotsa room. Lotsa pretty things to see. The vista can be appreciated all the more when you come from an overcrowded, squeezy high-rent place with lots of people (and I'm comparing San Diego to Idaho in my head right now). This analogy applies to your hard drive as well. Nothing beats an empty hard drive and the joy you'll find filling it up with interesting stuff. That is, until the hard drive gets full and you're screaming for more space. When that happens, DoubleSpace is the thing you seek.

DoubleSpace is a *disk-compression* program. Its purpose is to give you more room — to *double the space* of — your hard drive. It does this by magic, more or less. The point is, DoubleSpace gives you more room when you're cramped for space, and it works without your having to think about it.

✔ DoubleSpace is *not* installed by the Setup program that brought MS-DOS 6 to your hard drive. You must set up DoubleSpace yourself, a task which is covered later in this chapter. But before doing that, be sure to read the next section.

✔ Chapter 17 contains some philosophical notes on disk compression, if the concept boggles you.

When it's time to run DoubleSpace

Obviously, if you have more room on your hard drive, you can store more stuff. Even so, I don't recommend running DoubleSpace for greed's sake. If you have room on your hard drive now, great. Otherwise, you'll probably be in one of the following situations where compressing a drive with DoubleSpace would apply:

1. **Space on the hard drive becomes scarce.**

   This situation applies to everyone. Refer to the techy note "How much space is left on your hard drive?" to see if you're ready for compression.

2. **You have room on the hard drive, but not enough to install that massive software package you're eyeballing.**

   Software packages list both RAM and disk space requirements on the side of the box. Say you have a comfortable 15MB of space on your drive, but the bloated package wants 20MB. Time to compress.

3. **You have a laptop computer with a puny hard drive.**

   Laptops are engineered for weight and battery life. The trade-off is usually a doinky hard drive that barely has enough room to run Windows. The solution is to use DoubleSpace and get more room *now*.

It's not always necessary to run DoubleSpace. Remember, disk compression is a solution to a problem, not a glorious benefit everyone needs. Memory management, backing up, and optimizing your hard drive are important things to do. DoubleSpace? It's a solution for a problem. No problem, no need to bother with DoubleSpace.

Misconceptions about DoubleSpace

Using DoubleSpace has few consequences. Rather than dwell on them, the following check marks discuss common DoubleSpace misconceptions:

✔ DoubleSpace may slow down your system. This isn't true for very fast computers, but then again, people with very fast computers don't worry about sluggish stuff anyway. Mere mortals who buy bargain basement systems (or inherit them) should probably expect a slight decrease in disk performance with DoubleSpace installed.

✔ There are nasty rumors afoot about DoubleSpace being unreliable. These rumors are unfounded. With MS-DOS 6.2, Microsoft has taken extra pains to ensure the safety of your files on a compressed drive. (Besides, the clowns who claimed DoubleSpace was unreliable didn't do their homework, in my opinion.)

✔ DoubleSpace can't be undone; you can't decompress your hard drive once you start. You're committed. Oh well. Again, this isn't true. MS-DOS 6.2's DoubleSpace has a decompress option should you suddenly feel that you don't need extra room on your hard drive.

✔ DoubleSpace is incompatible with some programs. Sadly, this is true. If any programs do have problems, they'll be listed in the README.TXT file that comes with MS-DOS 6.2.

Installing DoubleSpace

Compressing a drive involves two steps. First, you must install DoubleSpace. Second, you compress. Both of these steps are handled together when you first run DoubleSpace on your PC.

Before you do anything, it's a good idea to back up your hard drive. Refer to Chapter 17 for information on using MSBackup, the section "Backing up the whole hard drive, all of it."

How much space is left on your hard drive?

To discover how much space you have left on your hard drive, use the DIR command. The very last line reads *xxxx* (or however many gazillion) `bytes free`. That value, typically in the millions of bytes, tells you how much room is left on the drive. When you get down below 10 megabytes, it's time to consider compressing.

The best way to examine disk usage statistics is to run the MSD program that comes with MS-DOS 6. Type **MSD** at the command prompt; then

type **D** when you see the main panel displayed. This action selects `Disk Drives`, and you'll see a second panel that describes the disk usage statistics for your PC. In one column you'll find the disk's `Free Space` (the room you have left) and in another you'll see the `Total Size`, or how many bytes of stuff the drive can hold total. When the two values are far apart (15MB free versus 80MB total size), it's time to compress.

To install DoubleSpace on your system, type **DBLSPACE** at the DOS prompt:

```
C> DBLSPACE
```

DBLSPACE is the DoubleSpace command, and it illustrates just how artfully you can compress the word DoubleSpace into an eight-character filename.

You cannot install DoubleSpace if you already have a disk-compression program on your PC. Consult with your guru and discuss whether you should keep the old compression program or switch to DoubleSpace. Refer any gurus to the DoubleSpace section in the README.TXT file for more information.

After you type **DBLSPACE**, press Enter. The DoubleSpace program runs and displays all sorts of information, graphs, and such. The following tutorial steps you through the installation and compression process with a minimum of grief.

1. First comes the `Welcome to DoubleSpace Setup` program. Read the screen carefully and then press Enter to move along.

2. At the next screen, the `Express Setup (recommended)` item should be highlighted. If not, press the up-arrow key to highlight it. Read the screen (though I've just told you everything you need to know) and press Enter.

3. Because you already backed up, the warning displayed next is of little consequence. Press **C** to continue.

4. Finally, to start compressing, type **C** again. This begins the compression process for drive C. Press C to compress drive C, see?

5. The first step is to run the ScanDisk program to ensure that drive C is up to snuff and is compatible with DoubleSpace. If any errors are reported, fix them and continue, reading the instructions on the screen as they're encountered. If the errors are of a drastic type, don't bother with DoubleSpace on the drive. Instead, consider buying a replacement hard drive of a larger capacity. A guy with lots of teeth at your local computer store has all the details.

6. Golly! DoubleSpace resets your computer. Don't panic. (And if it doesn't reset after a time, say a minute or two, help it along by pressing Ctrl-Alt-Delete.)

7. The compression screen finally appears, complete with a mediocre estimate of the time DoubleSpace will take to compress your drive, along with the handy thermometer motif. Hey, this may take some time — especially if you have a large hard drive brimming with files. Relax. Empty your waste basket. Have a cup of coffee. Drive to New Jersey.

8. Lo, after compression is done, the Defrag program is run to optimize the newly compressed drive. Lots of poking and plodding follow.

9. Finally, you see the resultant compression screen. On my system it says I had 30 megabytes free before DoubleSpace and a whopping 60 megs free afterwards. DoubleSpace lived up to its name and doubled the size of my hard drive.

10. Press Enter. DoubleSpace will reset once more and you're done.

- After installing DoubleSpace, run MemMaker to reoptimize your computer's memory. Refer to the section in Chapter 8, "Managing Memory."

- DoubleSpace takes a long time to compress files. To shrink all the files on a full hard drive, plan on sitting there for several hours. Or — here's a better idea — run DoubleSpace overnight.

- After DoubleSpace is done, you'll have a larger hard drive! Use the DIR command to see how many more `bytes free` you have. You can continue to use your computer as before. There's nothing more, nothing mental. Refer to Chapter 17 for additional information on working with hard drives and compressed drives in particular.

- Refer back to the README.TXT file that came with MS-DOS 6 for additional information on DoubleSpace — especially if you have any problems or questions. It may be a good idea to direct your guru to examine the information as it can be quite technical.

- DoubleSpace doesn't really double your hard drive storage space. No, it's really more like OnePointEightSpace. Don't be disappointed if you end up storing only a few more megabytes of information on your hard drive — not the "doubled" capacity DoubleSpace boasts of. The end result is still more storage than if you hadn't used DoubleSpace, so be glad.

New things to wonder about after DoubleSpacing

Running some of DOS's disk commands subtly changes when you work with a compressed drive. The following list touches upon a few of these changes:

- ✔ The ScanDisk program will now recommend that you check the "host drive" as well as the compressed drive. No problem; press Enter to select the Yes option and use ScanDisk as before. Refer to Chapter 17 for more information on using ScanDisk.

- ✔ Using ScanDisk on a compressed drive causes DOS to check a few more items about the drive. This is nothing to worry about; it's just DOS being careful with your files.

- ✔ When you back up your hard drive, back up the same way you did before. Don't bother with backing up the "host drive" or the CVF or anything more technical than that. (Chapter 17 contains information on backing up as well as info on ScanDisk.)

- ✔ Never ever delete any file that starts with DBLSPACE. I won't forgive you if you do this.

- ✔ The FDISK program will not recognize your compressed drives. You shouldn't be using the FDISK program, anyhoo.

- ✔ Do not use the FORMAT command on your DoubleSpace drive. Indeed, I recommend only using FORMAT to format floppy disks in drives A or B, not with any hard drive or compressed drive.

- ✔ Don't bother trying to use DoubleSpace to compress a RAM drive.

- ✔ There's no need to tinker with SMARTDrive when you have compressed drives on your PC. The version of SMARTDrive included with MS-DOS 6.2 is very keen on DoubleSpace. (SMARTDrive is discussed later in this chapter.)

Using the DoubleSpace program

Having a compressed, DoubleSpace drive on your PC means nothing new, nothing mental. But if you feel the urge, you can run the full-screen DoubleSpace program to manage and examine your compressed drives, as well as create other compressed drives. To do so, type **DBLSPACE** at the DOS prompt:

```
C> DBLSPACE
```

After pressing Enter, you'll see the full-screen DoubleSpace compressed disk management program, as shown in Figure 28-1. If you have a mouse, you can use it to access the menu commands and poke and prod around. Otherwise, the Alt key works to get at the menus; press Alt and the first letter of the menu item you want, such as Alt-T to get at the Tools menu.

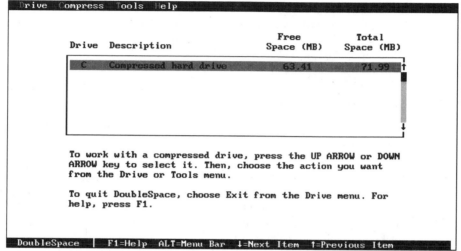

Figure 28-1:
The full-screen DoubleSpace program in all its glory.

✔ The full-screen DoubleSpace program will not run unless you've installed DoubleSpace on your computer.

✔ There are lots of interesting things you can do with the full-screen DoubleSpace program, most of which could fill an entire book. Fortunately, the program has a handy F1 help key to lead you through everything should you need help.

✔ Press Alt-D and then X to quit the DoubleSpace program. This action just quits the program; it doesn't decompress your hard drive.

✔ If you decide that DoubleSpace is not for you, highlight your compressed drive and select the Uncompress command from the Tools menu. But first — back up! Then, when you select the command, read the various panels displayed to continue. (I heartily recommend that you have your guru do this because uncompressing isn't a casual thing.)

Restoring an obliterated DoubleSpace drive

DoubleSpace is somehow gone. You start the computer and see nothing! Or you notice that all your files are gone. Or maybe you get an oddball error message and then a really boring DOS prompt. This should never happen to you, but if it does, you're not totally alone and lost in the wilderness. For goodness sake, put away that gun.

After losing a DoubleSpace drive, do not do the following:

1. Panic.

2. FORMAT.

3. FDISK.

Your first step should be to reset the computer. Remove any floppy disk from drive A. Press Ctrl-Alt-Delete. Pray to your chosen deity.

If that doesn't work, try using the UNDELETE command on your hard drive to try and rescue DoubleSpace and its associated highly secret files. Alas, the UNDELETE command was probably zapped with everything else. If possible, get a friend or your guru to build you a floppy boot disk with a copy of the UNDELETE.EXE program file on it. Then you can try the following command after starting your PC with that disk in drive A:

```
A> UNDELETE C:\*.*
```

That's UNDELETE, a space, C, colon, backslash, asterisk, period, asterisk. This plan may or may not work, depending on what went goofy with DoubleSpace and your hard drive.

Your second resort, and the one with the highest chances of success, is to reinstall MS-DOS 6.2 on the hard drive, reinstall DoubleSpace, and then restore from a recent backup diskette using MSBackup. This process is more involved, but not complex. And it works best when you back up often.

First, run the Setup program. Second, run DoubleSpace as discussed earlier in this chapter. Third, restore from your latest full hard disk backup, as described in Chapter 20's section, "Restoring from a backup." This will get you back to where you were the last time you backed up.

Day 2 — The Seaside SMARTDrive Disk Cache

Just up ahead you'll see the magnificent sea cliffs which just happen to be located by the disk drive ocean. Rumor has it pirates sailed these waters recently. Somewhere up in those cliffs they buried treasure and other booty. Yes, there must be a whole *cache* of stuff up there, which works for the pirates because they have so much trouble opening bank accounts.

MS-DOS 6 comes with a program that improves the performance of your disk drives. The SMARTDrive program is a disk cache (pronounced *cash*). What it does and how it does it aren't important. The end result of using SMARTDrive is that your disk drives seem faster — almost instantaneous at times.

- ✔ SMARTDrive requires extended memory to work. Refer to Chapter 8 for a discussion of extended memory.

- ✔ In addition to extended memory, you also need an extended memory manager (XMS) installed on your PC, such as DOS's HIMEM.SYS file. This can be done for you if it hasn't already; refer to "Managing Memory" in Chapter 8.

- ✔ The disk cache SMARTDrive sets up is different from any hardware cache your PC may already have. For example, your microprocessor may have a 256K cache, or your hard disk controller may have a cache.

- ✔ To see how much extended memory you have, run the MSD program that comes with DOS 6. Look by the `Memory` button just after the program starts, and you'll see a value such as `3328K Ext`. That means that you have 3328 kilobytes of extended memory in your PC (or whatever it says on your screen). You need at least 256K of extended memory to take advantage of SMARTDrive. (Refer to Chapter 21 for more info on MSD.)

Checking out SMARTDrive

The SMARTDrive disk cache is definitely not a pain to set up. In fact, the Setup program has probably done all the work for you. (See? This is so easy I don't know why I bother writing these books. . . .)

Start by running the DOS Editor, as described in Chapter 16. You'll need to edit your AUTOEXEC.BAT file. Here is the command to type that does that:

```
C> EDIT C:\AUTOEXEC.BAT
```

That's EDIT, a space, C, colon, backslash, and then AUTOEXEC.BAT. Press Enter. In moments the Editor appears on your screen with the contents of your PC's AUTOEXEC.BAT file displayed (see Figure 28-2).

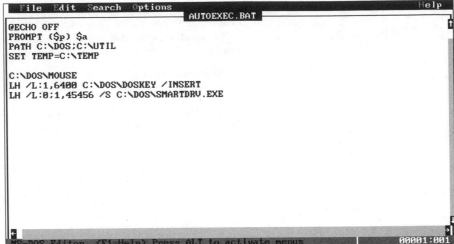

Figure 28-2:
The Editor
ready for
you to
monkey with
AUTOEXEC.BAT.

Scour the file, looking for the following text:

```
C:\DOS\SMARTDRV.EXE/X
```

That's the command that loads the SMARTDrive disk cache into memory. The command itself may look different. For example, Figure 28-2 shows the following:

```
LH /L:0;1,45456 /S C:\DOS\SMARTDRV.EXE
```

Cryptic stuff, eh? That LH and number stuff is extra PC spaghetti added by MemMaker as it massaged memory and found a proper hiding place for SMARTDrive. If you've run MemMaker (or a third-party memory manager), you'll probably see something similar hovering before SMARTDRV.EXE. Or if someone has stuck the SMARTDRV.EXE file in another directory, you may see it there instead.

And now the good news: Because you've found SMARTDrive in your AUTOEXEC.BAT file, you're done. There's nothing else to do here, other than swell with that PC-induced pride you get from knowing that something was already done for you. Ahhh.

- ✔ If SMARTDrive isn't to be found in AUTOEXEC.BAT, refer to the next section.

- ✔ Information on using the SMARTDRV command is found in the section coincidentally called "Using the SMARTDRV command."

- ✔ You need only *one* copy of SMARTDRV.EXE in AUTOEXEC.BAT. If you see several lines that contain the SMARTDRV.EXE program name, delete all but the first one. Run MemMaker again (see Chapter 8).

✔ Do not delete, edit, or otherwise mess with the information MemMaker sticks in front of SMARTDRV.EXE!

✔ SMARTDRV may also be found in your CONFIG.SYS file. Refer to the box "All about the Double Buffering nonsense" for more information.

Installing SMARTDrive

1. Are you in the Editor? If not, read through the previous section.

2. Make one last attempt to find the SMARTDrive command. Press Alt-S and then F to activate the Editor's Find command. Into the Find What box, type **SMARTDRV**. Double-check what you've typed and then press Enter.

3. If SMARTDRV, the SMARTDrive command, is to be found in AUTOEXEC.BAT, it will appear highlighted on your screen. If so, re-read the previous section. If not, you'll see a box displayed proclaiming Match not found. Press the Esc key.

4. Now you're going to add the SMARTDRV.EXE command to your AUTOEXEC.BAT file.

5. Press the Ctrl-End key combination. This moves you to the end of the AUTOEXEC.BAT file.

6. Press Enter. This starts you off on a new line.

7. Type the following:

```
C:\DOS\SMARTDRV.EXE/X
```

That's the letter C, colon, backslash, DOS, another backslash, and then SMARTDRV, a period, EXE and then /X. No spaces!

8. If you've installed DOS 6 into a subdirectory other than C:\DOS, substitute that directory's pathname for C:\DOS. Actually, if you're nerdy enough to do that, you've probably already made that correction.

9. Press Enter to end the line.

10. Save AUTOEXEC.BAT back to disk. Press Alt-F and then S to select the Save command.

11. Quit the Editor. Press Alt-F and then X to select the Exit command.

12. When you're back at the DOS prompt again, reset your PC. You must do this to "load" the new copy of AUTOEXEC.BAT and run the SMARTDrive disk cache.

- Refer to Chapter 16 for more information on the Editor and editing AUTOEXEC.BAT.

- SMARTDrive will not display superfluous text on the screen the next time you start or reset your computer. If you're eager to see such information, add a space and /V (slash-V, for *verbose*) to the SMARTDRV line in AUTOEXEC.BAT.

- After SMARTDrive is installed, there's nothing else to worry about. It works every time you turn on your computer.

- You should run MemMaker after adding the SMARTDRV.EXE command to your AUTOEXEC.BAT file. Refer to the section in Chapter 8, "Managing Memory."

- If your system already has a disk cache installed, contact your guru for help in removing it and replacing it with SMARTDrive. (Or just ask him or her if that's a sensible thing to do.)

Using the SMARTDRV command

To prove that SMARTDrive really does something for you, type the following at a handy DOS prompt:

```
C> SMARTDRV /S
```

That's the SMARTDRV command (O blessed be the eight-character filename!) followed by a space and then slash-S. After you press Enter, DOS displays a list of information and vital statistics about SMARTDrive. Of interest are two items near the middle of the list:

```
There have been 294 cache hits
and 126 cache misses
```

These two values show how well SMARTDrive is improving disk performance. The ratio of *cache hits* to *cache misses* tells you how much "faster" your disk drives have become thanks to SMARTDrive. Above, 294 cache hits tells you that 294 times DOS has relied on SMARTDrive for faster disk access. The relatively low cache misses values is another good sign that SMARTDrive has improved your disk performance.

- Don't let the "hits" and "misses" terminology throw you. Nothing is wrong with your system if you have cache misses. It just means that a lot of loose disk shrapnel is flinging around inside your PC. Wear eye goggles if this concerns you. (I'm kidding.)

All about the Double Buffering nonsense

Occasionally, the SMARTDRV.EXE command finds its way into your CONFIG.SYS file. Indeed, it may even be there already in the following format (or one similar):

```
DEVICE=C:\DOS\SMARTDRV.EXE\DOUBLE_BUFFER
```

The Double Buffer option has nothing to do with SMARTDrive's disk cache. Instead, it's a separate program designed to make life easier for certain hard disk technology and MS-DOS memory management (advanced concepts that NASA scientists are only now able to grasp).

Not everyone needs the preceding command in CONFIG.SYS. Only if you're using a SCSI or ESDI hard disk controller will this be necessary. If it concerns you, follow these steps and you'll be certain:

1. Add the preceding command to your CONFIG.SYS file. Refer to Chapter 16, "It tells me to update my CONFIG.SYS or AUTOEXEC.BAT file!" for the details.

2. After changing CONFIG.SYS, save it to disk and then, once you see the DOS prompt again, reset your system. Refer to Chapter 1 for more information on resetting.

3. Back at the DOS prompt after resetting, type **SMARTDRV** and press Enter.

4. In the SMARTDRV command's output, look at the third column under buffering.

5. If you see a yes in the buffering column, you need the SMARTDRV Double Buffering command in CONFIG.SYS. If not, you can delete that line from CONFIG.SYS.

Day 3 — The Defrag Jungle

It can be a real jungle out there. Wild. Untamed. A lot like a bad case of bed-head. But it's not your hair I'm talking about. It's your hard drive. Let alone, your hard drive becomes a messy place, thanks to the somewhat sloppy job DOS does storing files on your hard drive. The solution is to run a disk optimizer utility, such as the Defrag program that comes with MS-DOS 6.

Defrag is easy to use. Just type **DEFRAG** at the DOS prompt:

```
C> DEFRAG
```

Press Enter and you'll see the full-screen Defrag program displayed, looking similar to Figure 28-3.

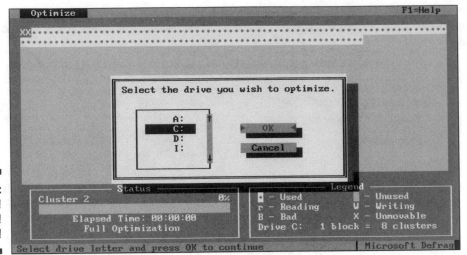

Figure 28-3:
Look, Boss!
Defrag!
Defrag!

To use Defrag, follow these steps:

1. Select a disk drive to optimize. Press Enter to optimize drive C, or use the up- or down-arrow keys to highlight a specific disk drive.

2. Defrag displays its *recommendation*. Thank you, Defrag.

   If Defrag proclaims No optimization necessary, press the Esc key and then Alt-X to exit and return to the DOS prompt.

3. Press Enter to select the Optimize button-thing on the screen.

4. Enjoy the pleasing graphical display as Defrag buffs out your disk. This may take some time.

5. *Dee-dee!* Defrag is done. Press the Esc key.

6. You may select to optimize another disk drive, configure, or quit. Select Another Drive if you have more than one hard drive. When you're done optimizing all your hard drives, select Exit DEFRAG.

   - Defrag is short for *defragmentation*. Fragmentation is what happens to your files as DOS stores them on a hard drive. It's not a negative thing; without it your hard drive would fill up quickly. Defrag combats fragmentation and gives you an optimized hard drive.

   - Running Defrag every once in a while improves disk performance. How often? About once a month should do it. Defrag isn't voodoo, so running it all the time doesn't make your hard drive spin with the uncontrollable fever of a hurricane.

   - You cannot run Defrag while you're running Microsoft Windows. Instead, quit Windows and type **DEFRAG** at a convenient DOS prompt.

Day 4 — The InterLink Isthmus

An isthmus is a narrow strip of land connecting two larger pieces of land. Or it's a narrow strip of land separating one huge body of water. The word is Greek and comes from the spot in Greece where the lower part (the Peloponnesus) is connected to the upper part (the Upperponnisos). Of course, long ago the Greeks cut a canal through it, so I guess my point is lost here. However, the isthmus concept ties in nicely with the InterLink program, which allows you to connect two PCs together for chatting and tea, using only a thin Greek-like cable.

DOS 6 comes with the InterLink programs, which allow you to connect two PCs together for file swapping, and disk drive and printer sharing. Yes, it's a lot like love. But while DOS comes with InterLink, you'll need to fish up the special cable to connect two PCs.

- ✔ Typically, you use InterLink to connect your desktop PC to a laptop model. However, Interlink can also be used to connect two desktop PCs.

- ✔ InterLink is a you-must-be-there program. You cannot use InterLink to connect to another computer over phone lines or through mental telepathy.

- ✔ InterLink actually works sort of like a mini-network. Not only can you use two computers' hard drives at once (for copying files or running programs), but you can also use the other computer's printer.

Finding that cable

The cable you need to use InterLink is called a *null modem cable*. Most computer stores carry several models. Be sure that the connectors on either end of the cable match the various rump connectors on the back of your two PCs.

- ✔ InterLink can talk using either serial or parallel ports. Serial ports are the most popular. Refer to Chapter 7 for more information on ports.

- ✔ You can also use a null modem *adapter* to connect two PCs for InterLinking. You need a standard serial cable, but you must plug the adapter into the cable and then into the second PC. Actually, getting the null modem cable is a better idea.

- ✔ If you're really nuts, you can build your own InterLink cable. Type **HELP CABLE** at the DOS prompt and then press the PgDn key a few times until you see `Pin Connections for a Serial Cable`. Strange stuff, eh?

Putting InterLink to the test

Setting up InterLink is the real hard part; using it is a snap. This is advanced stuff here, so I'll explain it in a sketchy manner to force you to get your guru to set things up for you.

Start by putting the INTERLNK.EXE device driver into your CONFIG.SYS file on the first PC. You'll need a line similar to the following:

```
DEVICE=C:\DOS\INTERLNK.EXE
```

Study the rules for editing CONFIG.SYS in Chapter 16. Remember to save CONFIG.SYS to disk after editing it and then reset your computer.

Next, connect the two PCs using the proper serial cable. Plug the cable into COM1 (the first serial port) on both PCs, connecting them.

Finally, on the second PC, type the INTERSVR command at the DOS prompt:

```
C> INTERSVR
```

After you press Enter, the second PC displays a "connection" screen. On the first PC, you'll now have access to the disk drives and printers on the second PC.

✔ You use the disk drives and printer on the second PC just as if they were part of the first PC's equipment list. You can copy files with the COPY command, run programs on the second PC's hard drive, and use its printer.

✔ To see a list of drive connections, plus the new drive letters for the first PC, type **INTERLNK** at the DOS prompt and press Enter.

✔ To break the connection, quit any programs you're running and log back to drive C on the first PC. Press Alt-F4 on the second PC. This breaks the connection. You may want to reset the first PC after doing this.

✔ No, you can't use both computers while they're InterLinked; you can only work with the first PC's keyboard and screen.

✔ Can you connect a Macintosh to your PC using InterLink? What? Are you daft?

✔ See? Isn't this technical stuff? Actually, InterLink is a specific program to solve a specific problem: exchanging files between two PCs. For example, if you just bought a PC and needed to copy all your old data files to it, you could use InterLink.

Day 5 — The Power Precipice

The last day of your MS-DOS 6 tour takes you to the Power precipice. A perilous place where laptop computers are heaved into the unknown blackness, empty and out of juice. Fortunately, the POWER command helps rescue these computers from an untimely death.

If you're on the road with a DOS laptop computer, you want your battery to last as long as possible. The POWER command may — it just may — be able to give you another, oh, say 5 to 15 minutes of extra computing time. Think of the work you'll be able to do!

Before you press on, note these two valid arguments *against* the POWER command:

1. It only works on laptop computers. Desktop PCs? Hey, no battery, no POWER command.

2. The POWER command works best with laptops that are *APM* (Advanced Power Management) compatible. If your laptop isn't compatible, the battery savings are scant.

   (OK, these aren't arguments "against" POWER. They're just two things you should take into consideration should you suppose that somehow the POWER command will open the floodgates of PC potency on any computer. Not so.)

Giving your laptop the POWER

To use the POWER command with your laptop, you must make a modification to your PC's CONFIG.SYS file. Refer to Chapter 16 for the details. The line you need to add to CONFIG.SYS is as follows:

```
DEVICE=C:\DOS\POWER.EXE
```

That's DEVICE, an equal sign, C, colon, backslash, DOS, another backslash, POWER, period, and then EXE. There are no spaces in that command. Double-check it and then press Enter.

- ✔ Alas, this just won't work to increase the battery life of your cellular phone. But, hey, get a life.

- ✔ Remember to save CONFIG.SYS to disk, exit the DOS Editor, and then reset your laptop. You must do this before you can start using the POWER command.

- ✔ It's a good idea to run MemMaker after resetting your PC. Refer to "Managing Memory" in Chapter 8 for the details and stuff.

Using the POWER command

After the POWER.EXE command is installed in CONFIG.SYS, you can use the POWER command at the DOS prompt to monitor how your laptop is consuming battery juice. For example:

```
C> POWER
```

Type **POWER** and then press Enter. You may see output similar to the following:

```
Power Management Status

- - - - - - - - - - - - - - - - - - - - - -

Setting =  ADV: REG

CPU: idle 51% of time.

AC Line Status : OFFLINE

Battery status : High

Battery life (%) :

100
```

The last line is the most important. It tells you how "full" the battery is. When the value drops down to 40 percent, you're running on near-fumes. (Like a gas gauge, it seems to stay at full, or 100 percent, for a long time and then drops rapidly.)

- ✔ If you don't have an APM laptop, the output you see will be brief and uninformative.

- ✔ When the laptop is plugged into a power socket, the battery information is not displayed. Like . . . duh!

- ✔ Alas, there's nothing you can do for a dwindling power supply. Try not to use your modem or, if you have one, a floppy drive. Those things use lots of juice. And if you have a "backlit" display on your laptop, shut it off. Sadly, that step only prolongs the inevitable. (I predict airplanes will soon come with power jacks for laptop users. Maybe only in first class.)

Day 6 — End of the Tour!

Hey, everyone! Thanks for taking the MS-DOS 6 Tour. Please take this time to fill in the response cards to tell us how much you enjoyed the trip, or let us know which areas could stand some improvement. Also, please keep in mind that at no time did someone climb on board and hand out "free" Cokes only to come back moments later and charge everyone a buck for them.

> ✔ May your journeys be without incident.

> ✔ *Booooooon* appetito!

Chapter 29
DOS Commands You Can Use (the Top Ten)

- -

In This Chapter

▶ CD

▶ CLS

▶ COPY

▶ DEL

▶ DIR

▶ DISKCOPY

▶ FORMAT

▶ MORE

▶ REN

▶ TYPE

- -

*T*here are a few DOS commands mentioned more than once in this book. I've added a few more to round the number out to ten.

You'll probably use other DOS commands with as much frequency as some of these. They're listed in the following chapter, along with every other DOS command whether you'll use them or not. But here are the ones most people find the most useful.

The CD Command

Purpose: To display the pathname of the current directory.

Sample: CD

Comments: Type **CD**, and you'll see the name of the current drive and directory — the pathname — displayed. That name tells you where you are in the maze of your hard drive structure.

Other purpose: To change to another directory.

Sample: `CD \WP51\DATA`

Comments: The CD command is followed by a space and the full name of the directory to which you're changing. The directory's pathname usually *starts* with a backslash but doesn't *end* with a backslash.

Where to look: "Changing Directories" in Chapter 2; almost all of Chapter 17; "Finding a Lost Subdirectory" in Chapter 18.

A longer version of this command is CHDIR. Both CD and CHDIR do the same thing; CHDIR was just designed for large bureaucracies, where typing must take longer to occupy time that would otherwise be spent being efficient.

The CLS Command

Purpose: To clear the screen.

Sample: `CLS`

Comments: CLS clears the screen, erasing the display and any embarrassing error messages that may be glowing therein. Simple enough.

The COPY Command

Purpose: To make a copy or duplicate of a file.

Sample: `COPY C:FILE1 A:FILE2`

Where to look: "Duplicating a File," "Copying a Single File," "Copying a File to You," "Copying a Group of Files," and "Moving a File," all in Chapter 4; you may also want to check "What Is a Pathname?" in Chapter 17 and "Wildcards (or Poker Was Never This Much Fun)" in Chapter 18.

The general rule here: First comes the location and name of the file you're copying, and then the location and name of the copy you're making. If you're already logged to the source or the destination, you can leave that location off, but if that's confusing, just give the entire location (the "pathname") for both halves of the command.

Give the entire pathname; for example:

```
C> COPY C:\WP51\DATA\FILE\ A:\FILE1
```

This command copies FILE1 from drive C to drive A. You *can* change the name of the copy — and if you're making a copy to the same place as the original, you *have to* change the name.

The DEL Command

Purpose: To delete one or more files, eliminating them from a disk and freeing up the space they used.

Sample: `DEL USELESS.TXT`

Or: `DEL *.BAK`

Comments: The DEL command totally zaps a single file (or a group of files if you use a wildcard). This practice is necessary to eliminate older files and to give yourself more disk space.

A handy trick to use with the DEL command is to tack on the /P (slash-P) switch. For example:

```
DEL *.* /P
```

This command directs DOS to prompt you, yes-or-no, for each file deleted:

```
C:\COMMAND.COM Delete (Y/N)?
```

Type **Y** to delete the file or **N** to save it from certain peril.

Where to look: "Deleting a File," "Deleting a Group of Files," and "Moving a File" in Chapter 4; also in Chapter 4 you may want to peek at "Undeleting a File." Check out "What Is a Pathname?" in Chapter 17 and "Wildcards (or Poker Was Never This Much Fun)" in Chapter 18; also see "The Perils of DEL *.*" in Chapter 20.

DEL has a twin brother, ERASE. Both DEL and ERASE do the same thing: ruthlessly kill files. The ERASE command was implemented for certain south-paw extremist groups because you don't need the right hand to type it.

The DIR Command

Purpose: To display a list of files on disk.

Sample: `DIR`

Or: `DIR C:`

Or: `DIR C:\WP60`

Comments: DIR is probably the most common DOS command, and it's the only way to look at the files you have on disk. You can see a list of files on any drive or in any subdirectory by following the DIR command with the drive letter or subdirectory pathname.

Where to look: "The DIR Command" in Chapter 2; "That Funny <DIR> Thing" in Chapter 17; "Using the DIR Command," "The wide DIR command," and "Displaying a sorted directory," all in Chapter 18.

The DISKCOPY Command

Purpose: To make an exact duplicate of a floppy disk.

Sample: `DISKCOPY A: B:`

Or: `DISKCOPY A: A:`

Comments: This command makes an *exact* copy of a disk. Both drives A and B have to be the same kind (physical size and capacity). If not (or if you only have one floppy drive), type **DISKCOPY A: A:**; DOS will copy the disk in drive A and then prompt you to swap in a blank disk for the copy.

Where to look: "Duplicating Disks (the DISKCOPY Command)" in Chapter 13.

The FORMAT Command

Purpose: To prepare floppy disks for use.

Sample: `FORMAT A:`

Comments: All disks must be formatted before you can use them. The FORMAT command must be followed by the drive letter (and a colon) of the floppy drive containing the disk to be formatted. *Never* use the FORMAT command with any drive letter higher than B.

Where to look: "Formatting a Disk" and "Formatting a Low-Capacity Disk in a High-Capacity Drive" in Chapter 13. Also look up "Reformatting Disks" in Chapter 13.

The MORE Command

Purpose: To view text files one screen at a time.

Sample: `MORE < FILENAME`

Comments: The MORE command is followed by a space, a less-than symbol (<), another space, and then the name of a text file you want to view. At the end of each screen you'll see the *more* prompt; press the spacebar to see the next screen. Press Ctrl-C to cancel.

Where to look: Refer to "Looking at Files" in Chapter 2; "The Tree Structure" in Chapter 17 discusses another interesting use of the MORE command; also look at the TYPE command in this chapter.

The REN Command

Purpose: To rename a file, giving it a new name without changing its contents.

Sample: `REN OLDNAME NEWNAME`

Comments: What's to comment? Just follow the DOS naming rules. DOS will object if you try to give the file the same name as another file in the same directory.

Where to look: "Renaming a File" in Chapter 4; also "Name That File!" in Chapter 18.

If you think REN is really the name of a cartoon character, you can use the longer version of this command, RENAME. Both REN and STIMP, er, RENAME do the same thing.

The TYPE Command

Purpose: To display a file on the screen, enabling you to read its contents.

Sample: `TYPE STUFF.DOC`

Comments: The TYPE command displays any file you name, though only files that contain readable text can be understood by humans. If the file displays as *garbage,* press Ctrl-C to cancel the TYPE command.

Where to look: "Looking at Files" in Chapter 2.

Chapter 30
Beyond DOS Commands You Can Use (the Other 50 or So)

· ·

In This Chapter

Here is a list of some more DOS commands. You may want to use some of these from time to time (but they didn't make the top-ten list in the previous chapter). The rest of these commands others can use. They're useful, but they won't be covered here as they are beyond the scope of the book.

Each command is briefly described. If necessary, a reference is made to the command elsewhere in this text. Otherwise, I just poke fun at it and leave it at that.

Full details on all the MS-DOS 6.2 commands are found in the on-line help included with MS-DOS — the HELP command. Refer to Chapter 21 for more information.

· ·

Commands You May Occasionally Use

BACKUP   This is the old backup command for DOS versions prior to 6.0. If you have DOS 6, use the MSBACKUP command instead; see Chapter 17.

CHKDSK   This command reports the status of a disk, how many files are on it, and how much of the disk is used by what. It can also check to see if there are lost file clusters, which you should immediately destroy. CHKDSK is covered in "Checking the Disk (the CHKDSK Command)" and "CHKDSK says I have lost files in clusters or something" in Chapter 17. This command has been supplanted by ScanDisk with MS-DOS 6.2.

COMP   The COMP command compares the contents of two files line by line and tells you if they're identical. This goes into detail beyond just comparing a file's name and its size by liiking at it using the DIR command. (This command is not included in DOS 6; use the more cryptic FC command instead.)

DATE   This command displays the current date (according to the computer, at least) and gives you the opportunity to enter a new date. See "The Date and Time" in Chapter 7.

DEFRAG — The DEFGRAG command is actually a disk tune-up program you should run every so often to ensure your hard drive is up to snuff. Refer to Chapter 28.

DBLSPACE — The DBLSPACE command runs your DOS Disk Compression Headquarters. Refer to Chapter 28 for everything you want to know about DoubleSpace.

EDIT — The EDIT "command" runs the DOS Editor program, which you can use to create and edit text files on disk. Refer to Chapter 16 for your editing pleasure.

FC — FC stands for *file compare*. Unlike the old COMP command, FC offers more detailed descriptions of the differences between two files, and it's not as chicken about looking at files as the COMP command was (and it's the only way to compare files under DOS 6).

HELP — This is the DOS 6 on-line help command, the one that lists the full details of all the commands covered in this and the previous chapter. Refer to Chapter 21 for all you want to know about getting help.

INTERLNK — The InterLink programs, INTERLNK and INTERSVR, are covered in Chapter 28. These commands allow you to swap files between two PCs using a simple cable you construct using loose hair strands and pieces of spaghetti.

MD — The MD (also MKDIR) command is used to make a subdirectory. Refer to "How to Name a Directory (the MKDIR Command)" in Chapter 18.

MEMMAKER — This is DOS's memory management command, painlessly covered in Chapter 8.

MODE — The MODE command configures a variety of things on your computer: the screen, keyboard, serial ports, printer, and so on. Refer to "Which Do I Have?" and "Funky Displays" in Chapter 9; "Controlling the Keyboard" in Chapter 10; and "The serial connection" in Chapter 11.

MOVE — The MOVE command moves a file or group of files from one place to another. It works like a combined COPY-DEL command; you first COPY files to another place, and then you thoughtlessly slaughter the originals. See "Moving a File" in Chapter 4.

MSAV   The Microsoft Anti-Virus command, MSAV, as well as information on fighting the viral plague, is divvied up in Chapter 28.

MSBACKUP   This command is used to archive files from your hard disk to several floppy disks. Its use is covered in Chapter 17.

MSD   The Microsoft Diagnostic program — a true PC privacy peeker — is discussed covertly in Chapter 21.

PATH   The PATH command creates the DOS *search path*, which is a list of one or more subdirectories in which DOS will look for programs to run. It goes in your AUTOEXEC.BAT file that runs when you turn on the computer.

POWER   The laptop PC power saving and management program POWER is touched upon in Chapter 28.

PROMPT   This command changes the appearance of the DOS prompt. Refer to "Prompt Styles of the Rich and Famous" in Chapter 3.

RESTORE   The RESTORE command is used to copy files from a backup disk back onto your hard drive — but only for the old BACKUP command. With MS-DOS 6.2, the MSBACKUP command handles this job. Refer to "I Just Deleted an Entire Subdirectory!" and "Restoring from a Backup" in Chapter 20.

SCANDISK   MS-DOS 6.2's ultra-keen disk check-up tool, ScanDisk will find and repair any disk maladies you may have, hard or floppy disks no problem. Refer to Chapter 17 for the full details.

TIME   This command displays what DOS thinks is the current time and gives you the chance to enter a new time whenever you want. Refer to "The Date and Time" in Chapter 7.

TREE   The TREE command displays a "visual" representation of your hard drive's tree structure — a map of your subdirectories. Refer to Chapter 17 for an example.

UNDELETE   This command rescues files back from the brink, safely recovering stuff you deleted too quickly. Refer to Chapter 4.

UNFORMAT   Another lifesaver, the UNFORMAT command undoes whatever it is the FORMAT command does to a disk. (Of course, being careful with the FORMAT command in the first place always helps.) See Chapter 20.

VER   The VER command displays DOS's name and the version number. Refer to "Names and Versions" in Chapter 3.

VOL | This command displays a disk's volume label. Refer to "Changing the Volume Label" in Chapter 13.

XCOPY | This is like a super COPY command; much faster and smarter than the plain old COPY command. You can use XCOPY as a straight-across substitute for the COPY command if you like. It even copies subdirectories! Wow, this modern age.

Commands You May See Others Use

APPEND | Weird command. Like the PATH command (listed earlier), this command enables DOS to look in other subdirectories to find data files. It's not really as keen as it sounds and generally causes more trouble than it's worth. An older command best avoided.

ASSIGN | The ASSIGN command forces DOS to ignore one disk drive, replacing it with another. For example, if you don't have a drive B, yet some idiot program insists on saving stuff there, you can use the ASSIGN command to tell the program to look on drive A instead. Programs can be so dumb. (This command is no longer included with DOS 6; you use the SUBST command instead.)

ATTRIB | This command changes a file's attributes, which describe how DOS can treat a file. Refer to "The File! I Cannot Kill It" in Chapter 4.

BREAK | The BREAK command turns special Ctrl-C and Ctrl-Break testing on or off. With it on, Ctrl-C may be a little more responsive; with it off, your computer runs faster.

CALL | This is a batch file command used in batch file programming. The CALL command runs a second batch file from within another batch file.

CHOICE | This batch file command waits for a certain key to be pressed. It's really quite cool if you're into batch files. Ignore it otherwise.

COMMAND | The COMMAND command is actually DOS, the program you use when you work on your PC (it's COMMAND.COM). Never delete this program.

DISKCOMP | This command compares two disks to see if they're identical. Because the DISKCOPY command is very reliable, this command is a colossal waste of time.

DOSKEY
The DOSKEY command runs a special keyboard enhancer that gives you more editing power and control over the command line. This can be a fun and useful tool, but it's a little too advanced for this book.

ECHO
This is a special batch file command that displays information on the screen, usually the line of text following ECHO. You can use this command to eject a page of paper from your printer; refer to "Form Feeding" in Chapter 11.

EMM386
This command controls DOS's expanded memory manager for 386, 486, and other advanced microprocessors. There's no point in messing with it, though official memory management information is presented in this book in Chapter 8.

EXIT
The EXIT command is used to quit DOS — actually, the COMMAND program that DOS runs (see COMMAND earlier). Refer to "How Do I Get Back?" in Chapter 20.

FIND
This command is used to find text in a file, or it can be connived into searching for text in a DOS command. A sample of this feat is offered in "Finding a Lost Subdirectory" in Chapter 18.

FOR
This is a special batch file programming command. Even in books I've written on batch file programming, it's been hard to explain what this command does. Best leave it alone.

GOTO
Yet another batch file programming command, which is only useful inside a batch file; there's really nothing to *go to* at the DOS prompt.

IF
IF is a special batch file command used in making decisions. For example: IF THE COMPUTER EXPLODES, I SHOULD WEAR A HAT. That's computer logic for you.

LABEL
The LABEL command is used to add or change a disk's volume label. See Chapter 13 for more information.

MEM
The MEM command tells you about memory in your computer and how it's used. Refer to "Conventional Memory" in Chapter 8.

PAUSE
This is a special batch file command that displays a `press any key` message and (surprise) waits for you to press a key before going on.

QBASIC   More than a command, QBasic is MS-DOS's free-of-charge Basic programming language interpreter. If you want to get into the Basic programming language, consider picking up a book on QBasic and teaching yourself to program. It's much more fun than playing with the DOS prompt.

REM   This is a batch file command that enables you to put comments or remarks into a batch file program.

RMDIR   The RMDIR command (also RD) is used to delete a subdirectory. The subdirectory has to be empty first.

SET   The SET command is used in two ways: First, by itself SET displays the contents of DOS's *environment*. Second, SET can be used to place items into the environment or to remove them. Yawn.

SHIFT   Another batch file command. This one does something so complex I'd have to tell it *twice* to Mr. Spock.

SORT   This command is used to sort the output of some other DOS command or text file.

SYS   The SYS command is used to make a disk bootable. It transfers the DOS system files to a disk so that disk can be used thereafter.

VERIFY   This command turns on double verification of all the information DOS writes to disk. With the command on, you'll be certain that the information is properly stored. On the down side, it slows down your computer. Normally, VERIFY is off.

Commands No One Uses More Than Once

CHCP   This is the *change code page* command, which enables you to switch in an alternate character set for the screen. (Sounds like fun, but setting up a PC to do that is complex and confusing.)

GRAFTBL   This is one of DOS's many *code page* commands. It loads a code page (foreign language character set) into the memory on your conputer's screen (graphics adapter). This command is no longer included with DOS 6.

GRAPHICS   The GRAPHICS command works with IBM and Hewlett-Packard printers, enabling them to accurately print graphics.

JOIN
: The JOIN command is used to fake DOS into thinking one of your disk drives is really a subdirectory. Weird. Also dangerous. (This command has been eliminated in DOS 6.)

KEYB
: The KEYB command loads a foreign language keyboard driver into memory, enabling you to type using special foreign language characters. (Ooo, la, la!)

NLSFUNC
: Yet another *code page* program. This adds *natural language support* to DOS, enabling foreigners to type in their own native lingo.

SETVER
: This command is used to fool some old DOS programs into thinking they're running under their favorite DOS versions. It's best that you leave this command alone.

SUBST
: The SUBST command is used to fake DOS into thinking a subdirectory is actually a disk drive. And dangerous, too.

Commands Not Worth Bothering With

DEBUG
: This is really a secret snooper type of program, intended for use by programmers and not mere mortals such as you or I.

DELTREE
: The DELTREE command is a powerful and merciless version of the tamer DEL command. Don't tempt fate by messing with this command. Even the experts don't use it without a garlic wreath, silver bullet, or recent backup handy.

EDLIN
: Yuck! This is DOS's old command-line editor. Refer tp Chapter 1, where I make my real feelings clear about using this cruddy old program. DOS 6 no longer includes EDLIN.

EXE2BIN
: This is a programmer's tool. (DOS used to come with another programmer's tool, LINK. Don't ask why. DOS dry.)

EXPAND
: This program is covertly used by the Setup program when it installs MS-DOS. There's no need for you to bother with it.

FASTOPEN
: This is a program used to speed up access to files on disk. I've heard nothing but problems with it, especially with switching floppy disks. Don't use this command.

FDISK

The FDISK command is used when you first set up a hard disk. It prepares the disk for formatting. Using this command after the disk has been prepared could damage your hard drive. Do not use this command; only let an expert play with FDISK.

LOADFIX

If you ever see the message `Packed file corrupt` when you try to run a program, don't panic. At the next DOS prompt, type **LOADFIX,** a space, and then type the name of the program again (plus any options or other doodads). That should fix the problem, and that's about all this command is good for.

LOADHIGH

This is a memory management command, along with its shorter version, the LH command. Because DOS 6's MemMaker command (Chapter 8) deftly handles this information, no need to dwell further.

PRINT

Although a logical person such as yourself would assume that the PRINT command printed files — and it does — the illogical truth is that it does a lot more, additional unnecessary stuff. Refer to Chapter 4 for information on printing files and avoid the ugly PRINT command.

REPLACE

Interesting command: It will search out and replace all files on the hard disk with newer versions on a floppy disk. Because most programs come with their own INSTALL or SETUP program, you rarely need to use the REPLACE command.

SHARE

The "something to do with networks" command. When you or your guru installs your network, this command may tuck itself inside your PC's CONFIG.SYS or AUTOEXEC.BAT file. If so, grand. If not, eh . . .

VSAFE

The lesser-half of MS-DOS 6's anti-virus brigade, VSafe is actually more of a pain than it's worth. Heed the rules offered in Chapter 21 on fighting the virus and you'll never have to bother with this meddlesome command.

Commands No One in His or Her Right Mind Uses

CTTY   The CTTY command is interesting, but typing it can disconnect your keyboard and monitor, forcing you to reset the computer in order to regain control. It's more of a curiosity than a command you can get any mileage out of.

RECOVER   This command is not as pleasant as its name may suggest. RECOVER tries too hard. Using this command can permanently damage all files on disk and instantly rob you of your subdirectories. Under no circumstances should you ever use this command. In fact, delete it from your hard disk. Fortunately, RECOVER is not included with DOS 6. However, you may still have a copy of this program on your hard drive, a leftover from an earlier version of DOS. If so, feel free to delete it.

Glossary

●●

386

Number that refers to all computers that have an 80386 microprocessor or brain.

80286

This is the number of a microprocessor or brain in an AT or 286 computer. It's one notch less than an 80386 and one notch greater than an 8086.

80386

This number refers to the microprocessor or brain in all 80386 computers. There are two types: the 80386DX and the 80386SX. The SX is simply a cheaper version of the DX model, with all the caffeine but only half the calories.

80486

This number refers to the brains found in an 80486 computer. It's a notch better than an 80386 system and will put a bigger dent into your wallet.

8086/8088

These two numbers refer to the first processors in the first line of PCs out the chute. Although a lot of these models were sold, and many are still up and running, few are sold today.

Alt-key

A key combination involving the Alt key plus some other key on the keyboard, a letter, number, or function key. When you see Alt-S, it means to press and hold the Alt key, type an S, and then release both keys. Note that Alt-S doesn't imply Alt-Shift-S; the S key by itself is fine.

applications

This is a term applying to computer programs, generally programs of a similar type. For example, you can have word processing applications, spreadsheet applications, and so on. There are several computer programs that fit into each application category. And everything is generally referred to as *software,* which makes the computer do its thing.

arrow keys

These are keys on the keyboard that have directional arrows on them. Note that some keys, such as Shift, Tab, Backspace, and Enter, also have arrows on them. But the traditional arrow keys are used to move the cursor. See *cursor keys.*

ASCII

An acronym for American Standard Code for Information Interchange. ASCII (ASK-ee) uses code values from 0 to 127 to represent letters, numbers, and symbols used by a computer. In DOS, you'll often see ASCII used to refer to a plain text file, one that can be viewed by the TYPE command and read by a human.

backslash

The \ character, a backward-slanting slash. Under DOS, the backslash character is used as a symbol for the root directory, as well as a separator between several items in a pathname.

back up

A method of copying a whole gang of files from a hard drive to a series of floppy disks (though other devices, such as tape systems, can also be used). It could also refer to a duplicate of a single file — an unchanged original — used in case anything happens to the copy you're working on.

baud

Part of the old computer cliché, *byte my baud,* it actually refers to a technical description of a *signal change.* With computers, people often use the term baud to refer to bits per second or bps, the speed of a modem. Baud comes from the 19th century French telegrapher, J.M.E. Baudot. See *BPS.*

binary

A counting system involving only two numbers, which in a computer are one and zero. Humans, which includes most of you, use the decimal counting system, which consists of ten numbers, zero through nine.

BIOS

An acronym for Basic Input/Output System. The BIOS is actually some low-level instructions for the computer, providing basic control over the keyboard, monitor, disk drives, and other parts of the computer. When the computer is on and running, DOS is actually in charge. But to use the computer, DOS will itself use the BIOS to "talk" with other parts of the PC.

bit

A contraction of *binary digit,* a bit refers to a single tiny switch inside the computer, which contains the values one or zero. There are millions of such switches — bits — inside the typical PC. They form the basis of all the memory and disk storage.

block command

Blocks are chunks of text in a word processor: a word, sentence, paragraph, page, or several words that the word processor treats as a group or block. Block commands manipulate a block of text somehow. Typical block commands copy, cut, delete, or perform a variety of functions on a whole group of words at once.

boot

The process of turning on a computer that, surprisingly enough, doesn't involve kicking it with any Western-style footwear. When you turn on a computer, you are *booting* it. When you reset a computer, you are *rebooting* it or giving it a *warm boot* (which sounds kind of cozy, you must admit).

BPS

An acronym for bits per second. It refers to the number of bits a modem can send over the phone line in one second. Typical values are 300, 1200, 2400 and 9600 bits per second. The higher the value, the faster information is sent. Note that this is the accurate term used to describe how fast a modem sends information; the term baud is often, though incorrectly, used interchangeably with bps.

byte

A group of eight *bits,* all clustered together to form one unit of information inside a computer. Conceptually speaking, a byte is one single character stored inside a computer. The word *byte* would require four bytes of storage inside your PC. Bytes are also used as a measure of capacity; see *kilobyte* and *megabyte.*

capacity

The amount of stuff you can store, the total number of bytes that can be stored in memory or, more likely, on a disk. Some hard disks have a capacity of 100 megabytes. Floppy disks have storage capacities ranging from 360K on up through 2.8MB. Some closets have a capacity for 24 pairs of shoes, though many women find miraculous ways to put more shoes into that tiny space.

CD-ROM

An acronym for Compact Disc-Read Only Memory. It's a special optical storage device that contains millions of bytes of information. Like the musical CDs, you can use the appropriate CD-ROM hardware to have access to the volumes of information stored on a CD disc. And just like a musical CD, you cannot record any new information on the disc; it's *read only.*

centronix port

See *printer port.*

CGA

An acronym for Color Graphics Adapter. The CGA was the first video system for the PC that offered both color text and graphics. The text was lousy and the graphics were only good for the chintziest of games. CGA was soon replaced by the *EGA* graphics standard.

circuit breaker

This is a safety device installed between a power source and delicate electronic equipment, such as a computer. If the power going through the line is too strong, the circuit breaker "blows." This shuts off the power, but in the process it stops nasty electrical things from invading your computer.

clock speed

The measure of how fast a computer's microprocessor, or brain, can think. It's measured in millions of cycles per second or megahertz (see *MHz*). The faster the clock speed, the faster the computer (and the more it costs).

clone

Oh give me a clone, yes a clone of my own, with the Y chromosome changed to the X. And when I'm along, 'cause this clone is my own, she'll be thinking of nothing but ___. Actually, *clone* is a term used to describe an imitation of an original. It doesn't appear much these days, but nearly all PCs are clones of the first IBM microcomputers, the original PC and PC/AT systems.

CMOS

This acronym refers to special memory inside the computer. The CMOS memory stores information about your PC's configuration, its hard drive, and it keeps track of the date and time. This is all maintained by a battery, so when the battery goes, the computer becomes terribly absentminded. CMOS. See MOS run. Run, MOS, run.

compatible

A term used to refer to a computer that can run DOS software. This used to be an issue a few years ago. But today, nearly all PCs are completely compatible with DOS and all its software.

console device

This is nerd talk for your screen and keyboard.

Ctrl-key

A key combination involving the Control (or Ctrl) key plus another key on the keyboard, typically a letter, number, or function key. When you see Ctrl-S, it means to press and hold the Control (Ctrl) key and type an S, after which you release both keys. Note that Ctrl-S shows a capi-tal S, but you don't have to press Ctrl-Shift-S.

conventional memory

This is memory DOS uses to run programs. Most PCs have the full 640K of conventional memory, also called *DOS memory* or *low DOS memory*.

conventional memory

This is a common term, so I've listed it twice.

CPU

An acronym for Central Processing Unit, CPU is another term for a computer's microprocessor or brain. CPU. Don't step in the PU. See *microprocessor*.

Ctrl

The name of the Ctrl key as it appears on the keyboard. See *Ctrl-key*.

cursor keys

These are special keys on the keyboard used to control the cursor on the screen. The four primary keys are the up, down, left, and right arrow keys. Also included in the cursor key tableau are the PgUp (page up) and PgDn (page down) keys, and the Home, and End keys.

cursor

The blinking underline on the screen. The cursor marks your position on the screen, showing you where any new text you type will appear. Cursor comes from the Latin word for runner.

data

Information or stuff. Data is what you create and manipulate using a computer. It can really be anything: a word processing document, a spreadsheet, a database of bugs your daughter has collected, and so on.

default

This is a nasty term computer jockeys use to mean the standard choice, the option or selection automatically taken when you don't choose something else. They should really use the term *standard*

choice instead. *Default* is a negative term, usually associated with mortgages and loans.

DIP switch

A tiny switch inside a computer, on the back of a computer, or on a printer. DIP switches are used to control the way a computer or printer automatically behaves, to tell the system about more memory, or to configure some doohickey to work properly. This only needs to be set once, twice if you weren't paying attention the first time.

directory

A collection of files on disk. Every disk has one main directory, the *root directory*. It can also have other directories or *subdirectories*. Files are saved to disk in the various directories. You view the files using the DIR, or directory, command.

disk

A storage device for computer information. Disks are of two types, hard disks and floppy disks. The floppy disks are removable and come in two sizes, 3½-inch and 5¼-inch.

diskette

This is a term applied to a floppy disk, usually to distinguish between it and a hard disk (which isn't removable). Diskettes are often referred to as disks. See *disks*.

display

The computer screen or monitor. The term *display* is rather specific, usually referring to what is displayed on the screen as opposed to the monitor (which is hardware).

document

A file created by a word processor. The term *document* means something you've saved with your word processor, usually a file that contains formatting information, various text styles, and so forth. This marks the line between a file created by a word processor (the document) and a plain text file, which lacks the formatting information (and can be viewed by the TYPE command).

DOS

An acronym for Disk Operating System. DOS is the main program that controls all of your PC, all the programs that run, and anything that saves information to or loads it from disk.

DOS memory

This is another term for *conventional memory*, the basic 640K of memory in a PC. See *conventional memory*.

dot matrix

A type of printer that uses a series of pins to create an image on paper. Dot-matrix printers are a cheap, quick, and noisy way to print computer information, not as slow as the old daisy-wheel printer, and not as fast, expensive, or as cool as a laser printer.

dump

A place where you take the computer after you're fed up with it. Actually, *dump* is an old computer term that means to wash out one thing and dump it into another. For example, a screen dump takes the information displayed on the screen and literally dumps it out to the printer. See *screen dump*.

eek! eek!

This is the noise a computer mouse makes. See *mouse*.

EGA

An acronym for Enhanced Graphics Adapter. The EGA was the second graphics standard for the PC, after CGA. It offered many more colors than CGA, plus it has the benefit of easy-to-read text. EGA has since been superseded by the VGA standard. See *VGA*.

EMS

An acronym for Expanded Memory Specification. The EMS, or more precisely, the LIM EMS (LIM for Lotus/Intel/Microsoft) is a standard for accessing extra memory on all types of PCs. This memory, *expanded memory,* is directly of use to DOS and most DOS applications. See *expanded memory*.

Escape

The name of a key on the keyboard, usually labeled "Esc." The Escape key is used by many programs as a cancel key.

expanded memory

This is extra memory in a PC, useful to DOS and lots of DOS applications. To get expanded memory you must add expanded memory hardware and software to your PC. (For a 386 system, you need only the software.) But, once installed, your computer will have access to lots of extra memory, which can be put to immediate use by many applications.

expansion card

This is a piece of hardware that attaches to your computer's innards. An expansion card expands the capabilities of your PC, enabling you to add new devices and goodies that your computer doesn't come with by itself. Expansion cards can add memory (such as *expanded memory*), a mouse, graphics, a hard disk, or external devices like CD-ROM drives, scanners, plotters, and so on.

expansion slot

This is a special connector inside most PCs that enables you to plug in an expansion card (see preceding entry). The typical PC has room for five to eight expansion cards, allowing you to add up to that many goodies.

extended memory

This is extra memory in an 80286 or 386 computer; it's not *expanded memory*. Extended memory is primarily of use to operating systems other than DOS. On an 80286, it's better to have expanded memory. On a 386 system, you can add extended memory — as much as you like — and then convert it to the more usable expanded memory using special software.

field

A field is an area on the screen where you enter information. It's part of database-speak: A file is a collection of records; records contain fields; fields contain elements. For example, a folder full of employment applications is like a file; each application is a record; and the fill-in-the-blanks items on each application are fields.

file

A collection of stuff on disk. DOS stores information on disk in a file. The contents of a file could be anything: A program for DOS, a word processing document, a database, a spreadsheet, a graphics image of Claudia . . . , you name it.

fixed disk

An old, IBM word for a hard disk. The word *fixed* refers to the fact that a hard disk cannot be removed, unlike the floppy disk. See *hard disk*.

floppy disk

A removable disk in a PC, usually fitting into a 3½-inch or 5¼-inch disk drive. Refer to *disk* or *diskette*.

font

A typesetting term used in computer desktop publishing or word processing. The term really should be *typeface,* or a specific style of text. For example, many books use the Cheltenham typeface or font. Other fonts are usually available, depending on your printer or the software you're using. (The term *font* actually refers to a style of typeface: bold, italic, and so on.)

form factor

This is a heavy-duty term that really means the size of something. Typically, you'll see form factor used to describe a disk drive. Essentially it means what size the disk drive is, what kind of disks it eats, and how much information you can store on the disks. When you see form factor, just replace it mentally with the word *dimensions*.

format

The process of preparing a disk for use by DOS. All disks come naked out of the box. For DOS to use them, they must be formatted and prepared for storing files or information. That's done under DOS by the FORMAT command.

free

Nothing is free.

function keys

These are special keys on the keyboard, labeled F1 through F10 or F12. Function keys perform special commands and functions, depending on which program you're using. Sometimes they're used in combination with other keys, such as Shift, Ctrl, or Alt. (WordPerfect takes this to the max, with up to 42 combinations of function keys to carry out various actions in the program.)

geek

A nerd with yellow Chee-tos between his teeth. See *nerd*.

gigabyte

This is a perilously huge number, typically one billion of something. (And that's billion with a *b*.) A gigabyte is one billion bytes or 1000MB (megabytes).

graphics adapter

This is a piece of hardware that controls your monitor. There are three common types of graphics adapters on the PC: monochrome, EGA, and SVGA. The graphics adapter plugs into an expansion slot inside your PC.

hard disk

A high-speed, long-term storage device for a computer. Hard disks are much faster and store lots more information than floppy disks.

hardware

This is the physical side of computing, the nuts and bolts. In a computer, hardware is controlled by the software, much in the same way an orchestra plays music; the orchestra is the hardware and the music is the software.

Hayes-compatible

A type of modem that works like the original Hayes Micromodem, or at least that shares similar commands. Getting a Hayes-compatible modem guarantees that your communications software will work with it.

Hewlett-Packard

HP makes calculators and special scientific devices, but it's their computer printers that make them popular with the PC crowd. A Hewlett-Packard laser printer will be compatible with just about every piece of software out there. I say this for two reasons: I personally don't have an HP printer and it's a real pain. And I want to be nice to them so they'll send me a freebie.

hexadecimal

This is a totally nerdy way to count: in base 16, where you have the numbers 1 through 9 and then the letters A through F to represent values 11 through 15. The number "10" in hexadecimal is 16. Why bother? No reason, unless you're a programmer or know someone who speaks programmer lingo.

IBM

International Business Money or something like that. They made the first original IBM PC, which formed the platform on which the modern PC industry was launched. Some 60 million PCs later, IBM no longer plays a leading role in the industry, but it still makes quality computers (mostly for the Mercedes crowd).

I/O

An abbreviation for Input/Output, the way a computer works. Computers gobble up input and then spit out output. This is also what the Seven Dwarfs were singing when they went down into the mines.

icon

A religious symbol or painting. However, when you run Microsoft Windows, an icon is a teensy, tiny picture that represents a program. For example, Word for Windows has a pretty icon that looks like a big blue *W* stamped over a newspaper. That's how Windows presents programs to you: pretty pictures or icons. (DOS uses ugly text and — heck — the Phoenicians were doing that 7,000 years ago!)

i486

This is a common way of describing the Intel 80486 microprocessor. They write "i486" on the top of the chips, so many folks write "i486" when they refer to that microprocessor. See *80486*.

K, KB

Abbreviations for *kilobyte*. See *kilobyte*.

keyboard

The thing you type on when you're using a computer. The keyboard has a standard typewriter-like part, plus function keys, cursor keys, a numeric keypad, and special computer keys.

kilobyte

One thousand bytes or, more accurately, 1024 bytes. This is equal to about half a page of text. Note that kilobytes is abbreviated as K or KB. So 24K is about 24 thousand bytes (more or less).

laptop

A special, compact type of computer, usually running off of batteries, that you can take with you. Laptops are popular additions to a desktop system, allowing you to compute on the road. They are, however, considerably more expensive than regular computers.

laser printer

A special type of printer that uses a laser beam to create the image on paper. Most laser printers work like a copying machine, except that they use a laser beam to help form the image instead of smoke and mirrors. Laser printers are fast and quiet, and they produce excellent graphics.

LCD

An acronym for liquid crystal display, a type of computer screen particular to laptop computers. Most LCDs are compatible with a desktop system's VGA display, though they're limited to displaying black and white or shades of gray.

load

To move information (a file) from disk into the computer's memory. Only after you've loaded something, say a worksheet or document, into memory can you work on it. See *save*.

M, MB

An abbreviation for megabyte. See *megabyte*.

macro

A program within a program, usually designed to carry out some complex function, automate a series or commands, or make life easier for anyone who doesn't want to hassle with a program's complexities. Macros exist in just about every application — even DOS — to make routine things easier. (Under DOS, the macros are called *batch files*.)

math coprocessor

This is a special companion chip to a com-puter's microprocessor, specifically designed to perform complex arithmetic and to do it faster than the microprocessor can by itself. The math coprocessor chip is numbered similarly to the microprocessor, except that the last digit is a 7 instead of a 6. Note that the 80486 microprocessor has its math coproces-sor built in.

megabyte

One million bytes, or 1024K. A megabyte is a massive amount of storage. For example, *War and Peace* could fit into a megabyte with room to spare. Typically, hard drive storage capacity is measured in megabytes, with about 40MB being a popular size.

memory

Where the computer stores information as it's worked on. Memory is temporary storage, usually in the form of RAM chips. The microprocessor can only manipulate data in memory. Once that's done, it can be saved on disk for long-term storage.

memory-resident program

This is a special type of program that stays in memory when it's done. Memory-resident programs do one of two things. First, a memory-resident program will add to or modify some function of DOS. A mouse driver, a printing program, a program allowing you access to more memory, and so on are examples. Second, memory-resident programs can be pop-up utilities, that is, programs activated by pressing special key combinations that then appear on the screen — as if by magic. These include pop-up editors, calculators, printing-control programs, and so on. Borland's SideKick was probably the best example of a pop-up memory-resident program.

menu

A list of commands or options in a program. Some menus are displayed across the top or bottom of the screen, giving you one-word commands or choices. Some fill the screen, asking you "what next?" Some menus are graphical pull-down menus that display a hidden list of items or commands. Fun, fun, fun.

MHz

An abbreviation for megahertz. This refers to how fast a computer's microprocessor can compute. The typical PC zips along at 20MHz. The typical human brain, scientists have discovered, works at about 35MHz — or 40MHz after six cups of coffee.

microprocessor

The computer's main brain, where all the calculations take place and the control center for the entire computer. Microprocessors are also called processors or CPUs. They're given numbers such as 80286, 80386, and so on. (Refer to the numbers at the start of this glossary.)

modem

A contraction of *modulator-demodulator,* a modem is a device that takes electronic information from your computer and converts it into sounds that can be transmitted over the phone lines. Those sounds can be converted back into electronic information by the other computer's modem.

monitor

The computer's display or video system. The monitor is like a TV set, showing you information. It's actually only half of your computer's video system. The other half is the graphics adapter, plugged into an expansion slot inside your PC.

monochrome

A type of computer display that shows only two colors, black and white (or green and white). Some monochrome systems will display shades of gray, substituting them for the various colors.

motherboard

This is the main circuitry board inside your computer. The motherboard contains the microprocessor, some memory, and expansion slots into which you can plug additional goodies.

mouse

This is a small, hand-held pointing device primarily used in graphics programs to manipulate stuff on the screen. A mouse has two parts: the hardware part, consisting of the mouse unit itself connected to a mouse card in your computer (or a serial port), and the software part, which is a program that controls the mouse and allows your applications access to it.

MS-DOS

This is the long, formal title for DOS, the Microsoft Disk Operating System.

nerd

Someone who enjoys using a computer. No one reading this book should be a nerd, though one day you may become one. There is no cure.

network

Several computers hooked together. When your computer is on a network, you can share printers with other computers, easily send files back and forth, or run programs or access files on other computers. It sounds neat, but in practice a network can be a hassle to set up and a pain to maintain. See *NBC.*

on-line

To be on and ready to go. When a printer is on-line, it's turned on, contains paper, and is all ready to print.

option

An item typed after a DOS command that isn't required. You type an option after a command to control the way the command performs. Most options typed after a DOS command are in the form of *switches,* which are slash characters typically followed by a letter of the alphabet.

parallel port

See *printer port.*

pathname

The full, exact name of a file or directory on a disk. The pathname includes the drive letter, a colon, and all directories up to and including the directory in question and a filename. Pathnames are an extremely specific way of listing a file on disk.

PC

An acronym for personal computer. Before the first IBM PC, personal computers were called *microcomputers,* after the *microprocessor* — the computer's brain. The *PC* in IBM PC means personal computer and since the time the IBM PC was introduced, all microcomputers — even non-DOS computers— have been called PCs.

PC-DOS

This is the IBM-specific brand of DOS, the Personal Computer Disk Operating System. The differences between this brand of DOS and MS-DOS are slight, and you can run PC-DOS on non-IBM computers.

Pentium

The official name Intel gave to the "586" microprocessor. This is to keep all the knock-off goofs from calling their chips the 586 (but they'll do it anyway), since Intel can't copyright numbers.

peripheral

Any item attached to the outside of the computer, such as a printer, a modem, or even a monitor or keyboard.

pixel

An individual dot on the computer's display, used to show graphics. A graphic image on a computer is made up of hundreds of dots or pixels. Each pixel can be a different color or in a different position, which creates the image you see on the screen. The number of pixels horizontally and vertically on the display give you the graphics *resolution*.

pixel dust
That thin layer of dust that coats your montor. It's deposited there nightly by the pixel fairy.

port
Essentially, this is a connection on the back of the computer to which you attach various extern items (*peripherals*). There are two primary ports on each PC, a *serial port* and a *printer port*, though what the keyboard and monitor plug into could also be considered ports.

printer
This is a device that attaches to your computer and prints information. A printer is necessary to give you *hard copy,* which is printed output of the information inside your computer.

printer port
This is the connection on the back of the PC into which you plug a printer cable, thereby attaching a printer to your computer. Most PCs have the ability to handle several printers, though you need to add special hardware to give your system the extra ports. The printer port is also known as the *parallel port* or sometimes you'll hear some dweeb call it a *Centronics port*.

program
This is a special file on disk that contains instructions for the computer. Under DOS, all programs are stored in files with their second part named either COM, EXE, or BAT. To run a program, you need to type in only the first part of the filename.

prompt
This is the ugly C> thing you see when you use DOS, telling you to "type that ridiculous command line here." The DOS prompt is the most familiar of all the prompts. Other programs may use their own prompts, each of which is designed to show you where information is to be entered on the screen. Handy.

RAM
An acronym for random access memory, this is the primary type of memory storage in a PC. RAM = memory.

redundant
See *redundant*.

resolution
This refers to the number of dots (*pixels*) on the screen. The higher the resolution, the greater the number of dots vertically and horizontally, the finer the graphics image your computer can display.

RGB
This is an acronym for red-green-blue, or the three primary colors. These colors are used in all computer displays to show you all colors of the rainbow and from which graphics are created. In the old CGA days of computing, RGB also referred to a type of monitor for use with a PC.

ROM
An acronym for read-only memory. These are special chips on the computer that contain instructions or information. For example, the computer's BIOS is stored on a ROM chip. ROM chips are accessed just like regular RAM memory, but unlike RAM they cannot be changed; they're read-only.

root directory
The primary directory on every DOS disk. Other directories, or subdirectories, branch off of the root directory. The symbol for the root directory is the single backslash (\).

RS-232
This is a technical term used to describe a serial port. See *serial port*.

save
The process of transferring information from memory to a file on disk for permanent, long-term storage.

screen dump
An ugly term for taking the information on the screen and sending a copy of it to your printer. A screen dump is performed on a PC by pressing the Print Screen key, which may be labeled Print Scrn, PrtSc, or something along those lines. Note that the screen dump does not include graphics screens, and if your printer can't handle the special IBM characters, then God-knows-what will happen.

SCSI
An acronym for small computer system interface, it's like a very fast and versatile serial port. I only mention it here because it's pronounced "scuzzy" and I think that's cool.

serial port
A special type of port into which a variety of interesting devices can be plugged. The most common item plugged into a serial port is a modem (which

leads some to call it a modem port). You can also plug a computer mouse, a printer, a scanner, or a number of interesting devices into the serial port. Most PCs have one or two serial ports.

shareware

This describes a category of software that's not free, yet it's stuff you don't have to buy before you try it. Generally, shareware consists of programs written by individuals and distributed hand to hand through user groups, national software clearing houses, or via modem. You try the software and, if you like it, you send the author the required donation.

slide rule

Whoever is on top of the ladder gets to go down the slide first.

software

This is what makes a computer worth having. It's the vast collection of programs that control the hardware and enable you to get your work done. Software controls computer hardware.

source

The original from which a copy is made. When you copy a file or duplicate a disk, the original is called the source. The source drive is the drive from which you're copying. The destination, or the location to which you're copying, is referred to as the target.

string

In computer lingo, this term applies to any group of characters. A string of text is a line of text, a command you type, or any other non-numeric information. Don't let the term throw you, or force you to insert twine or yarn into the disk drive.

subdirectory

A term for a directory in relation to another directory. All directories on a disk are subdirectories of the root.

SVGA

An acronym for Super Video Graphics Array; the next generation VGA. Turn the computer off and you get mild-mannered Clark Kent VGA.

syntax

The format of a DOS command, the things you must type, the options, what order they go in, and what they do. When you goof up and specify something out of order, DOS tosses you back a Syntax Error. Not fatal, it just means you need to find the proper syntax and retype the command.

tab stop

Just like on a typewriter, a tab stop on a computer is the location where characters will appear after you press the Tab key. Sometimes, the Tab key simply produces eight spaces. In most word processors, you can set tab stops at specific positions on a line of text.

tab shooter

Someone you employ to make a tab stop real fast, or a whimpy drink made with tequila and a popular diet drink.

target

The location of a copy or duplicate of an original file. A target can be a filename, a subdirectory, or a disk drive — the final destination of the file. Copying things on a computer is a lot like archery.

text editor

A special type of word processor that creates or edits only text files, often called ASCII, unformatted, or nondocument files. A text editor lacks most of the fancy formatting features of a word processor. Oh, you might want to look up *ASCII* since I mentioned it here. (Not that it helps much.)

toggle

Something that can be on or off; a single switch that's pressed once to turn something on and again to turn it off. This term appears when describing something you can do in a program that turns a function on and then doing it again turns it off.

TSR

An acronym for terminate but stay resident. Believe it or not, that's an MS-DOS program-mer's function, not anything any human being will use. Yet it's a quick-and-dirty term that can be used to describe *memory-resident programs.*

user

The person who operates a computer or runs a program. The computer is then the usee.

V20

A special, faster type of 8088 chip, usually found in some of the cheaper laptop computers. See *8088/8086.*

V30

A special, faster type of 8086 chip, found in some lightweight laptop computers. See *8088/8086.*

VGA

An acronym for Video Graphics Array, the current top-of-the-line in PC graphic systems. VGA offers you stunning color graphics, great resolution, and crisp text, much better than its predecessor, EGA. A SuperVGA (also known as *SVGA*) is available that extends the powers and capabilities of VGA.

window

An area on the screen where special information appears. It can be a graphic window, à la Microsoft's Windows program, or it can be a text window, outlined with special graphic text characters.

word wrap

The capability of a word processor to move a word from the end of one line to the beginning of the next while you're typing. Word wrap enables you to type an entire paragraph of text without having to press Enter at the end of each line.

write protect

A method of protecting information on disk from being accidentally changed or erased. This is done by putting a write protect tab on a 5¼-inch disk, or by sliding the little tile off of the hole of a 3½-inch disk. Once that's done, the disk is write protected and you cannot change, rename, delete, or reformat it.

WYSIWYG

An acronym for what-you-see-is-what-you-get. It refers to a program's capability to display information on the screen in exactly the same format in which it will be printed. Sometimes this works, sometimes it doesn't. Generally speaking, if a program is WYSIWYG, what you see on the screen will be close enough to what you get when it's printed.

Index

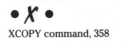